One Simple Idea

One
Simple
Idea

**Turn Your Dreams into a LICENSING GOLDMINE
While Letting OTHERS DO THE WORK**

STEPHEN KEY
with Colleen Sell

New York   Chicago   San Francisco   Lisbon   London   Madrid   Mexico City
Milan   New Delhi   San Juan   Seoul   Singapore   Sydney   Toronto

1 2 3 4 5 6 7 8 9 0 DOC/DOC 1 2 1 0 9 8 7 6 5

ISBN: 978-1-259-58967-6
MHID: 1-259-58967-6

e-ISBN: 978-1-259-58478-X
e-MHID: 1-259-58478-7

Library of Congress Cataloging-in-Publication Data

Key, Stephen, author.
   One simple idea : turn your dreams into a licensing goldmine while letting others do the work / Stephen Key. — Revised and expanded edition.
      pages cm
   Includes index.
   ISBN 978-1-259-58967-6 (alk. paper) — ISBN 1-259-58967-6 (alk. paper)
   1. Inventions—Marketing.   2. Entrepreneurship.   3. Inventions.   4. New business enterprises—Management.   I. Title.
   T339.K49 2016
   658.1—dc23
                                                                    2015028850

McGraw-Hill Education books are available at special quantity discounts to use as premiums and sales promotions, or for use in corporate training programs. To contact a representative, please visit the Contact Us page at www.mhprofessional.com.

To Janice, my wife, my life

Contents

Preface

The Ferriss Effect

BACK IN 2003, when I first started teaching my "10 Steps to Bring Your Idea to Market" course, a guy who didn't look much like a student started showing up at my classes. Unusually fit, he wore leather from head to toe and carried a motorcycle helmet. Long after everyone else had settled down, he would walk in and scan the room for the perfect spot to sit and focus. Thus positioned, he would cock his head and fix a penetrating look at either my partner Andrew or me as we spoke from the front of the room. I got the sense he was absorbing every story, statistic, and strategy we shared and was turning them over in his mind.

At the end of class, students would mill around deferentially, eager to ask questions. But Tim Ferriss didn't waste time on small talk.

"Let's go out for gin and tonics," he proposed. "I need to know more."

I waved him off at first, but he persisted. He wanted to learn how I had become my own boss with tens of thousands of people whom I didn't know working for me. Eventually, I went out for those drinks, in part just to shut him up. Tim has got to be the most persistent individual I've ever met, and he drilled me about what I do and how he could apply my experiences to his business. You see, Tim had created a dietary supplement, Brain Quicken, and like many entrepreneurs, he had also launched a company to manufacture and market it. Now he wanted to do what I do: get a licensee to manufacture and market his idea *for* him so he could kick back and collect royalty checks.

Eventually, Tim took off to travel the world, calling in periodically for more advice about how to turn his company from a time-sucking machine into a passive income generator. One day in 2005, he called me from Argentina, where he was studying tango, to announce he was writing a book. He asked me to read what he had written thus far.

Tim's book came to be titled *The 4-Hour Workweek*, and it quickly climbed to the number one spot on the *New York Times* Best Sellers list. The lessons Tim learned from my classes helped him form the book's underlying philosophy. In it, he coins the term "lifestyle design" and describes me as a member of "a quiet subculture of people called the 'new rich'"—people who have escaped the rat race and discovered how to live the life they want to.

Teaching had begun as a side project, but a few months after Tim's book came out, a flood of new students began signing up for our course. "Wow," I said to my wife one day after I got home, "We're going to have to start taking this seriously."

Thanks to what I now call "the Ferriss effect," the number of my students keeps growing. I have now taught people from more than 30 countries, including Australia, Bolivia, Costa Rica, Chile, Norway, Iceland, Singapore, and Canada. The strategies I teach can work for anyone anywhere.

My students hunger to pick up where *The 4-Hour Workweek* leaves off, which is what my classes and this book do. For the last 30 years, I've designed my lifestyle by "renting" my ideas out to large corporations. What I do and how I do it is simple, even if it isn't always easy. However, it is easier today than it has ever been before because of a phenomenon called "open innovation," which anyone at all—regardless of education or background—can take advantage of.

One of my life's passions is teaching others my road map for jumping into the innovation stream and becoming their own boss. I've condensed my teachings into these 20 chapters. Whether people learn this road map from me or figure it out for themselves, I believe many, many more people will begin designing their lifestyles this way in the future.

Although Tim came to me for help at first, he ended up returning the favor.

Tim, next time you're in town, drinks are on me.

Acknowledgments

FIRST AND foremost, I want to thank my wife Janice for allowing me to pursue my dreams. I don't think there is any greater gift one can give. I know it hasn't always been easy living with Peter Pan, yet you continue to be the most remarkable, smart, and beautiful woman I have ever met. I want to thank my children, who have also had to put up with me over the years. Your dad has never had a traditional job, but you've all been patient with me throughout the ups and downs. I am so proud of each of you and what you have accomplished.

James Shehan, you make me look so good. You've been an incredibly loyal assistant and friend. I thank you for that. I don't know anyone who possesses all of the skills and talent that you do. I'm constantly impressed by your genius. And you put up with me, too—which may be the most challenging task of all! I look forward to the next 10 years.

I need to thank my business partner, Andrew Krauss, for helping me start this journey. I don't think I would have begun mentoring inventors if it weren't for him. Andrew grew the Bay Area's Inventors' Alliance into one of the most active and well-established associations in the country, which is how I met him. Together, we designed the inventRight 10-step system. I have never known anyone who is so giving of himself. Your dedication to the inventing community is remarkable. Andrew, we are truly a team. I appreciate everything you do.

Linda Pollock, I want to thank you for being my absolute first student and believing in me and supporting me all these years. You have become a true friend.

My mentor, Stephen Askin, has been incredibly supportive of me as well. You gave me my first opportunity to succeed when I was just beginning my career. Everyone else thought I was crazy, but you believed in me! Your guidance and encouragement gave me the confidence I needed. I have watched you continue to mentor other individuals with all your heart and soul. Thank you.

Tim Ferriss, you helped spread my message across the world as you spread your own. I can't thank you enough for that.

My literary agent, Kirsten Neuhaus—thank you for teaching me how to write a book and for holding my hand throughout this journey.

I want to thank my editor, Gary Krebs, for understanding my vision and for helping me focus my material. You are truly great at what you do.

Colleen Sell, you are more than a collaborator. You went beyond the call of duty in helping produce this book. You understood the content as well as my voice. Thank you for being such an integral part of our team.

John Kimball, my father-in-law, you've been tough on me over the years, but through it all you have been my biggest supporter. You are my second father. I've enjoyed our Friday evening talks more than you will ever know. Thank you for your wisdom.

And finally, I would like to thank my father. The business principles you instilled in me are the ones I continue to live by and share with my students. These are the principles that have made me the man I am today. I've followed my passion, Dad. Life *is* too short, and I've been enjoying it all I can.

Foreword

I REMEMBER GETTING the call like it was yesterday. The head of McGraw-Hill Education's San Francisco office called me and asked if I would like to write a book. He had discovered my coaching business online and thought it had a growing audience.

I can barely put two sentences together, so I was very flattered. At that point, I had been teaching inventors how to bring their product ideas to market through licensing for more than a decade. McGraw-Hill Education wanted me to write about the 10 simple steps that were (and still are) the foundation of our yearlong program. At the time, Andrew and I scratched our heads. Were we really going to give away all of our content for the price of a hardback book?

But I remember hearing from trusted sources that if you have really great content, and you share it with the world, people will follow you. I asked Tim Ferriss, my former student and author of the bestselling book *The 4-Hour Workweek*, for his advice. His only comment was, "If you're going to write a book, write it like it's your last. Don't hold anything back." Tim, once again, I want to thank you for your spot-on advice.

I poured everything I knew into the first edition of this book, *One Simple Idea: Turn Your Dreams into a Licensing Goldmine While Letting Others Do the Work*. And, something seems to have worked. Since *One Simple Idea* was published in 2011, it has been translated into five other languages and is still a top seller on Amazon.

But what gives me the most pleasure, by far, is hearing from people who have licensed their ideas simply by reading this book. They haven't wasted their money paying for expensive patents. Sometimes they haven't even built prototypes. They relied on the 10 simple steps outlined in this book to get it done. They and I know this works.

Why a revised and expanded edition then?

I'm excited to report that things have changed a great deal in four years. The opportunity for creative people to profit from their ideas has never been greater, because open innovation is that much more popular. Companies all over the world are hungry for your ideas! This edition contains new details and an even greater level of specificity when it comes to licensing your ideas. I wanted to give you the latest, cutting-edge strategies that my students are using to sign licensing deals—so even more of you can license your ideas using this book as a guide. For example, it includes the new strategies my students are using to get in to potential licensees, like video sell sheets. It details how to get in by attending a trade show—cheaply. It will teach you how to work with freelancers to bring your ideas to life with 3-D computer graphics. It explains what the new patent rules mean for you, as well as how to use intellectual property strategically from a business perspective. It further lays out how to negotiate so that everyone wins. It's never been easier to stay current, to be inspired by what other creative people are doing, and to find the right home for your idea.

I've never been more excited about what I do for living, and that's due large in part to the response that *One Simple Idea* has received. I want to share every bit of what I know about this process so you too can sit back and enjoy getting the biggest companies in the world to work for you—instead of the other way around. I had no idea the licensing lifestyle would resonate with so many people. But then again, why wouldn't it?

Introduction

How One Simple Idea Led to
the Life of My Dreams

Hi, my name is Stephen Key, and I am a successful entrepreneur and licensing expert. I don't have a degree in engineering, marketing, or business. I don't own a big company, nor am I employed by a big company. Instead, companies work for me—bringing my product ideas to life while I sit back collecting royalty checks, creating new product ideas, and enjoying the life of my dreams with my beautiful wife and our three children. I wrote this book to show you how you can do the same thing and reap the same kinds of benefits.

But before I tell you how to bring your ideas to life, let me tell you a little more about me . . . because I have a feeling we're a lot alike. From an early age, I dreamed of being an entrepreneur. But I didn't want to go to college for four or six or more years to study how to create and manage a business. I didn't want to run a business with a lot of employees, overhead, debt, hassles, and headaches. I didn't want to live to work, as so many business owners and professionals do. Instead, I wanted to work to live—and to live well. More than anything, I wanted to create stuff. Have fun! See the world! Have a family! Enjoy life!

That's exactly what I've been doing for more than 30 years. I just wish someone would have told me the secrets of the game—the secrets I'm going to tell you in this book—when I started out on this journey.

My first foray into entrepreneurism began when I handmade soft sculpture designs and sold them at art shows and state fairs across California. That's when I learned my first big lesson in product design: when the rent is due and you're hungry, if the product you've spent several hours making doesn't sell, you quickly move on to something else.

Before long, I taught myself how to make patterns and began freelancing for the biggest plush animal toy companies in the world, like Dakin, Inc. Then I got my first "real job"—you know, the kind with a regular paycheck—at a start-up company called Worlds of Wonder (WOW). I figured I could work at WOW during the day and do my freelance projects at night, doubling my earnings. As it turned out, I spent far more time overseeing the manufacture of products than I did designing them. Still, as head of the design group at WOW, I was involved in the design (not the creation, but the manufacturing and design) of several hit toys, such as Teddy Ruxpin, the world's first talking teddy bear, and Lazer Tag, the top-selling toy of 1986. But I would often look at the new product ideas that came in and think, *I can do better than that!*

So after two years I left WOW to start my own toy creation, design, and licensing company. For a while, to pay the rent, I continued to do freelance design work for toy manufacturers, including Disney, Applause, Dakin, and WOW, among others. Then I began focusing solely on creating and licensing my own ideas.

I've licensed more than 20 ideas for products in such diverse fields as the toy, beverage, music, novelty, and pharmaceutical industries. Celebrities Michael Jordan and Alex Trebek have served as pitchmen for two of my products. Collectively, my creations have sold more than a half billion units and generated billions of dollars of retail revenue. I have served as a consultant on the reality show "American Inventor" and been featured on the CNBC show "The Big Idea with Donny Deutsch." I am invited to speak at U.S. Patent and Trademark Office events, Stanford University, IDEO (one of the world's top design firms), and elsewhere, and I teach my "invent right" strategies to thousands of people.

My product ideas range from the simple to the silly to the lifesaving. In my view, good ideas are those that sell—plain and simple. I dreamed up a Valentine's Day dart with a suction cup and a flag reading, "I'm stuck on you." That idea brought me $10,000 in advance income with zero up-front investment. I reenvisioned the plain gray guitar pick as a blank slate for new colors and designs like skull shapes and paisley patterns, to name a few. I even made lenticular picks specifically for Taylor Swift. This simple insight upped a 25-cent purchase to a $1 purchase and has sold 20 million picks.

One of my favorite early ideas was a small basketball backboard designed to look like a basketball player with his arms outstretched. Ohio Art licensed that idea from me and sold more than one million Michael Jordan Wall Balls the first year! One of my most successful ideas is the Spinformation rotating label, which adds 75 percent more information to bottle labels. The label has sold more than 400 million units worldwide and has won more than 15 accolades, including a Gold and a Bronze at the Edison Awards. In its newest incarnation, the Spinformation label as sold by Accudial Pharmaceutical, Inc., is helping prevent the estimated 30,000 cases of medicinal over- and underdosing of children nationally.

On any given day, I've got six new ideas out to different companies. Like my students, I'm still creating.

I've had a fantastic time creating new product ideas and "renting" them to manufacturers. It's fun. It's exciting. I'm never bored. I never run out of ideas. I never have to worry about going to work for someone else. And I never worry about money, even though I don't claim to be good with money in the conventional sense.

I have many friends who spend all their time trying to figure out how to increase their wealth. They're obsessed with investing in the market and paying less in taxes. I could not care less. Money for money's sake doesn't interest me. When the stock market crashed, I was unaffected; I wasn't in it. When the recession hit, it didn't impact me. Two of my children attended the University of California, Berkeley, and my youngest graduated from the University of Oregon. I paid for all of their college educations, comfortably.

Our home in Modesto, California, though lovely, was a tract house in a nice but nondescript neighborhood. We owned it outright. Although our home was not lavish, it was by our choice, and we did not live a "practical" lifestyle. The cars we drove, all purchased with cash, were probably too expensive. And it probably wasn't practical for us to take the kids out of school and for me not to go into the office for a month so we could go to Africa, or for six months so we could travel the United States together.

Two years ago, my beautiful wife and I moved to Glenbrook, Nevada—the oldest settlement on Lake Tahoe. We are delighted to have made such great friends here already. Janice and I walk several miles around the neighborhood often, stopping to gaze out across the lake and take in the colorful sunsets. I, of course, can do my work anywhere. And I'm happy to report that the view from my home office has never been better!

Sometimes, I still can't believe that I've been doing this for more than 30 years and making a living at it—a good living. It wasn't easy at first. It has taken a lot of hard work, and I've learned a lot along the way. I have made a lot of money and lost some as well. But I've had a ball.

Anybody can do what I've done, including you. Like I said, I don't have a background in sales or marketing or engineering. All I have are ideas. Some of my ideas are great; some are OK; some are lousy. It doesn't matter whether your idea is big or small. It doesn't have to change the world. It doesn't have to be the next best thing since sliced bread. And you don't have to quit your day job to start creating and licensing ideas. All it takes is *one simple idea*—and the ability to translate that idea into a product that consumers want and that a company will want to make and market for you.

I've been doing this for many years, and I've taught thousands of other people how to "invent right" too. Now, with this book, I'm sharing this amazingly simple strategy with you, so that you, too, can live the life of your dreams by creating great product ideas and licensing them to companies.

"If you can dream it, you can do it."

—Walt Disney

One
Simple
Idea

PART ONE

The Power of One Simple Idea

How would you like to wake up every day eager to go to work? Better yet, how would you like to work for yourself—focusing on what you want and love to do? Even better yet, how would you like for your entrepreneurial enterprise to give you the time, energy, money, and freedom to live the life of your dreams?

All you need is one simple idea . . . and a simple strategy for bringing your ideas to market.

How You Can Create the
Life of Your Dreams

A RE YOU a creative type who is always envisioning new and better ways to do things? Do you constantly think of ways to make things more efficient or enjoyable, more aesthetically pleasing, or just plain more fun? Do you often see ways to improve or enhance the products and services you use regularly, or ways to give them more pizzazz? Have you ever wished that *you* could be the one to bring those ideas to life . . . and actually make a living doing it?

Or are you one of the millions of people worldwide who are unemployed? Do you want a livelihood that can't be snatched away tomorrow through a single stroke of bad luck, like a layoff or illness? Or are you one of the many millions more who are underemployed, struggling to make ends meet and bored to tears in a dead-end job? Do you need to find a way to supplement your day job without running yourself ragged? Do you dream of having a job that doesn't squander your talents and limit your earning potential?

Or perhaps you're like me. You know life is short, and you don't want to waste it working just to pay bills and to build up your retirement account. You want to work in an industry that interests you, to do work you're passionate about, to have the means and the freedom to pursue your personal interests, to spend quality time with family and friends, to travel—to enjoy life.

That's what I wanted. And that's exactly what I've been doing—dreaming up ideas, licensing them to companies, and living the life of my dreams. That's right. I *rent* my ideas to other companies. While they're making and marketing the stuff I've dreamed up, I'm collecting the rent for those ideas and doing what I love to do: create.

Every day, tens of thousands of people all over the world are working for me: box boys, cashiers, truck drivers, printers, fabricators, accountants, marketing execs, sales reps, researchers, human resources administrators, and presidents and CEOs of companies like Ohio Art, Nestle, Jim Beam, Toys"R"Us, Walgreens, Walmart, and others all are laboring on my behalf. They take care of the research and development, production, marketing and sales, customer service, accounting, and everything else that goes into producing and selling my creations . . . so I don't have to. My creativity fuels their production, and I leverage their immense power. I have found a way to make the system work for me rather than the other way around.

You can, too. All it takes is one simple idea—one that's ripe for the marketplace.

The reason I can do this—as well as you and anyone else, regardless of where you live—is a trend called "open innovation" that is reshaping the business world. In the past, most new product and service ideas came from inside a company or from a big design firm. Rarely would these big corporations even consider ideas from an "outsider" like me—a regular guy with no credentials in engineering, marketing, or design, but with a creative bent and a penchant for dreaming up cool stuff. Now for the first time in history, companies are realizing that maybe, just maybe, they don't have all of the world's smartest and most creative people working in their companies. They have finally grasped that they can, and must, find new and innovative ideas from the outside.

You can find many academic books on the subject of open innovation, but this is the first book to explain why open innovation is important to you and how you can use it to become a successful entrepreneur—as you'll learn in Chapter 2. Today, companies need help. They need people like you and me. It doesn't matter if you're a stay-at-home mom, a truck driver, an aerospace engineer, or a teacher. It doesn't matter whether you have a Ph.D. or are a high school dropout. To play the biggest, most exciting game in the world—coming up with new or improved or jazzed-up products and services—your credentials are irrelevant. All you need is a simple idea and a simple strategy for bringing that idea to market.

Is It Really That Simple?

Oh, here they come . . . all those "but" questions buzzing around in your brain. I knew they would, and I understand. What I just said and what I'm about to tell you flies in the face of conventional wisdom. Later, I'll explain how my strategy turns conventional wisdom on its head and traditional methods of innovation into the dinosaurs they are. First, though, let's get those nay-saying questions out of the way.

But Don't I Need to Start a Company?

You no longer have to start a company to experience the entrepreneurial thrill of innovating. As you'll learn in Chapter 3, licensing your ideas lets you focus on the most exciting part of any business and leave the tough stuff, like manufacturing, marketing, and distribution, to others.

In fact, it's never been a better time to be an innovator who *doesn't* want to start a business. There are more opportunities for us to succeed today than ever before. To my delight, innovation is *popular*. Nearly eight million people tune in to watch entrepreneurs pitch their ideas on ABC's *Shark Tank* every week. Crowdfunding—whose campaigns are being breathlessly reported on by the media—has become a powerful catalyst for product development that shows no signs of slowing. In fact, a World Bank report projects that the global market for crowdfunding could surpass $96 billion a year by 2025. And companies whose explicit goal is to take concepts, prototypes, and nearly finished products and get them on the market—like Quirky—have risen at a rapid rate. These opportunities will be discussed at length in Chapter 20.

My students and I—as well as many others I have never met—provide living proof that The American Dream has far from expired. In fact, it is more alive, more accessible, and far more exciting today than it ever has been in the history of our country. You'll read many of our stories and learn all about this exciting new world of innovation and how to be a part of it throughout this book.

But Do I Need to Quit My Day Job?

Absolutely not. In fact, I strongly recommend that you do *not* quit your day job—until and unless you have the passion to create and license ideas as a profession, a few successes under your belt, *and* sufficient royalties coming into your bank account. As I always tell my inventRight students: licensing is a numbers game. Most people have to come up with a lot of ideas before one gets licensed. It will also take time to find a licensee and for the licensee to bring your idea(s) to market.

The great thing about licensing ideas is that it doesn't have to be a 40-hour-a-week job, even for those who are ready, willing, and able to do it "full time." When you're first starting out or if you're doing this as a hobby or to supplement your day job, you can do it in as little as 10 hours a week or less using my 10-step strategy for creating and licensing ideas.

But Don't I Need a Patent?

Well no, and maybe yes. In my experience, you do not have to put your financial security at risk to innovate. You don't have to take out a mortgage on your home or empty out your retirement savings to get a patent on your idea. You do not need patents to license ideas, and product cycles churn so quickly that you will lose your opportunity if you spend the years and tens of thousands of dollars it takes to get a patent.

Besides, if you think a patent guarantees you protection, you're crazy. First-to-market owns the shelf space. That's the best protection you can have. In Chapter 10, I'll show you the smart way to play the patent game. I have more than 15 patents myself. For now, just realize that patents are not nearly as important as you think they are. It really depends on the idea or invention. Read Chapter 10 to help you decide!

But Isn't It Really Hard to Do This?

Back when I first started licensing my ideas to big companies, it was much harder to do than it is now. Today, the pace of business is so fast and products come and go so quickly that companies simply do not have the ability to do it all on their own. Consequently, many companies have opened their doors to independent product developers like you and me—a movement called "open innovation," which you'll learn more about in Chapter 2. The 10-step process that I teach my inventRight students and that I've outlined in this book makes it easy for anyone to create and license ideas.

But What If I Don't Have Any Ideas?

Everyone has ideas. You're a consumer, right? By virtue of being a consumer, you have plenty of opinions about all the products and services you buy and use at home, at work, and at play. So you do have innovative ideas. It's those ideas that companies desperately want and need. It's those ideas that can help you go into business for yourself without having to start and run a company with a lot of overhead, equipment, and people. You just need to learn how to translate those ideas into a marketable product and how to get your ideas into the right hands and in the right way. That's what this book is all about.

But if dreaming up product ideas is truly not your thing, you can still get into the innovation game by becoming a connector—a product scout—someone who brings other people's ideas to companies that want and need them.

Whether you're a creator or a connector, these ideas do not have to be mind-blowing. They don't have to change the world. No reinventing the wheel here, I tell my students. Companies can make huge gains from small, incremental changes and from slight improvements to existing products.

I've been swimming in the innovation stream for more than three decades, so I know where and how to look for ideas. In Part Two, I show you how to brainstorm ideas and pick the best ones to develop for licensing. I also tell you where and how to find products and industries in need of refreshing.

But How Do I Start?

My dad spent his entire career at General Electric. He was a project manager, and he loved his job. He never thought about it as having to go to work. He was just doing what he loved. When I was struggling back in my twenties, making and selling soft sculpture toys at craft fairs, Dad told me, "Find what your passion is. Make it your career, and you will never 'work' a day in your life."

That's where I tell my students to start: *find your passion*. Are you interested in sports? Then look there for simple ideas—existing products you can improve upon. If your passion is gardening or pets or monkey-wrenching or parenting or music or home improvement, start there. When your work is your passion, it propels you forward. And it's fun!

I work a lot because I love what I do. But like my dad, I never feel like I'm working. Sometimes all I do for long stretches is make sure my checks are being deposited.

I like to think I took Dad's advice to heart and went one better. Although my father loved his work, he wasn't in control of it. When he was laid off, his years of loyalty were powerless against much larger economic forces. Today, I get to love my work and know that I don't have all my eggs in one basket. They're scattered about in dozens of different baskets. Even better, there's an endless supply of eggs out there for me if I need them. They're available to you, too.

I love being my own boss. I love coming up with new products. I love the life that creating and licensing products has enabled me and my family to live. And I'd love to help you do the same. All it takes is one simple idea.

So start with one simple idea that you're passionate about. Then follow my 10 simple steps to bring your idea to market.

My Introduction to a New Way of Innovating

When I was in college, I didn't have it in me to be like those ultra-driven business students. I wanted to relax and have fun and make things. In fact, after my dad gave me his piece of golden advice about finding my passion, I realized that if I could come up with good ideas and make things with my hands, I would be the richest man in the world, in every sense of the word.

I switched from business classes at Santa Clara University to art classes at San Jose State University, even though I couldn't paint or sculpt as well as my classmates. A few years later, I began making my own stuffed toys by hand sculpting them. I sold them out of a booth at fairs around the state of California. My favorite part was watching my funny creations make people smile. To the world I was looking like a pretty big loser, but I loved every minute of it. I just didn't love the fact that I needed more income to do the things I wanted to do with my life, like get married, buy a home, and raise a family.

Around this time, I had another conversation with my father. This time Dad gave me his second most important piece of advice, one that he didn't follow personally but saw his employer, General Electric, put into action. This is what he told me:

- Find something that doesn't require your presence.
- Find something that doesn't require your hands.
- Make sure it has a "multiplying effect."

At first I didn't understand what he meant. But over the ensuing couple of years, I figured it out.

Here's what happened next: I knew I needed to break out of the fair circuit, so at age 27 and with a background in art, I talked myself into my first job with a start-up toy company called Worlds of Wonder (WOW). Within a year, I found myself on the manufacturing and design team that helped bring the company's most popular toy ever to market, the original storytelling teddy bear, Teddy Ruxpin. Kids were entranced by his animated ability to talk and blink his eyes. Parents could pop a cassette into his back, and he would rivet kids to their seats by telling them stories. In 1986 alone, Worlds of Wonder sold five million Teddy Ruxpins.

For a brief while, we became the fifth largest toy company in the world. All of a sudden, my future was looking bright.

You wouldn't have known that if you'd seen me after I'd stepped off a 13-hour flight to Hong Kong. Haggard and wild-eyed with jet lag, I felt like I'd just landed on the moon. The tropical heat and humidity hit me like a ton of bricks. I stumbled into my hotel room and collapsed. The next day I traveled across the border to our factory in mainland China, which was working around the clock to fulfill the demand for our bears. My job was to make sure every one that came off the line looked beautiful. The bears meant money, and we had to keep them coming. My boss had given me a parting directive in no uncertain terms: "Never stop the production line."

Standing on that production line watching bear after bear pass me by, I kept thinking about a man named Ken Forsse. Ken created Teddy Ruxpin and licensed it to Worlds of Wonder. Everyone knew he was making millions of dollars in royalties. Those numbers pinged about in my head as I watched the workers' hands move rapidly over soft brown fabric.

Something about this equation was inspiring. The man with the idea, the one who was making lots of money, wasn't even there. We only saw him when we needed approval. He wasn't the one standing halfway across the world in a frenetic factory far from home, like me.

I finally understood what my dad was talking about and what the multiplying effect could mean. I suddenly realized I didn't want to be the guy on the line, working day in and day out. I wanted to be the other guy. Like Ken, I wanted to be the smartest guy in the room, the one collecting the checks while others were working for me. That single thought changed my life—just as so many of my ideas since then have.

When I got back to California, I decided to show my own ideas, my *own creations* for toys to our company president. He smiled and listened politely, but later my boss reprimanded me for taking my focus off our existing product lines. I knew right then I had to quit. Fortunately, by then I had years of experience as a freelance designer and a network of potential clients to fall back on. I knew WOW needed me, so I hoped it would be my first client—and it was. I also had the support of Janice, my girlfriend and future wife, whose salary could take care of us financially until I got my feet on the ground as an independent product developer. And so with that support as my springboard, I launched Stephen Key Design, LLC, and set out to create, develop, and license my own ideas.

Flash forward to spring 2000. It's a sunny day in Boca Raton, Florida. I am standing in front of yet another production line and watching as my Spinformation label is being affixed to thousands of bottles of herbal supplements at the Rexall Sundown production facility. Watching that production line made me oddly nervous; any breakdown would mean an interruption in my income. I couldn't help but smile. Finally, I was on the right side of that upside-down equation.

This production line was printing money for me just as it had for Ken years earlier. The best part was that I didn't even have to be there. I'd only dropped by that day because I wanted to. I'd become the smartest guy in the room. By renting out ideas to others, I'd finally fulfilled my dad's prescription. I didn't have to be there for an idea to reach customers. And by getting some of the world's largest companies to work for me, I'd set in motion an awe-inspiring multiplying effect.

The crazy thing about this story is that the label itself wasn't even *my* idea. I just figured out how to manufacture it, something no one had done before. The point is: you don't even need to have your own ideas to do this.

So how did I manage to become an outsider who successfully licenses ideas? The answer is simple: I have always enjoyed making products that bring a smile to people's faces. Somehow I just knew I could license my own ideas. When I went down to the store and looked at the products there, I knew I could do better. I was not impressed with the existing products on the shelf. I'd also worked for a company and watched it license ideas from creative people like Ken Forsse.

My attitude set me apart from classic inventors. In the early days, I didn't network much with other product designers. I still don't think of myself as an inventor, because I have never really identified with that word. I don't fit the typical image of an inventor. I'm a social creature and not one to squirrel myself away in a garage to tinker. But since other people tended to call me an inventor, I decided to check out different inventors' associations.

In a bizarre stroke of fate, the first meeting I attended was held in an old classroom of mine at Santa Clara University. As the meeting went on, I felt confused. I wasn't experiencing any of the problems these people were obsessed with. Inventors often start by seeing a problem and visualizing a solution. That's all well and good, but that orientation leads many of them to fixate on the problems themselves.

After the meeting ended, I showed a few of the other attendees some of the products I had licensed, which I had brought with me (not really knowing how this all worked). A crowd grew, which piqued the interest of the association's president, who had been leading the meeting—Andrew Krauss. At that time, the inventors in his group were struggling to succeed. He had never met anyone who had simplified the process like I had. Andrew and I started talking, and it became clear to us that there was a need for a program, and we should be the ones to develop it. Ultimately, we decided we could do a better job of teaching creative people how to profit from their ideas together, and the rest is history.

Many of the inventors' association meetings I have attended since then have been gobbled up by debates about finding investors and spending years and thousands of dollars on patents. I tell my invent-Right students not to waste their time on prototypes and patents. When you license, it's not that complicated. To successfully license, you don't even need big ideas. Small ones will do. Slight or incremental changes translate most rapidly and most profitably to market. And to find them, you do not have to be an inventor.

First and foremost, I am a consumer. I'm the kind of guy who likes to go to stores and look around at all the fun stuff you can buy. Maybe this describes you. Do you like to shop for electronic gadgets? Cosmetics? Toys? Tools? Kitchenware? Or any other kind of stuff? If so, you are qualified to dream up ideas for new and renewed products and license them.

Welcome to the New World of Innovation

You may have heard it said that inventors are our most valuable resource. I say ideas are our most valuable resource. If we are going to solve some of the world's most vexing problems, from saving the environment to curing diseases, the answers are going to come through new thinking. Very few products are manufactured in the West anymore, but we do produce exceptional ideas. What a lot of people don't realize is that there is a new and much simpler way to get those great ideas from conception to market. And anyone can do it—including you. Especially you, if you're a creative type who dreams of being an entrepreneur steering your own ship and controlling your own destiny.

One of the best things about this new world of innovation is that today you can build a career, or at least a hobby, out of the single most exciting aspect of any business: creating ideas. All you need is a passion for good products or services.

Now I'm going to explain something to you that most "experts" just don't get. My livelihood and the courses I teach are based on a single word you have heard before and read in these very pages, but may not understand: *licensing*. Despite being relatively unheard of, licensing is a huge industry. For example, in the United States, it is worth $500 billion to the economy. That's bigger than the cell phone and magazine publishing industries combined. In 2013 alone, Samsung paid Microsoft *$1 billion* in royalties. The opportunity is enormous—and unlimited.

In basic terms, licensing means taking your idea, your "intellectual property," and giving someone with a lot of powerful resources the privilege of using it for a price. You set the terms by which you extend this privilege. In return, the user gives you a rent check, also known as a "royalty" check, four times a year. These quarterly royalty checks, and sometimes one-time advances on future royalties, are the means by which you will generate income. Sometimes a royalty check is $1,000. Sometimes it's $10,000, or $100,000, or $1 million. I have students who bring in millions in royalty income. I have many others who make $30,000 to $40,000 a year for each of their three licenses for a total annual income of $90,000 to $120,000. Not bad.

Still with me? If you graduated from a top business university or college, you may not be. Graduates of top institutions have been mercilessly drilled in the ways of the Old World, the world of manufacturing. That means they can't separate the concept of renting their ideas—or anyone else's—from an unexamined conviction that they have to go out and start their own company to do so. They don't know there's another way to be entrepreneurial. They have invested a tremendous amount of tuition and mental energy into figuring out how to raise money from venture capitalists or angel investors or how to get a loan from a bank or the Small Business Administration or a wealthy aunt. Or they may already be bootstrapping to fund their company's growth through cash flow. To keep on growing, they will have to become expert at managing people, sourcing material, running faster and more efficiently than their competition, generating cash flow, minimizing their tax bill, and keeping down costs like rent, electricity, payroll, and legal fees.

There's nothing wrong with doing all that work if you have the passion and aptitude for it. But maybe you don't. Even if you do have what it takes to launch and run a company, your business may still fail miserably, regardless of the merit of your idea. Businesses owned by well-educated and competent people fail all the time, sometimes because the owners were unable to complete all those complex tasks as well as they'd hoped. Sometimes it's because they put all their eggs into one basket, focusing all of their resources on a single product or brand. And sometimes it's because their idea wasn't so great after all, which is often the result of creating a product for which there isn't a substantial market. These are the sad stories you won't find recounted on the pages of business magazines.

I'm acquainted with a professor at one of America's top universities. He developed a product and raised millions from investors to start a company, only to discover 10 years later that there was still no market for it. He wishes he had figured this out before he invested not only his own lifeblood and resources but also his investors' resources in a venture that was doomed to fail from the outset. It's a fitting commentary that this individual, though highly intelligent and entirely well-meaning, is no longer an entrepreneur, but a professor teaching others.

If he had used my system for creating and bringing ideas to market, he might have discovered the flaws in his strategy long before so many resources were lost. If you decide to start a company to bring your ideas to market, you can still use my road map for rapidly testing the marketability of an idea to save yourself years and, literally, millions of dollars worth of trouble.

Not long ago, I was invited to talk to students at the renowned School of Design at Stanford University. Aspiring engineers and industrial designers come there from all over the world to learn the most cutting-edge technologies and techniques. They pay a fortune in tuition for the privilege of learning how to turn their brilliant ideas (and many of them are, indeed, mind-blowing) into market successes. But they are so focused on doing it the old way that they couldn't hear me when I started explaining what I do. Instead, they looked at me as if I had a third eye. (Although, afterward, many of them called me asking for advice.)

Another time, I spoke to the employees of one of the premier industrial design firms in the country. I doubt I will be asked back. Naturally, companies want to hang on to their best people. In effect, I showed all of their brilliant designers the keys to escape the prison of employment. I explained exactly how to bring their ideas to market and cut their employer out of the process.

The amount of time and resources devoted to educating some of the smartest minds out there about the Old World way of bringing products to market is so exhaustive, so overwhelming, that many very bright people just can't conceive of there being an easier way to do this. I suspect that to them, licensing seems like cheating. After all, they're already accustomed to working long hours and getting little sleep, to spending a lot of money, and to working very, *very* hard. They can't imagine that there is another way to realize their entrepreneurial dreams that might be . . . easier, faster, simpler.

That's exactly what the licensing lifestyle can be: *simple*. And it all begins, and continues, with *one simple idea*.

2

The Beauty—and Opportunity— of Open Innovation

FOR MORE than a decade I've been teaching other people how to license their ideas—now it's your turn. And your timing couldn't be better! Licensing your ideas has become easier than ever, thanks to social media and the new tools and strategies that enable you to bypass the prototype and patent processes (which you'll read about in Chapter 11). But the most significant element driving the modern licensing wave is the innovation-driven global marketplace that has changed the way companies do business.

Companies of all sizes and in all industries have realized that to stay in the game, in some cases just to stay alive, they must innovate continually and quickly. Given the exorbitant costs of traditional research and development (R&D) and the economic constraints facing almost every company today, few can afford to develop all of their products and processes internally and at the pace required.

Besides, although many "insiders" are reluctant to admit it, today many of the most innovative and successful ideas come from the "outside"—from people like you and me, the ones who actually buy and use all this stuff. As I'm sure you've noticed, there are more products in the market all the time—exponentially more every year.

Finally, and this is crucial, it is often much faster and more economical for a company to bring to market a licensed product *based on a simple idea*—an improvement or enhancement to an existing product—than it is to start at square one in R&D and go through the whole long, complicated, and expensive process of coming up with and developing an idea themselves.

So licensing our ideas is really just good business for companies. It reduces their R&D costs. It accelerates their product development time. And it creates a multiplying effect: essentially getting other people to develop ideas for them for free.

The concept of a company licensing an idea from outside its own walls, otherwise known as *open innovation*, was unheard of when I first entered the licensing game. Twenty years ago, Procter & Gamble (P&G) would never have given me the time of day. Now, P&G—the largest consumer products company in the world—is among the vanguards of the open-innovation movement. In 2001, after dismal earnings the year before, P&G set a goal of sourcing at least half of its new products from the outside. A few years later, the company reached that goal. Many of the iconic brands you associate with P&G today are products of its open-innovation program, including Swiffer Dusters and Mr. Clean Magic Eraser. Strategic partnerships were responsible for 8 of the last 11 Febreze innovations. As Jeff Weedman, a P&G vice president involved with the company's open-innovation strategy, has said: "We don't care where good ideas come from as long as they come to us."

P&G is not alone. Today, the world's most enlightened corporations, including Black & Decker, Ford, Kraft Foods, Samsung Electronics, IBM, Intel, Philips, Unilever, and thousands upon thousands of others, have opened their doors to outside innovators. Today, when my students call potential licensees to pitch them on their ideas, an overwhelming majority of companies are familiar with open innovation. They know how to process their calls—which wasn't necessarily true as recently as five years ago. Increasingly, companies have systems in place for reviewing new ideas. Online submission forms are becoming more and more popular. But that doesn't mean that every company that professes to embrace open innovation actually means it or is employing policies and practices that are friendly to independent product developers. I'm confident they will soon enough, though.

In 2005, Professor Henry Chesbrough introduced the phrase "open innovation" to the world when he published his book *Open Innovation*.

This is what he had to say about the growth and future of the phenomenon in a recent publication:

> *When I wrote* Open Innovation *in 2003, I did a Google search on
> the term "open innovation," and I got about 200 links that said,
> "Company X opened its innovation office at location Y." The two
> words together really had no meaning. When I conducted a search
> on that same term in 2012, I found 483 million links, most of which
> were about this new model of innovation. . . . As the future unfolds,
> I expect universities to become more welcoming of this trend. Public
> policies will be adapted to support this movement. And the innova-
> tion capabilities of organizations around the world will no longer
> stop at the boundaries of the organization. Instead, open innovation
> practices will extend to suppliers, customers, partners, third parties,
> and the general community as a whole.*

Henry continued on to explain that he thinks that "designing and
managing innovation communities" is going to become increasingly
important to the future of open innovation: "Open innovation was
first understood and implemented as a series of collaborations between
two organizations to open up the internal innovation process. Today,
though, we see many instances in which the concept is being used to
orchestrate a significant number of players across multiple roles in the
innovation process."

The Global Churn

Innovation is driving the global economy. A hot new product comes
out in the United States or the United Kingdom, in Japan or Germany,
and thanks largely to the Internet, it's soon selling in all four corners
of the world. No sooner does the latest product or process hit the
market than someone, somewhere is upping the ante: creating a new
and improved spin-off; adapting it for new applications or for
new demographic, geographic, or niche markets; making it better,
fancier, simpler, cheaper, prettier, or "greener"; or improving it in some
beneficial and simple way.

The Opportunity

It used to be that a country's manufacturing capacity determined its dominance in the global economy: the higher a country's gross domestic product (GDP), the bigger its share of the global market. Not anymore. Today, the countries that dominate the world economy are the ones that produce the most ideas. In other words, the more *intellectual property* a country controls, the bigger its slice of the global market pie.

Intellectual property is the legal ownership, by a company or individual, of an *intangible asset*, a creation of the mind—an idea. Intellectual property encompasses many types of intangible assets, including musical, literary, and other artistic works; ideas, discoveries, and inventions; and words, phrases, symbols, and designs. The owner of intellectual property has the right to produce and market the creation, or to grant someone else the right—the license—to produce and market it.

The reason the United States still owns the biggest share of the global market is because U.S. companies own or control most of the world's intellectual property. Although little manufacturing is actually done in the United States, the country's GDP remains the largest in the world and not by a small margin. It is nearly twice as large as China's (the second largest GDP in the world) and four times as large as Germany's and Japan's. So the United States is responsible for most of the world's innovation *and* sells most of the goods and services derived from those innovations around the world.

Not only does the United States control the lion's share of the world's intellectual property, but it is also a huge market for the tangible manifestations of those ideas. The United States is a major, if not *the* major, consumer of products, services, processes, and technologies on the planet. And we don't just buy and use innovations created by American minds and companies. We also consume innovations from minds and companies around the world.

So today's innovations are coming from all over the world and are consumed all over the world. The innovation wheel just keeps churning, forcing companies to innovate constantly and quickly. To keep up, many companies have opened their doors to outside innovators. That has created a world of opportunity for independent product developers like you and me.

The Beauty

Not only does the global churn of open innovation provide entre-preneurs and independent innovators like you and me with a huge opportunity, it also gives us a distinct advantage. Why? For these three reasons:

1. We're close to the market.
2. We're creative and motivated.
3. We're quick on our feet.

First and foremost, as consumers we know what we like and don't like. We know what's out there in the market. We also know what *isn't* out there and should be. As entrepreneurs we thrive on creating new ideas and improving on existing ideas. We're motivated to bring our ideas to market, to share them with the world and to benefit per-sonally from them. Since we don't have a big company to run and worry about, we can turn on a dime to bring those ideas to life (so that a licensee can quickly bring them to market). We don't have the overhead and the hierarchy to impede our creativity and progress. We don't have to form a committee, or jump through hoops, or finance a long, drawn-out process to develop a product, build a prototype, get a patent, and secure the buy-in of different departments and investors.

Now here's the beauty of this new world of open innovation: it doesn't require big ideas. You can have a simple idea or a simple improvement to a product that's already out there. Piggybacking on existing products gives you a real advantage. You don't have to educate the world about your idea. You don't have to create a market for it, because there already *is* a market for it. You don't have to invent or reinvent something brand new. Because a simple improvement or a small incremental change to an existing product is often the easiest, fastest, most cost-effective, and most profitable way for companies to bring a new product to market, it's also your shortest, fastest route to licensing success.

You might think companies would have come up with these simple ideas themselves, but they often don't. I truly believe that sometimes these big companies are so close to *what is* that they don't even consider *what if*. It sometimes appears as if they wouldn't know a good idea if it hit them on the head. With all their departments and committees, I think it's hard for them to think outside the box or even right beside the box, which is where many of the most doable and profitable ideas are situated. In many of these companies, one person knows one thing and another knows another thing, but nobody is familiar with the entire process—nobody has the whole story.

As a consumer and an innovator, you not only have a larger perspective, but you also know how your idea fits into the big picture. You know the market, and you start at the beginning of the innovation process: with an idea.

There are so many ideas out there waiting for you to find them. You just have to look at things a little differently. Take a close look at the products you use at home and at play and see in the ads in magazines. Keep your eyes open and look for a simple improvement that you feel passionate about. If you're passionate about a new idea, chances are you'll be able to "innovate right" and get a company passionate about licensing it.

That brings me to another beautiful thing about open innovation: it's a one-size-fits-all strategy. Companies of all shapes and sizes are potential licensees for your idea. That said, a midsize company is usually the ideal candidate to license your idea. Midsize companies have enough money, and they are most likely to view licensing an idea as an opportunity to become number two or three in the market. Small companies are the least likely to have the capital and other resources to bring your idea to market. And although some really big companies do license ideas, they are more likely to *buy* ideas that are developed outside their walls than they are to *rent* them. That's because very large companies are risk averse. Scaling up is a challenge for them because implementing the slightest of changes to their product lines results in major ripple effects. They'd prefer for someone else to take on the risk of bringing a new innovation to market and to buy ideas that have already proven themselves in the market. That's been the traditional mode of development for a long time now, and that is why it is usually best to pursue the second and third largest players in a market rather than the largest player. When a big corporation is interested in an idea created by an independent product developer or a design firm, it typically wants to purchase the idea (patent) outright. Likewise, if large companies are interested in an idea that a smaller company has developed, they typically just buy the other company.

So I suggest that you find a midsize player in the market and show it how licensing your idea can make it number two or even number one. But don't rule out any company based on size alone. Any company that sells in your product category is a potential licensee; you just need to find the right company to license your idea, which you'll learn about in Chapter 15.

First to Market Wins

The same forces that are fueling the global churn of innovation—technology, the Internet, consumerism—have also shortened the "legs" of those very innovations. Today, new products sweep in and out of the market at a dizzying pace. The life cycle of any given product is shorter than ever, and the window of opportunity to get an idea to market is shrinking. In this environment, the first to market wins.

It's All About Shelf Space

Forget prototypes! Forget patents! Forget venturing!

What matters most in today's innovation-driven global economy is *shelf space*—getting your idea in front of consumers before someone else beats you to it. The easiest and fastest way to get your idea to market is to license it to a company that already has shelf space at Walmart, Kroger, Best Buy, Cabela's, Home Depot, Toys"R"Us, or wherever consumers shop for whatever you dream up.

Of course, your idea doesn't have to be for a consumer product. It can be for a product or process purchased and used by businesses, governments, scientists, and so on. Personally, though, I think dreaming up ideas for consumer products is fun, and the opportunities for innovation are endless. Consumer spending accounts for 60 to 70 percent of the total U.S. economy, even during economic slumps, and 40 percent of consumer spending is discretionary and driven by desire, not necessity. Figures in the United Kingdom and Canada tell a similar story. When consumers want something, they want it now, not years from now. Consumers in the commercial, government, and scientific sectors are no more patient.

Say you go the conventional route of bringing an idea to market. While you're spending all your time and money building prototypes and getting patents, writing a business plan, raising capital, setting up and running a company, and muscling your way into retailers and wrestling shelf space away from established companies, you can believe that someone else is going to bring your idea, or something close enough to it, to market. Bam! Your window of opportunity has just been slammed shut.

Licensing your ideas to established companies puts your idea on the fast track to market. It gets you shelf space *now*. Plus, it shifts all the costs and risks of bringing your idea to market to the licensee, and there are *always* risks associated with bringing products to market, especially new ones.

The Tao of Now

Successful companies of all sizes know the importance of shelf space. They also know shelf space for "me too" products is extremely limited, that some wholesalers and retailers want nothing whatsoever to do with them. They know many consumers feel the same way: they want only the real deal, the name brand, the first to market.

So to secure shelf space for their products and to ensure continued shelf space for future products, smart companies strive to continually innovate, to be *first movers*, to always stay ahead of the competition. By being the first to market, they grab shelf space, and with it, market share. To keep and grow their shelf space and market share, they continue to innovate, continue to be first to market.

These companies realize that open innovation—licensing ideas from the outside—enables them to be first to market and to fill their shelf space with products consumers want. Believe me, these companies want your ideas. They *need* your ideas. They benefit from your ideas. More important, licensing your ideas benefits *you*. It enables you to be a first mover: to get your idea on the market before someone else comes out with a similar idea.

The conventional method of bringing an idea to market—building a prototype, getting a patent, building a company around it, and so on—takes so much time, money, and effort that, in my opinion and experience, it just doesn't make sense for most ideas. When you license your idea to a company, everything is already in place. You just plug into the company's product line, and you're ready to rock and roll. The company takes care of manufacturing, marketing, sales, distribution, customer service, and all that other business. You collect royalty checks, *and* you still own the idea.

Licensing is the easiest and fastest way to get your idea on the shelf . . . and to start generating income for you.

HOW A SIMPLE SCREW MADE MILLIONS

Dwight Deveraux contacted me several years ago, wondering whether I could help him with his idea. A former guitarist for the 1980s pop-rock band Tommy Tutone (you may remember the group's Billboard Top 40 hits "867-5309/Jenny" and "Angel Say No") and a guitar aficionado, Dwight had developed a "locking stud" that kept a guitar's bridge from falling off when replacing the strings and also improved the intonation and "sustain" of the strings. He had run the idea by a luthier, or guitar maker, Kurt Laubhan, and Kurt helped him build a prototype. A friend of a friend referred Dwight to me because he had some questions about whether he should protect his idea, how to go about doing so, and how to bring his idea to market.

I met with Dwight at his home—something I never do, but I did this time because he was both a friend of a friend and my neighbor, and he had a physical impairment that limited his mobility. He explained that with existing technology, when you removed the strings to replace them, the bridge (the metal plate on the guitar's body that raises the strings above the surface of the instrument) often would fall off. As you replaced the strings, you had to hold the bridge

continued

in place with one hand while attaching new strings with the other. This made restringing a guitar difficult and time consuming, and when the bridge fell off, it often scratched the guitar's surface.

Then Dwight showed me how his idea solved this problem: First, you replaced the two screws (called studs) on either side of the wraparound bridge with the special "locking" screws that Dwight had designed. To replace the strings, you loosened the studs enough to remove and replace the strings, but the screws stayed locked in place, preventing the bridge from falling off. Once you had replaced all the strings, you tightened the studs, tuned your guitar, adjusted the pressure of the studs on the bridge to achieve the perfect intonation, and were ready to play within a few minutes.

His idea was so simple. Dwight wondered: *Did it have value? Could he protect it?* Absolutely, I assured him. In fact, his idea was simply genius!

I then explained my process for developing, protecting, and licensing ideas. I connected Dwight with the right attorneys, told him the right questions to ask, and gave him my road map for licensing his idea—the same one I've used successfully. The same one you're learning about in this book.

In 1998, Dwight started licensing his locking screws to guitar component manufacturers. Peter Wiltz, Dwight's longtime friend and a renowned guitar tech who toured with artists such as Bruce Springsteen, the Eagles, and the Rolling Stones, was instrumental in getting Dwight's locking studs into the hands of the world's top guitarists. Today, Dwight's company, TonePros, both manufactures the locking studs and licenses them to manufacturers—to the same companies that supply parts to the top guitar manufacturers in the world, such as Gibson and Fender. TonePros locking studs are distributed to more than 30 countries on four continents.

Dwight has said that his playing career "does not rival the success of TonePros." His simple idea has enabled him to live a very comfortable lifestyle, to continue being an integral part of the music industry, and to make a major contribution to the instrument he loves.

In one way, Dwight's story is unique. Few of us have the resources, skill set, and desire needed to successfully manufacture, market, and distribute our ideas. In another way, Dwight's story is similar to mine and to that of anyone who has created and licensed an idea. And it could be your story, because a huge component of Dwight's success is that he came up with a simple idea that he was able to license to other companies that had a *much* bigger share of the market than his little company did.

Today, thousands of companies around the world—from midsize manufacturers to megacorporations—are looking for the same kind of simple ideas. The need and opportunity for open innovation has never been greater. With the tools and techniques you'll find in this book, it has never been easier to create and license ideas. Now is the perfect time for you to jump into the open-innovation game!

3

CEO or CIO—Which Hat Fits You Best?

IDEAS ARE a dime a dozen. So goes the old maxim. There is a hard truth to that. An idea has little value in the real world until it is actually *in* the real world—selling in the marketplace, benefiting consumers in some way, and generating revenue for whoever owns and manufactures it. There are basically two ways to get your idea to market: do it yourself or get a company to do it for you.

Doing it yourself means starting a new business, or if you already own a business, adapting and expanding it to develop, manufacture, market, sell, and distribute the product or process. That's the chief executive officer (CEO) hat. Of course, with most start-ups, the founder/owner of the company wears multiple hats: CEO, chief operating officer (COO), chief financial officer (CFO), vice president (VP) of product development, VP of marketing and sales, director of distribution, director of human resources, and many more. With the manufacturing route to market, you assume all the responsibilities, risks, and costs. You also reap all the profits—or eat all the losses, as is often the case.

With licensing, you are the chief innovation officer (CIO) of your *idea* rather than the CEO of your *business*. You wear one hat: the creative one. Your primary focus is to bring your idea to life and license it to an existing company that brings it to market. The licensee, rather than you, assumes all the responsibilities, risks, and costs of manufacturing and selling the product. The licensee pays you a percentage of sales, or a *royalty*, to rent your idea.

Neither approach is superior or inferior to the other. With some ideas, manufacturing the product yourself is the better way to get your idea to market. With other ideas, licensing is the better route. In fact, I believe licensing is a much better, faster, easier, and cheaper route to market for *most* ideas conjured up by entrepreneurs, independent product developers, and regular people who use products every day and come up with innovative ways to improve them. For people like me, whose interests and capabilities align more closely with creating new products than with running a business, licensing is also a more gratifying way to get an idea to market.

Let's face it, not everyone is cut out to be a CEO. Not everyone has the abilities, resources, and desire to start, manage, and grow a business. But everyone can come up with a simple idea that companies will want to produce and consumers will want to buy.

Of course, not all ideas are created equal, either. Some ideas are too complicated or too new or too expensive for a company to want to take on, leaving you no choice but to bring it to market yourself . . . or to let it go. On the flip side, some ideas are or seem so easy to make and sell that you'll want to do it yourself, and sometimes that works out just fine.

CEO or CIO: how do you decide which hat fits you and your idea? Well, that depends largely on your interests, capabilities, resources, and the idea itself. It also depends on the market. There is no simple formula for delineating the ideal scenario for licensing versus the ideal scenario for manufacturing. But you can keep this formula in mind as a rule of thumb:

Simple idea + existing technology + 3 or more players in the market = license

Unique idea + new technology + 1 or 2 major players in market = manufacture

Knowing what's involved with each approach will also help you determine whether manufacturing or licensing is the best route to market for your idea.

It's also worth noting that it is possible to license an idea that you yourself have been manufacturing. My friend Nancy Tedeschi did exactly that. Nancy came up with the brilliant idea to reinvent the screw by adding a long snap-off piece—thereby enabling those who wear glasses the opportunity to quickly fix their eyewear. When I met her, I told her that I thought she should try to license the idea, but she was absolutely sure she wanted to bring the product to market herself. She didn't think starting a business would be difficult, and she wanted to reap all the profits.

Nancy has been very successful. She invested $250,000 of her own money to get her business up and running, and today, retailers including Walmart, Office Depot, and Ace Hardware sell her repair kits. Still, three and a half years after she embarked on bringing the SnapIt Screw to life, she changed her mind—and decided to license the idea to her distributor. The learning curve was unexpectedly steep and "excruciatingly painful," she says. "I was a rookie; I knew nothing. And I had to know everything about everything, make all of the right decisions at the right time, and that resulted in a lot of pressure and stress." Needless to say, she's happy to let someone else take over all of the day-to-day tasks of running a business. She recently began selling the SnapIt Screw in European markets and plans to license the idea there as well.

If you have an idea that companies are passing on, bringing it to market yourself first and licensing it later on is always an option.

Manufacturing 101

Starting a manufacturing company requires a lot of expertise, money, work, and time, no matter how simple your idea may be. Unless you've done it before and unless you're already a major player in the market, it typically takes years and hundreds of thousands, if not millions, of dollars to get a company going and a new product to market—and even longer to turn a profit, if you ever do. According to the U.S. Small Business Administration (SBA), one-third of new "employer enterprises" (businesses with employees) fail within the first two years and more than half fail within the first four years. But even if your business is among the 66 percent that make it past the two-year mark and the 34 percent that make it beyond four years, you still have to go through the same start-up process and take on the same risks as the businesses that ultimately fail. And it's not a walk in the park.

Here are the major steps involved in bringing your idea to market yourself:

- **Study the market.** The absolute first thing you'll need to do is determine whether there *is* a market for your product as well as who your target customers are, who your competitors are, and what your product offers consumers that your competition does not.
- **Develop the product.** This typically involves designing the product and the packaging, building and testing prototypes, and filing a patent.
- **Determine how to manufacture the product.** What materials, processes, technologies, skilled labor, facilities, and equipment will be required to produce and distribute your product? Who are your potential vendors? What local, state, and national rules and regulations will you need to comply with? Manufacturers pay 81 percent more in regulatory costs than do other types of businesses; you'll need to know these requirements and costs up front.
- **Write a business plan.** This comprehensive document proves on paper that a viable market exists for your product, that your business is capable of producing and selling the product, and that you can sell enough of the product to be profitable and to be attractive to potential backers. It must include a production and distribution plan, a marketing and sales plan, and a slew of financial data and projections.
- **Put up and raise capital.** Getting even a small manufacturing company up and running is likely to cost hundreds of thousands of dollars—more than most people can get from investors, mortgaging their homes, or borrowing money from banks, friends, and relatives. Not surprisingly, inadequate funding is the leading cause of business failure.
- **Launch the company.** You'll need licenses, insurance, facilities, and at least a few employees. You'll also need to purchase

equipment and materials to make, package, and distribute your product.

- **Sell the hell out of the product.** When you're the new kid on a block dominated by heavy hitters, this is much easier said than done. No matter how brilliant your idea and how many resources you throw at advertising, marketing, trade shows, and sales—and you'll need to do all of that—it is always tough to break into a market, much less to grab a big-enough share of it fast enough to survive.
- **Keep up with the market.** Remember the global churn you read about in Chapter 2? Well, that whirling dervish is always on your tail, forcing you to stay abreast of market trends or to go out of business. Innovate or become obsolete: that's the new rule of the game.

Any way you cut it, manufacturing is a tough row to hoe, and it isn't for everybody. But when it works for you and your idea, it gives you maximum control of the product, the process, and the profits.

Licensing: Easy as 1-2-3

The first phase in the licensing route to market is actually the same as in the manufacturing route: *study the market*. The more you know about the market, the more likely you are to design a product that companies will want to license and consumers will want to buy. Do some market research. Do some comparative shopping.

At the very least, you must find the answers to these six critical questions:

1. Who are my competitors? Identify both the major players and the smaller players.
2. How does my idea compare and contrast with other products in the market?
3. What value does it offer that the other products do not?
4. How large is the market?
5. Who are my primary customers?
6. What are my potential sales?

The second phase in the licensing process is to *develop your product*, or what I like to call "bringing your idea to life." This involves translating your idea into a bona fide product and proving that it's doable, valuable, and sellable. As with manufacturing, this may require building and testing a prototype and filing a patent. But it doesn't have to. Not if it's a simple idea: an improvement, enhancement, or incremental change to an existing product with a proven market. Not if it's a simple idea that uses existing technology. Instead of a prototype, a concept drawing or a computer model will likely do the trick. (You'll learn all about prototypes and other ways to model your ideas in Chapter 10.) You should also know the basics of manufacturing the product so that you can speak intelligently about it to potential licensees.

You will need some sort of intellectual property protection for your idea, but filing a patent is not your only option. I am not an attorney and cannot give legal advice, but here is what has worked for me as well as thousands of other independent product developers: file a provisional patent application. It will give you patent pending status for one year without huge expenditures of time and money, and you can even file it yourself. (I tell you how in Chapter 10.)

The third phase is to *secure a licensing contract*. This involves identifying potential licensees and picking the right one, which is what Chapter 15 is about. It also involves getting your foot in the door and licensing your idea to those companies—which I cover in Chapter 16. The important thing to remember is that you're selling the *benefit* of your idea, which you can usually accomplish with a good concept drawing (or computer model), a hard-hitting benefit statement, and a great sell sheet, which I talk about in Chapter 12. Then it's simply a matter of cutting a great deal, and I tell you how to do that in Chapter 17.

In fact, I wrote this book to show you how easy it is to license your ideas. It's certainly a whole lot easier—and in my opinion, a lot more fun—than launching a company to bring an idea to market. I know this to be true from my own firsthand experience—in licensing more than 20 of my ideas and manufacturing one, and only one, ever.

MY ONE FORAY INTO MANUFACTURING

About five years ago, a longtime friend of mine named Rob came to me with a proposition. We both knew a guy who was making a slew of money selling a guitar pick with the image of an alien head printed on it. Rob wanted to do something similar. I thought about it for a minute, because the last thing I wanted to do was get into a business. But this was a creative challenge. So I said, "Why not?"

The first thing I did was go to the mall to check out the images kids liked. One of the stores I browsed was Hot Topic. Now, if you're familiar with Hot Topic, you can imagine how out-of-place a 50-year-old man looked in a dark store that was blasting loud alternative rock music and filled with teens and tweens wearing black clothing, every imaginable part of their bodies pierced. But it worked. I noticed that the most popular products in the store had skulls on them. One sticker in particular stood out: it was in the shape of a skull, but the chin came to a point. Instantly, it looked like a guitar pick to me. The light went on: rather than just printing an image on the surface, why not change the shape of the pick, too? Just a little bit. As long as the picks were the standard sizes and thicknesses and were in the basic shape of a rounded triangle, why couldn't they be shaped like skulls, or hearts, or alien heads—or for that matter, Mickey Mouse (which by the way, we eventually licensed from Disney)?

We had some skull picks made and took them to the largest music trade show in America, where we gave away the Grave Picker, as we called it. Our booth was packed. I knew then and there we had a hit.

But I also knew from market research I had done that the two companies dominating the market would never license my idea, because it was too novel and the owners were guitar players. You see, guitar picks had been the same shape for 80 years. I do not play the guitar, but Rob does. At first, he thought my idea was nuts, too. But then he saw that it worked, and he knew it would sell. Because he had had a music store for 15 years, he also knew all the distributors. We figured the picks would cost only pennies to make, and we even knew a guy in town who could make them for us. A million picks could fit

continued

under my desk, so storing inventory wouldn't be a problem. I could do the designs; Rob could do the selling. How hard could it be?

Hard. Very hard. I've never worked harder in my life. I worked six long days a week. I had to wear many different hats. It took about a quarter million dollars to get the company up and running. We had no idea it was going to cost that much and be that much work. Making and selling a few guitar picks out of your garage is one thing. But to be successful, we had to produce and sell large volumes. Our picks ended up in more than 10,000 stores worldwide. HotPicks became a big player in a small industry in a short period of time. I had a blast! I got to work with some great bands and great people, like Taylor Swift and her family. And I had complete control.

But it took $250,000, a time frame of more than a year, and a lot of blood, sweat, and tears to get there. In comparison, I can develop a product for licensing in less than 30 days and for under $500—something I had already done successfully 20 times . . . and had a fantastic time doing it.

With HotPicks, I had stopped being creative and was just running a business. It got to be not so much fun. So I sold the company to Rob and some investors and went back to innovating and licensing my ideas, which fits me to a tee.

As you can see, I learned firsthand that licensing takes a heck of a lot less time, effort, and money than launching and running a manufacturing company does. Dollar for dollar, hour for hour, and task for task, licensing is a cheaper, faster, and easier way to get your idea to market. True, you lose some control, but you gain the freedom to create even *more* great ideas. You also have the freedom to live and work wherever you choose. Even though you get a smaller share of profits, you have a *lot less to do* and a *lot less to lose*. And licensing can be very lucrative. Just ask the thousands of people, like me, who are enjoying the licensing lifestyle.

You can, too. All you need is one simple idea.

PART TWO

Find Your Million-Dollar Idea

Do you frequently think of ideas for new and better products and wish, *If only I could make a living doing this!*

Have you ever felt frustrated because you can't find the perfect product and wondered, *Why doesn't someone come up with a product that is exactly what I'm looking for?*

When you hear about someone who has come up with a simple idea that forever changed his life for the better, do you think, *Why can't I do something like that?*

Well, you can. Anyone can. Great ideas are everywhere, hiding in plain sight. You just need to know where to find them and how to mine them.

4

Look for Marketable Ideas

Most people innovate backward. They develop a product to solve a problem that bothers them personally without first confirming that it bothers the market universally. They dream up a product without first identifying who will use it, how, and why. They conjure up a clever idea—thinking, *Man, this is going to be mind-blowing! Nothing like it out there!* Then they build a prototype, file a patent, and start making and marketing it—without first identifying the market, qualifying the market, or even knowing whether there *is* a market for it.

Not surprisingly, most of those ideas fail. In fact, most ideas that are patented never make more than or even as much money as the cost of the patent itself. Why? Primarily because the designer innovated for the sake of innovation rather than for the benefit of the market.

There is a better way to innovate. It is this simple: instead of creating a new market for your idea, create an idea for what's missing and needed in an *existing* market. In my experience and the experience of countless others, the fastest, easiest, and most profitable road to licensing success is with an evolutionary idea, not a revolutionary one. It's with giving a new twist, a small tweak, or a unique value to a proven product. It's with a simple idea.

But don't mistake simple for mundane. In today's global churn, where innovation is the order of the day, creativity is king. Whatever your idea is, it has to stand out in the marketplace. It has to offer something that competitors don't offer *and* that consumers want. It has to have that touch of creative genius.

Don't let that scare you, though. Virtually anyone can come up with a simple but creative idea that has great licensing potential. Sure, coming up with novel ideas comes naturally to some people. They look at a glob of bread dough and see Play-Doh. They see a child trip over his untied shoelaces and instantly think, *Velcro fasteners!* They look at an ID tag that's slipped off a dog collar and think, *pet microchip!* But most people need to look harder and longer at many things for an idea to materialize.

No matter how creative you are or are not, there are tools and methods you can use to find marketable ideas.

A Few Practical Tips

Ideas can come from many different places and at any time. I get some of my best ideas when I'm driving and, of course, when I'm shopping. For some people, their most creative ideas come when they're taking a shower or bath or while going for a walk. Some prefer retreating to a quiet place that blocks out distractions; others are more creative in the thick of things, where their ideas can cross-pollinate with whatever is going on around them.

Nobody creates in a vacuum, though. Everybody needs inspiration and information to come up with marketable ideas. Trust me, you'll be doing a lot of researching, brainstorming, gathering information, asking questions, making observations, taking photos, sketching out your ideas, and checking out lots of different things. So you'll need some basic tools for collecting all of that information.

Here are a few simple suggestions:

- Keep your iPad, BlackBerry, or other mobile note-taking device, or even a small paper notebook and a couple of pens, with you wherever you go.
- Take a small digital camera or a smartphone shopping with you. As they say, a picture is worth a thousand words. With a smartphone, you can take a photo of an interesting product and add a few notes about it in a heartbeat.

- Keep a small audio recorder in your car so you can record your ideas without looking away from the road to jot them down. If the shower or bathtub is your creativity hub of choice, keep the recorder within arm's reach (but don't get it wet). Again, a smartphone that has the ability to audio record and replay is a great all-in-one tool for researching marketable ideas.
- Keep a drawing pad and some pencils wherever you brainstorm and work on your ideas. Some people can draw their ideas electronically on a computer or mobile device. I prefer to sketch out my ideas by hand.
- Keep all the information for your ideas in one place. That includes anything that inspires you or helps stimulate your creativity. The free program Evernote can help you keep track of what you find online.

And, you'll need access to the Internet. When I began inventing for the marketplace decades ago, I did most of my research by visiting retail stores in person and walking their aisles. Today, the Internet is your best market research tool. The amount of information on the web is astounding, and most of it is free. Although I personally think that in-store visits are invaluable to a product designer, I rely heavily on information I find online. These days, there are many more products available online than there are in stores, and doing market research via a computer will help you cut down on the time you spend studying a category.

OK, now that you've got the basic tools of the trade in place, it's time to find a market that gets your creative motor running.

Study the Marketplace

It's one thing to create a product you like. It's quite another to design a product that consumers like and will buy. Companies are only interested in licensing ideas they're convinced will sell. To be convinced of that, they must see not only how the idea fits into the market but also how it is unique. If there are too many products similar to yours and your idea doesn't offer a truly unique value, the market may be too saturated to allow room for your idea. On the other hand, if there are no products similar to yours out there, there may not be a viable market for your idea.

That's why it's vitally important to study the market. It is the best way to figure out which market you want to work in, brainstorm ideas that will sell in that market, and design your idea *for* the market.

The most marketable ideas are those that solve problems, address needs, or satisfy desires. In other words, they provide value that consumers are willing to pay for. When I came up with the idea for the Michael Jordan Wall Ball, I knew kids didn't need it. It didn't solve a problem; there were other indoor basketball games on the market that worked fine. But there weren't any indoor basketball hoops with Michael Jordan's image on them, and I knew kids would want one.

Large companies spend millions of dollars on market research trying to identify consumer wants, needs, and problems and to generate ideas for meeting them. I just went to Toys"R"Us and walked the aisles. I love basketball, so I checked out all the basketball stuff. I looked at what was on the shelves and tried to imagine ways to make a small change that would have a big impact. I also observed how kids responded to the basketball products on the shelves, and it didn't take long to see that they loved anything with Michael Jordan on it.

Of course, my shopping excursions only planted the seed of an idea. I had to do more market research to germinate that idea: to figure out how to design it, how much it should cost, who might license it, and so on. Doing market research didn't cost me anything. All it took was some ingenuity and some of my time.

You can and should do the same thing. You should study the marketplace, first to find a market or product category to design for and then to come up with an innovative idea *for* that market. You can't rely on assumptions and guesses; you need real-world information. If you come up with an idea without studying the market first, there's a good chance that you'll reinvent a product that already exists, which is a waste of time.

As you go about studying the marketplace, these are some important goals to keep in mind.

- Discover what markets are hot and emerging trends. Check out websites, blogs, social networking groups, online forums, trade and consumer magazines (I read *Wired* and *Fast Company* religiously), TV shows, and industry newsletters that focus on or cover market trends. Go shopping, look at new products, and ask store managers which items are hot.
- Learn as much as you can about a specific market: customer demographics, the companies providing most of the products, the range of products within the market, and so on.
- Check out existing products in the market: assess their features and functions, strengths and weaknesses, prices and popularity.
- Evaluate how your idea stacks up against the competition; figure out your idea's unique value proposition: what it offers that comparative products do not.
- Figure out where your idea fits into the market: determine who will buy your product, how they will use it, where they will buy it, and how much they might pay for it.
- Find out how your idea might be manufactured and packaged.
- Determine the manufacturing price point as well as the retail price point.

To gather this information, you don't have to go through the long, complicated, and expensive market research process that companies go through. There are simple ways for you to study the market—and they're free.

Go Shopping: Become an Expert in a Micro-Category!

If you're fishing for a market that's rich with innovation opportunities, cast a wide net and see what you come up with. Start getting your feet wet by going to the mall and big-box general retailers, like Walmart and Target, and walking the aisles. Go to specialty stores that carry products you're interested in or curious about as well. Take your time and really look at the merchandise. Ask the store manager or store clerks which products are new, which are selling well, and which are duds.

Take note of products customers are drooling over and buying—and which they're passing over.

If you find yourself being drawn to a certain product or product category, focus on that area of the store. Examine the products more closely. Check out variations in design, quality, size, packaging, and price. Notice which products have the most shelf space and the most prominent displays. Take notes and photos of products that pique your interest or that you sense offer innovation opportunities. You can do additional research by browsing consumer magazines and catalogs.

However, you don't have to go to a brick-and-mortar store to do your market research. It used to be that you could view the entire world of consumer products by visiting a few retailers and examining their shelves. That's no longer true. Today's marketplace is far more complex than it was 20 years ago—which is why I encourage my students to do the bulk of their research from the comfort of their own laptops. Major retailers have online stores, of course, but there are also innumerable online specialty stores and shopping hubs.

I'm going to tell you how to do the same kind of market research I just described over the Internet, rather than in a retail store. Let me start out by saying that the goal of studying the marketplace in the way I am about to describe—which is what I instruct my students to do—is to *become an expert in a micro-category*. What do I mean by micro-category? Well, a category like school supplies is far too large to become an expert in. But becoming an expert on binders, for example, is doable in a relatively short amount of time—between one and three hours. That's more than enough time for you to determine whether or not you want to move forward in that micro-category. If you attempt to study too large a category, you may become overwhelmed. So make sure to focus in on a narrow micro-category. By the time you finish, there's a good chance that you will know more about binders than someone who works at Office Depot.

As you go about studying the market, here are several questions you will want to answer about the category you select:

- **What is selling well?** Determining what is selling is easy: if you see the same product or similar products over and over again, it's selling. The same goes for specific features. If you observe that most products have the same feature, that's a feature you should plan on including in your innovation as well.

- **What are the benefits of the products that are selling?** Why would a consumer buy one product over another? What value does a product offer relative to another?
- **What are the price points of these products?** What's low? What's high? If most binders are retailing for about a dollar, and you come up with an idea for a binder that is going to retail for $5, that may be a problem. It might not. The point is that you should be aware of this information up front.
- **Do you notice that there are certain groups of products?** If so, start grouping similar products together.

Start out by identifying a general category that intrigues you and that you are interested in. Spend 15 to 30 minutes looking broadly into that category before narrowing your focus on a micro-category. Does the category still intrigue you? Are you excited? If so, what products are you most interested in? Look into that micro-category. (If the category no longer interests you and/or you don't think that you are capable of coming up with anything for it, don't sweat it. Simply move on and start over with another micro-category.)

You have two excellent Google search tools at your disposal: Google Images and Google Shopping. Plan on using your computer browser to bookmark important web pages as well as having a pen and paper nearby to take notes. There's something about scribbling my thoughts down in print that helps me be more creative.

First, go to http://www.google.com/images. This search engine will generate literally thousands of images of products available for sale, historical items, advertising and marketing programs using your type of product, and a myriad of other images—even artwork, movies, and music group logos. Click on Settings to access its "Advanced" search feature and type in a few keywords. When you first start searching, it's a good idea to keep your terms broad. The best way of studying the market is to start out broadly and then get more specific. Eventually, I suggest you search for as specific a product as you can describe.

You don't want to start with too narrow a search, though, because you might miss something that sparks an idea, but you do eventually want to get as close to your exact micro-category as possible.

Let's continue on with the binder example. Type in "binder" and start scrolling. Your goal is to learn as much about the items you see as possible. What are they made of? How much do they cost? Where are they sold? Who manufactures them? As you scroll through the images of binders, click on the products to learn more about them. The image you select will become larger, and a link to its source will appear. In many cases, when the image links to a web page, I find out more valuable information. The web page may be a blog post reviewing the product or a retailer that is selling the product. As you click through, start making observations. What separates different products from one other? What is unique about the different binders that you see? What benefits do they offer? What types of consumers are buying and using binders?

After I do a Google Images search, I do a Google Shopping search. Google Shopping searches allow you to filter by price, which is helpful. Click on a product and check out its reviews. What are consumers saying? Do they have any complaints about the product? Amazon.com is a great resource for doing market research because you can read what consumers have to say. Read the reviews of similar products. It's like a free focus group. You may find some nugget of information that gets your brain churning about how to improve a product right away.

After you've written down your observations, think about how you can add value to the micro-category. Are there any obvious holes? Can you make a slight tweak to something that is selling well?

You can learn a lot in a short amount of time by doing market research this way. Never assume you know everything about a micro-category simply because you use a certain product. You aren't an expert until you do the research. You will find products via Google Images you've never seen before in stores—I guarantee it! When you invent for the marketplace by studying the marketplace, you set yourself up for success. To put it simply, you're much more likely to come up with a good idea—and be able to license it!

Check Out the Movers and Shakers

There are usually three or four big companies that produce most of the products in a given market. To identify them, just check the products you research in stores or online; the manufacturer's name is stamped somewhere on the product, its packaging, or both. Then go to the websites of those manufacturers and review their product pages or online catalogs. Go to their media pages and read any new product releases or articles. Some manufacturers have online stores with retail prices and product descriptions. Some have product pages with wholesale pricing lists.

Other good places to research comparative products and product trends are catalogs, trade magazines, trade organizations, and trade shows. It seems like every trade show has a section with new products, and every trade magazine, industry blog, and trade association website covers new products. Industry experts who lecture and give workshops always talk about where their industry is going.

Watch and Listen

Many of the top design firms, like IDEO, and even some design schools are advocating "innovation through observation." *Innovation through observation* is observing how people use products at home, at work, or at play to identify their wants, needs, and desires. And it works. Companies routinely come up with new products by observing consumers, conducting focus groups and surveys, and asking the right questions. As previously mentioned, I created the Michael Jordan Wall Ball after just one day of observation.

You can do the same thing. In fact, going shopping to check out comparative products is a form of market observation. But you can go even further with this concept. You can observe people actually using a product similar to yours and watch for ways to improve or enhance it. You can solicit users' opinions and ask pointed questions, listening for cues about how to give your idea an added value or a unique sizzle that other products don't have.

For example, if I was interested in hammers, I could go to a construction site and observe carpenters using a hammer. I could go to a friend or a small business owner in my community who builds cabinets or furniture. I could spend a few hours shadowing people as they use a hammer, or better yet, several different hammers. I could ask them what sizes, styles, and name brands of hammers they use; what they like and dislike about each; what's missing; what material their ideal hammer would be made of; and what it would look, feel, and perform like.

When observing, here are some innovation opportunities to watch and listen for:

- Small details that are easy to overlook but equally easy to improve upon
- Flaws or gaps in form or function
- Inefficiencies and inconveniences
- Boring or outdated materials and styles
- Differences in the way different people use or view the product
- Unconventional use of the product
- Other products that people use for the same or a similar purpose
- Potential applications of existing technology

Whether you observe by shopping or by watching and talking with potential consumers of your product, make sure to record your findings. Take notes. Take photos of the products. And take heed of what you've observed. Because, and this is really important, you must be willing and able to adjust your idea to fit the market. Otherwise, consumers won't buy it, and if consumers won't buy it, companies won't license it.

Discover Sleeping Dinosaurs

Finding a sleeping dinosaur simply means finding an opportunity to update or spruce up something that has been around, relatively unchanged, for a long time. It's taking a classic product and breathing new life into it. It's making a small change that packs a big wallop.

For example, when I was at Worlds of Wonder (WOW) in the late 1980s, Paul Rago was the vice president of marketing. Before that, he had been a schoolteacher. Paul came up with ideas by looking at how kids play traditional childhood games and then updating them. One day he decided to take a look at a game kids have been playing forever: tag. "What can we do to update tag?" he asked himself and his team of engineers. "Is there any technology we can apply to tag?" Sure enough, they came up with Lazer Tag, using infrared technology. It was a huge hit and quickly became the top-selling toy for WOW.

Paul Rago applied that same approach to a couple of other things, with amazing results. He looked at all the things kids used in school and created ways to make them fun and fashionable. He looked at the basic backpack and duffel bag, really functional items, and said, "Let's make them denim." It was such a simple change that it's amazing no one else had thought of it, especially considering that denim was really popular with kids at the time. Everything was denim—jeans, jackets, shorts, shirts, shoes. Why not bags? It was Paul who asked that question and acted on it. Sack-It became one of the top-selling bags in the world.

He did the same thing with other back-to-school products, creating a whole new product line at WOW called Class Act. Among those designs were cool organizers for lockers and a little recording device for leaving a message for a friend, instead of writing a note and slipping it in his or her locker. Paul brought creativity and technology to a category of products where none had existed before.

Like Paul, you can find those sleeping dinosaurs and revitalize them by making them current. Just look at a product that's been around for a while in a new light. Envision how it would look and work if you jazzed it up or applied new technology to it. Just revamping a sleeping dinosaur a little bit can breathe new life into it, giving consumers an added value and incentive to buy and giving companies a way to boost profits.

Another great example of a former sleeping dinosaur is the guitar pick. Picks had remained essentially unchanged for decades—forever really—until my business partner and I decided to reinvent them. At the time, picks were boring. We observed that they had little to no personalization. They came in solid colors and didn't have any graphics; when you went to buy them at a music store, you had to rummage around for the one you wanted in a fishing tackle box. After determining that changing their shape wouldn't affect how guitarists played with them, we had fun. We modified picks to look like ghouls, vampires, devils, and other eerie characters to appeal to the heavy metal crowd. Eventually, we became a Disney licensee and printed picks with images of Mickey Mouse on them. We debuted a line of picks for young girls with bright colors and patterns called "Girls Rock." We even made customized picks for Taylor Swift. Needless to say, they were a hit. We sold tens of millions of picks and won "Best in Show" at NAMM two years in a row. And the idea truly couldn't have been simpler.

5

Get Creative!

CREATIVITY PLAYS a big role in all aspects of bringing an idea to market. It enables you to come up with novel ideas and to develop those ideas into marketable products. It helps you find fast, easy, inexpensive, and effective ways to prototype your idea. It definitely comes in handy when you're creating your one-line benefit statement and your sell sheet. Your creativity is also an asset when it comes to protecting your idea, figuring out whether it's doable, finding potential licensees, and getting a company to say yes to your idea.

Everyone is creative. Being creative is simply looking at something from a different perspective. It's turning something upside-down and looking at it through a child's eyes, seeing no limitations, seeing only possibilities. Creativity comes naturally to children; they look at the world with wonder and with no boundaries. Everything is new; anything is possible. I remember, as a kid, thinking I could fly—first by flapping my arms, and then, later, by building a jet pack and strapping it on my back.

I believe a streak of childlike creativity resides inside each of us. We don't really lose our creativity as adults. It's just that bearing the weight of the world on our shoulders—all that responsibility we carry around all the time—causes our creativity to be shoved into a small dark corner. But everyone is or can be creative. You just need to tap into that childlike creativity within.

I also believe creativity is a process that anyone is capable of developing. Creativity is about problem solving. It's about wondering how and why, and thinking outside the box. It's about examining what is and asking *what if*. I've found that creativity improves with practice—through constantly looking "differently" at many different things.

I also believe that passion drives creativity and that creativity should be *fun*.

Follow Your Passion

My dad's advice to me when I was trying to figure out what to do with my life—"find what you're passionate about"—makes sense not only when it comes to finding your profession, but also for finding design ideas. There is no better place to look for opportunities to design new and better products than in areas that are of interest or importance to you. I love the toy and novelty gift markets, and that's where many of my most successful ideas have come from. When I read about how many over-the-counter medications lack crucial information, some-times with dire consequences, I was inspired to create one of my most successful innovations, the Spinformation label.

Maybe you're passionate about child development or the envi-ronment. Maybe gardening is your thing, or fishing. Maybe you're a tool nut or a pet lover. Maybe you're into kitchen doodads or electronic gadgets. Whatever turns you on, turn to *that* to find a market or product category for which you might want to design a product.

Is there a store or type of store that you frequent even when you're not buying anything? A catalog you pore over? A hobby or trade magazine you read, including the ads, to find out what's new and interesting? A trade or product show you attend to keep up on the latest and greatest trends? As you go about your normal routine, keep your eyes and mind open for potential markets for your yet-to-be-discovered ideas.

Who knows? Maybe you'll find an idea that combines two things you're passionate about, like home improvement and the environment, pets and electronics, or fishing and child development.

Browse the Mall, Magazines, and Internet

Oftentimes when I'm looking for a new idea and my creativity seems to be blocked, I will visit the local mall. I'll go into the stores and look at all the merchandise, not only stuff I might be interested in developing or purchasing, but everything. I'll sit in the middle of the mall and watch people shop in the stores. I'll observe what types of products they are purchasing and what products they're drawn to. I'll go into some of the stores and talk with the manager and employees. I'll ask them what's hot and what's not, what trends they are noticing in buying habits. Often they will spill their guts and give me way more information than I needed. Sometimes they even tell me how their sales have been doing for the last week or month. This type of inside information can be important when developing new products.

That is how I came up with my idea for a fun, interactive cup for kids. I went into the Disney store at my local mall and asked the manager what the store's most popular product was. He said it was the colorful cups. I saw that some of the plastic cups had a double-layer outer wall. The back layer was a color (red, blue, yellow, etc.), the front layer was clear plastic, and there were sparkles between the two layers. I immediately thought of other images and games you could put between the two layers of plastic, which kids could play by rotating the outer layer of the cup: different dresses for Minnie Mouse; a numbers game with 101 Dalmatians; and Sesame Street characters spelling out names. I had actually come up with a similar idea for paper cups a couple of years before, but it was too expensive to manufacture, so I had put it aside. Now I realized the idea could be adapted for plastic cups. I looked on the bottom of the cups in the Disney store and saw the manufacturer's name, Trudeau. The manufacturer licensed the idea from me, and for five years my rotating character cups were sold in every Disney store and theme park worldwide.

Another place I go to get my creative juices flowing is the bookstore. I go to the magazine aisle, look at all of the trendy entertainment and fashion magazines, and check out what the celebrities are wearing or using. I can spend hours at a time reading those magazines, and sometimes doing so sparks an idea that's a simple but unique twist on a hot product. These days, there is also an abundance of engaging podcasts that get my brain going by posing thoughtful questions, relating the stories and experiences of unique people, and providing answers to questions I hadn't even thought of.

And of course, I also browse the web to spark my creativity—it is the largest library in the world, after all. Reading the news as well as my favorite blogs keeps my finger on the pulse of what's going on in the world, which I think is important. What do consumers care about? What are they looking for? How are attitudes and norms changing? Good inventing doesn't happen in a vacuum.

In addition to broadly examining popular culture, I focus in more closely on the industries that matter to me. I consistently innovate for the packaging industry, so I read packaging trade publications every so often. I look at design publications for the same reason.

I think it's easier to find inspiration today than it ever has been. For example, a project I worked on recently had to do with promotional cups. I typed "creative cups" into Google and started clicking on the thousands of images that popped up. Suddenly and with little effort on my part, I had access to creative and fun designs from all over the world.

When I first started out, the Internet didn't exist, so I had to rely on visiting the mall and bookstores. I still think there's a lot of value in getting away from your computer and out of your home to spark your creativity, but today I am often inspired by what I discover online. So, you don't have to leave the comfort of your home to get started.

Make a Game of It!

Just sitting at your desk and attempting to pull ideas out of your head is not the most effective way of generating a creative idea. Sometimes you need to feed your brain to stimulate creative thought. There are a number of ways to do that: go shopping, watch a current movie, take a walk, read a magazine, or go to a crowded café and people watch. In fact, making new friends always helps me; they usually have an entirely different perspective. Another way to poke your creativity is to change your habits: take an alternate route to work, listen to a new radio station, read a magazine, or shop at a new store.

When you're in idea-brainstorming mode, don't worry about whether your ideas are good or bad. Don't force or restrict the process. Just let your inhibitions and your mind go. Let the child in you come out. Make a game of it.

The following are three fun games I play to come up with ideas: Mix and Match, What If… and Solve It. Remember, when you play these games, there are no good or bad ideas. You're only playing, just exercising your creative muscle. If a good idea comes out of it, fantastic. If not, it's still good practice, and you might resurrect that idea one day and reinvigorate it into something even better. If you want to design and license your ideas, you'll need to come up with lots of ideas. So whatever you can do to keep the ideas flowing, do it.

Mix and Match

Pick two different items. Imagine how you might combine these two items to make a completely new product. For example, one of the most popular products right now is the camera phone. Someone simply combined a cell phone with a digital camera. When playing Mix and Match, I recommend combining two products that are normally found together—at least when you're new to this. It's usually much easier to find ways to combine two products used in the kitchen than it is to combine a product used in the kitchen with a product used in the garage.

That said, it is entirely possible to mix and match two products that seemingly have nothing in common—that is, until someone looks at them differently. For example, John Osher's SpinBrush—an electric toothbrush that cost a fraction of what electric toothbrushes at the time cost—was inspired by the Spin Pop, a lollipop that twirls in your mouth when you push a button on the figurine "handle." Toy candy meets dental hygiene. Now, *that's* a winning game of Mix and Match!

What If . . .

This is one of my favorite design games to play. I look at a product and ask, "What if this product did something totally different?" For example, I might look at a hammer and ask, "What if this hammer could hit a nail straight every time?" One of my students, Todd Basche, asked: "What if a combination lock had letters, instead of numbers, so you could spell out your secret code?" He now has a successful product, Wordlock, which is sold in tens of thousands of stores around the world.

Another great example of What If... (and this has changed an entire industry) is Netflix. In the old days of Hollywood Video and Blockbuster, consumers were charged hefty late fees if they did not return their video rentals on time. Someone asked, "What if there were no late fees?" and Netflix became viable. Now, new companies are asking, "What if consumers could just order a movie from their living room?" Questions are powerful!

Solve It

To play this game, I observe problems that I or other individuals face every day and try to come up with solutions to those problems. For example, after reading an article that stated there is never enough space on product labels to fit all the required and desired information, I solved the problem by inventing Spinformation, which increased the labeling space by 75 percent. The concept is simple: it's two labels, one on top of the other, both held in place with a fixed band. The bottom label is stationary; the top label is a thin plastic film with a clear window on it. The top label spins around the container revealing the information on the base label through the window.

Solving problems is the most common way that inventors and product developers come up with ideas. They see a problem in their own lives and try to solve it. You need to be careful, though, because what you think is a problem may not be a problem for everyone, or there may already be a solution to the problem out there that you are unaware of.

Observation is the best way to use this game. Observing and talking to others is a great way to identify a problem with a broad scope, which you can then come up with a unique solution for. That way, instead of innovating for yourself, you're innovating for the market, which is the most direct path to licensing your ideas.

PLAYING WITH A $20 MILLION SLEEPING DINOSAUR

If you go to the outdoor water toy aisle of any retailer, you'll see an array of squirt guns of varying sizes, shapes, colors, dimensions, and blasting power. That was not the case 20-some years ago when Lonnie Johnson created the Super Soaker, the first pressurized water gun. At the time, all squirt guns were the same basic, tired design they had been for decades.

Lonnie, a NASA scientist and an inventor by trade, was actually working on a design for a Freon-less heat pump that used water as a working fluid, propelled by jets. When one of the jets accidentally shot a stream of water across the bathroom where he was doing an experiment, he thought, "This would make a great water gun."

Within a year of its debut in 1990, the Super Soaker was the top-selling toy in the United States. And this new twist on an old toy earned Lonnie Johnson about $20 million in royalties.

Lonnie took a sleeping dinosaur and reinvigorated it by playing Mix and Match with a classic water toy and advanced water-jet technology. Of all his inventions, Lonnie ranks the Super Soaker as one of his top three favorites.

Coming up with great ideas and bringing them to market can, and should, be fun. If, like Lonnie, you follow your passion and use your creativity during each of the 10 steps outlined in *One Simple Idea*, you'll enjoy the game and win it!

6

How to Pick Winners

OK, YOU'VE followed your passion, studied the market, poked some sleeping dinosaurs, identified a few hot markets, and brainstormed a slew of intriguing ideas that are buzzing around in your head like a swarm of bees. Now you need to hone in on the best ideas. After you do that, you'll narrow your focus even more and pick one simple idea to work on—the one that lights a fire in your belly because your research and gut tells you it's a winner.

The Four Characteristics of a Winning Idea

You're going to have a lot of ideas, and you need to be able to quickly distinguish between the winners and the losers. I still get lots of ideas, and I love all of them! But I'm very selective about which ones I pursue. I only work on potential winners, and I make that determination quickly.

If you want to be successful at this, you, too, need to be able to quickly assess an idea to determine whether it's worth moving forward with before you say, "OK, now I'm going to work on this." At the end of the day, it's not about how big or small, how complex or simple, or how unique or clever your idea is. It's about which idea is going to take the least amount of work *and* has the highest probability of success.

Many people struggle with this. They come up with a bunch of ideas, and they can't decide which one to work on first or they try to work on several at the same time. You can't work on all 10 of your ideas at once! It is more productive to focus on one idea at a time when you're just starting out.

I also recommend taking a simple idea all the way through the entire development and licensing process before beginning to work on your other ideas. It's just so much easier and faster to bring an idea to market that is an enhancement, improvement, or unique takeoff on a proven product. Once you've gotten your feet wet, you'll be more efficient with your next idea. As you get some successes under your belt, you'll get better and faster at zeroing in on whether an idea is marketable and on how to design it to fit the market.

So especially in the beginning, it pays to stick with simple ideas in a proven market. More complicated ideas take longer to develop and can present you with some real challenges. You don't want your first few ideas to hang you up. That will just discourage and frustrate you. You want to get going, get through all the steps, and get your ideas in front of the right people and into the marketplace so you can start collecting royalties.

This is a good time to point out a few arenas that are particularly challenging. I'm talking about the software industry, the packaging industry, industries that have only one or two major players, and ideas that require educating the consumer. You should think twice about trying to license an idea you have for the software industry unless you have worked in it as well as have a technical background. Even then, though, I would caution you against it, because the industry is very rapidly changing, and intellectual property on software is currently very difficult to obtain. (Tech companies are up in arms suing one another over infringements at the moment.) I know firsthand that to successfully license an idea to the packaging industry, you really need to have prior knowledge of manufacturing. Industries that have only one or two major players (and not anyone else) can be hard to break into, because they control the market. They don't have any incentive to innovate. And finally, you should know that companies don't want to have to educate the consumer about an idea because it's extremely expensive and time-consuming. An easy idea to license is one that you can explain in a sentence and the person gets it. If you have to spend a lot of time explaining your idea to someone, more likely than not you have a problem on your hands.

On the other hand, there are some industries that my students have had a lot of success with. I'm talking about the pet, kitchen/household, hardware, novelty gift, and direct-response television industries. Companies in these spheres are very actively looking for your ideas!

Let's move on. Whenever I come up with an idea I'm interested in, I give it this four-step litmus test to see if it's a potential winner worth pursuing further:

1. Does it solve a common problem?
2. Does it have a wow factor?
3. Does it have a large market?
4. Does it use common production methods and materials?

Does It Solve a Common Problem?

The idea with the best chance of success is one that virtually anyone can look at and immediately understand how it solves an everyday problem, satisfies a prevalent need or want, or fills an obvious void in the market. As a rule of thumb, the more universal the problem and your solution, the easier it is to license it.

Companies don't want to have to educate the market about a product or create a new market for a product. They're like me: they like ideas that are simple to explain and whose unique value is obvious. They want ideas that consumers will take one look at and say, "I get it. I love it! I see how it benefits me. I want it."

Don't assume there's a need for your idea, and don't base your determination on guesswork. Study the market and do whatever homework is necessary to determine whether your idea solves a common problem. Confirmed and well-defined needs are a lot easier to license than maybes. Take, for example, a simple idea for unclogging household drains that my good friend Gene Luoma came up with. Everyone has sink, shower, or tub drains in his or her home, and every drain gets clogged at one time or another. Gene studied products for unclogging drains on the market and came up with a better solution for this common problem.

He observed that when a drain gets clogged, most people reach for a plunger. When that doesn't work, they pour in liquid or crystal drain cleaners, which don't always work and, as Gene noted, are both expensive and toxic. He learned that some people try to unclog drains with a coat hanger, which rarely works, or with a plumber's snake, which only works if you know what you're doing (if you don't, you can damage the plumbing). As a last resort, he learned, people just call in a plumber, which is *very* expensive. And a plumber may not be available for hours or even days.

Gene created an effective alternative to the other options for unclogging drains that were available in the market. The Zip-It Clean is a long, flexible plastic gadget with barbs on it that, when placed down the drain and rotated back and forth, grabs the hair and other gunk and removes it when pulled out of the drain. It's become a huge hit! That's because Gene designed an innovative solution for a problem that is nearly universal. He studied the market to determine what was missing and wisely based his design off of that.

Does It Have a Wow Factor?

How does your idea stack up against its competition? Is it going to stand out in the crowd? Does it have one clear and exciting benefit that other comparable products don't and that consumers want? As I've said, a small change to an existing product is often the most marketable, but it still has to sizzle. It has to grab the attention of potential buyers and make them want to open their wallets. It has to wow potential licensees, dazzling them with some outstanding feature they know will give them a competitive edge and making them want to license your idea.

Again, never assume that the market is as crazy about your idea as you are. Do some comparison shopping, talk with store clerks, observe customers, and verify that your idea has a wow factor that sets it apart from the competition.

Does It Have a Large Market?

When I develop a product, I want all the major retailers for that product category to sell it, and I want them to sell a lot of it, because an idea with that kind of potential market really motivates potential licensees. Sometimes I work on ideas with a smaller market, but only if I think I can find a licensee for it relatively quickly and easily. Often, it takes as much time and work to license a big-market idea as it does to license an idea with a moderate-sized market, so it just makes sense to put most of your time where the most money is. Before you decide to move forward with an idea, you should find out whether the potential market for your idea is big enough.

Estimating the size of the potential market for your idea is easy: just study the market. Find out whether the product category is a growth category, whether comparable products are selling well, and how similar products are priced. Get a profile of the industry or product category, including what is selling, who is buying, what they're paying, whether sales are increasing or declining, who the major players are, any up and coming trends, and so on. You can find this information through search engines, shopping, industry experts, trade associations, trade magazines (media kits often include industry profiles), marketing think tanks, and other resources.

Does It Use Common Production Methods and Materials?

Once you've piqued a potential licensee's interest in your idea, the first two questions the licensee will ask are, "How will it be manufactured?" and "How much will that cost?" In Chapter 9 you'll learn how to find and give the right answers to those two critical questions. But for now, to decide whether to even work on the idea, you need to get a feel for how doable and affordable it is to produce. That's easy enough to find out. If your idea can be manufactured using technology, materials, manufacturing equipment, and production processes that already exist, then it's definitely doable. If those methods and materials are already being used widely in your product category, then your idea is probably affordable—and profitable—for a potential licensee to produce.

Again, this is where your market research really pays off. In addition to your own findings, it really helps to cultivate a network of industry experts that you can call on. Among your network, you may even find a mentor to help guide you through difficult dealings.

Find Someone Who Has Done It Before

My father used to say, "Whatever you do in life, find someone who has already done it, get as close as you can, and learn as much as you can." I didn't know it then, but that was great advice. And it's one of the best pieces of advice I can give to anyone who wants to license his or her ideas.

So many people try to do this on their own, with no input from an insider who really knows the market. Frankly, I think that's crazy. I've been developing and licensing products, and I can't tell you how often I'll be working on a new idea and very quickly realize that I don't have all the information. So my first step is always to study the market. And my next is to find experts in that field and pick their brains.

If your idea is a gag gift, find someone who designs, makes, or sells novelty items or who has firsthand knowledge of that industry, such as a trade magazine editor or a trade association leader. If your idea is a kitchen gadget, find an expert in that product category. If your idea is a cool twist on a punching bag, find a leader in the sporting goods industry. Find out who the major players are and what they have to say about what's going on in the market. Read trade magazines. Visit the websites of the top designers and manufacturers in the field. Go to trade shows where they are presenting, sit in on their lectures, and talk with them.

Talk with them? Yes, talk with them. I realize that asking a stranger for help can seem intimidating, even impossible. But it is possible. There *is* someone out there who is willing and able to give you advice and information. Many people who have achieved success are glad to share what they've learned. They're in a position to help, and they want others to succeed too. Some pros are even willing to take on a protégé, to be your mentor—to show you the ropes. A knowledgeable and accessible mentor will be invaluable in helping you assess the viability of your idea and then develop it for the market.

You just need to find these experts and ask for the help you need. The worst that can happen is someone will say no. Keep looking until you find someone who is ready, willing, and able to give back.

How to Find a Pro

To find a pro who might be able and willing to answer my questions, I go online and search for an expert in that field. For example, if I were working on a healthcare product, I would look for someone who has written an article, given a seminar, or been a speaker at a trade show or conference geared toward the healthcare products industry. I might call the editor of a trade magazine or a trade association and ask for the name of someone who really knows whatever product category I'm working in. I might go to a trade show and look for someone to network with there.

When I find someone who has the experience I'm looking for, I start out by trying to establish a relationship with that person. Whenever you reach out to someone you want help from, take the time to craft a meaningful, well-written, and *brief* message. Always remember to stroke the expert's ego first. Why have you decided to reach out to him or her in particular? Let the person know. Compliment pros on their successful products and acknowledge their expertise. Have you read something they have written? State that. Flattery will get you far. Then, explain who you are in one or two sentences. Make sure that the expert you reach out to can speak to your questions. I sometimes receive messages asking for my opinion regarding subjects I am not an expert on, which confuses me. Don't make any demands and don't ramble. When I receive long e-mails asking for help, I don't read them, because I feel like my time is being wasted. The best relationships start off slowly! And finally, use e-mail to make a request if you can. (It's fine to ask for someone's contact information over social media, but I would save a serious conversation for a more serious medium.) Experts want to help you. Make it easy for them to do so.

I am always able to find someone who is willing, able, and qualified to give me the information, advice, or opinion I need—or at least direct me to someone else who might.

Go for the Gold

When seeking out mentors and industry experts to learn from, make sure their expertise is relevant to your idea. Be wary of information that comes from someone who does not have experience in the industry or product category you need. The person best able to help you along your journey is someone who has done it before, who has had success developing and licensing products in the same field as your idea.

Nothing beats having a two-way dialogue with a real person who has walked the walk. I think this is so important, because in anything you do, there are always twists and turns. Questions come up. Challenges arise. So do opportunities. It is so helpful to be able to ask someone who knows the ropes, "Hey, what do you think? . . . What should I look out for? . . . What do I need to know? . . . Who might be interested in licensing my idea?" And sometimes, it just helps to "talk shop" with someone who's walking the same path that you're on.

How My Mentor Changed My Life

I was fortunate to meet the man who would become my mentor when I was in my early twenties and first starting out as a product designer. One day someone came up to my booth at the Sausalito Art Festival and said, "Your products should be everywhere, and I know just the guy who can do that for you. His name is Stephen Askin. He has a showroom in Los Angeles called 'What's New.'"

So I called and asked to speak with Stephen Askin. Sixty seconds later, he was on the line. I told him that the name of my company was Softies and he needed to see my products. He said, "Sure. Come on down." I made the six-hour drive to L.A. with my father. When I walked into the showroom, my heart thumped wildly in my chest. It was filled with soft sculpture toys and novelty items—the exact items I had been creating.

Stephen Askin represented artists from across the United States. That day his company was getting ready for its big trade show, which drew retailers from across the country. Stephen nodded toward my boxes and said, "Let's see." When I started pulling out my handcrafted animals and characters, his eyes lit up. He told me he loved them, and he told his staff to put them in the showroom for retailers to order. An hour later, I was in his office signing a contract.

Dad and I sat in funny chairs that had feet for legs, one of which was wearing cowboy boots, the other tennis shoes. Stephen Askin sat across the desk from us wearing funny eye glasses and a Deely Bobbers hat that bobbed dollar signs in front of his face. Everywhere we looked, we saw toys. My father, a tenured executive at General Electric, was shocked. I felt right at home. I had found someone who believed in me and my products.

It was one of the best days of my life, and it changed my life forever. Stephen Askin took a chance on me. He took my phone call, he gave me a big break, and he advised me every step of the way.

Later, when I couldn't keep up with all the orders that were coming in from retailers across the country, he stepped up to the plate again. "Teach my workers how to make your products using our equipment, rather than by hand. Then we'll take care of the manufacturing and distribution for you." Looking back, I guess that was my first licensing deal.

Among the many things I have learned from Stephen Askin over the 30 years he's been my mentor is the importance of designing a product so that it can be produced at the right price point and retail for the right price point. Today, with more than 20 licensed products under my belt, I still run ideas by him. We still talk on the phone whenever I need some advice from my favorite mentor. He still works in an office filled with toys and novelties. And he still wears funny glasses and Deely Bobbers.

Although it wasn't exactly what my father had in mind, Dad was spot on: find someone who is doing exactly what you want to do, and learn from him or her. Find a mentor!

Experts Have Limitations, Though

However, let me be clear: when you're looking at all the ideas you've brainstormed trying to figure out which ones to pursue, it's not enough to ask an industry expert what he or she thinks. You're not looking for someone to simply evaluate your idea—what you're after when you contact an expert is *insight*. The reality is, some industry experts wouldn't recognize a good idea if it walked up to them, introduced itself, and had "million-dollar idea" written all over it. Sometimes, because you're *not* an expert in a field, you are able to look at things differently and see simple ideas with mega marketing potential that "experts" might overlook. But once you get an idea that fires you up, you need to gain some expertise in that field so you can make good decisions about whether and how to move forward with it.

What you need is a clear snapshot of the playing field. What are the hot products in the market now? What are their features, benefits, and price points? How are they packaged and displayed? Which companies manufacture them? Where are they sold? How well are they selling? Who is buying them? How are sales industrywide? For that product category? What are the emerging trends in the field?

All of this information can be obtained by studying the market using the techniques discussed in Chapter 4.

Trust Your Gut

People ask me all the time, "Stephen, what do you think of my idea?" If I know the market, I'll give my opinion. But it's just that: an opinion.

Now, there are consultants who charge people to evaluate their ideas. I believe that's nonsense. For one thing, the only opinions that really matter are the opinions of potential licensees. And if you do this right, you've thoroughly evaluated the idea yourself (which is what Chapters 4 through 10 of this book are all about), plus you've gotten *free* advice from someone who has successfully done what you're trying to do. So beyond that, you just need to trust your gut.

One thing almost all product developers do, myself included, is run their ideas by family and friends. And that's fine. Just make sure to take their opinions with a grain of salt and not to heart. They are consumers, after all, so their opinions may well have merit. But they do not have industry expertise. Even if they are familiar with an industry or product category, they haven't done the research you've done on your idea. So hear them out, but trust your research and your gut.

I learned the importance of this with one of my early ideas. Every night, after we had put the kids to bed, my wife and I would slip into bed and I'd bring out my big sketch pad and show her my ideas. It was a fun time for us to talk and laugh—and Janice always laughed at my bad ideas. I would always start with the worst idea and save the best for last. Well, one night after showing her and laughing with her about my bad ideas, I brought out the best idea I had come up with that day. I had spent several hours researching, thinking about, and tinkering with the idea. I had even made a crude prototype: it was the Michael Jordan Wall Ball that I discussed earlier in this book. I made it with cardboard, a photocopy of a poster of Michael Jordan I had bought for $5 or so, and some tape.

So I showed it to Janice, fully expecting her to tell me what a great idea it was. Instead, Janice looked at me and said, and I quote, "Steve, the chances of you licensing this idea are one in a million. Forget about it, go do something else." Ouch!

Janice is one of the smartest people I know. She went to Stanford University and has an MBA from The Kellogg School of Management at Northwestern University. She has had an impressive career in marketing and product development, and even has experience in the toy industry. In fact, I met her at Worlds of Wonder, where she brought to market the company's biggest-selling toy ever, Lazer Tag. Before that, she was at Clorox, and she went on to be the vice president of marketing at E. & J. Gallo Winery, one of the highest-ranking women in the company's history. So I respect her opinion very much, and I was crushed for a few minutes there.

But I had done my market research. I had gone to Toys"R"Us and saw that all the indoor basketball backboards were square and boring. I noticed one with a small photo of Michael Jordan on it, from Ohio Art, so I knew it had the Michael Jordan license, but the picture was really small. I'm a basketball player, and I know the toy industry. *This is terrible*, I thought. *Michael needs to be bigger. This needs better graphics. It needs to be more exciting.* I knew it could be manufactured at the right price point. I just *knew* I had something.

So the very next day I sent off my idea to Ohio Art. In fact, I believed so strongly in my idea that I sent it by next-day delivery service. Three days later, Ohio Art put a licensing contract in the mail to me.

Soon, it was on store shelves everywhere, including the coveted end-cap display at Walmart. It was on the front of the Wheaties box as a premium. One Saturday morning, my wife and I were sitting in front of the TV watching cartoons with our three kids, and the Michael Jordan Wall Ball commercial came on. As Michael Jordan looked into the camera and said, "This is the best-looking backboard I've ever seen," I looked over at Janice, smiled, and gave her a little I-told-you-so look.

An idea my brilliant and knowledgeable wife said had a one-in-a-million chance of getting licensed—an idea that took me less than a day to come up with, about 15 minutes to prototype and send out, and about a week to license—ended up selling for 10 years and earning me more than $250,000 in royalties.

So be careful about the input you get from other people, even people whose opinions you value.

At the end of the day, if you've done your market research and if your idea passes the four-point litmus test, you can trust your gut that you have a potential winner. But before you put your idea to the ultimate test—submitting it to a potential licensee—there are a few simple things you should do to prove and protect your idea, which you'll learn about in Chapters 7 to 11.

PART THREE

Prove Your Idea

You've come up with an idea you're passionate about. Your market research has convinced you that the idea has the markings of a winner. Now you're eager to get it developed, get it to market, and start getting royalties!

Whoa! Hold on a minute.

Have you done the research, analysis, and design work needed to prove your idea will sell? To prove your idea is doable? To prove it can be sold at a price and made at a cost that is profitable?

Before you pour your blood, sweat, and tears as well as a lot of time and resources into building a fancy prototype, patenting your idea, and trying to find licensees, you should evaluate your idea and do a little more homework so you can give the right answers to those deal-making, or deal-breaking, questions.

7

Will It Sell?

THE CONVENTIONAL method of developing and licensing a product goes something like this. You come up with an idea and sketch it out. You spend six months to a year and thousands, if not tens of thousands, of dollars building a prototype, during which you run into all kinds of problems and repeatedly go back to the drawing board to iron out the kinks, fix the prototype, or build a new one, until you get it right. You file a patent application, which costs thousands of dollars and takes days, weeks, or months to do, depending on how much research and how many design adjustments you need to do. Once the design meets your satisfaction and the patent is filed, you wait two or three years until the patent is issued. By then, four to five years have gone by and you're wondering, "Now what do I do?"

Twenty or so years ago, I looked at that scenario and said to myself, "That doesn't make any sense. That is not for me." I knew I wanted to make a career out of coming up with ideas, out of being creative. I wanted to see my ideas on store shelves. That was my goal. But if I had to spend more than $10,000 every time I had an idea? Well, there was no way I would fulfill that goal. My wife would never allow it! You see, I knew that inventing was a numbers game.

When I worked at Worlds of Wonder, we were often presented with 20 or more ideas at a time to consider—meaning we looked at hundreds of ideas every year—and only a handful actually became products that were sold in retail. Why? More often than not, it was because the idea didn't hit all the market targets. It wasn't unique enough. It was too far removed from the norm. It didn't have a wow factor. It wasn't the right price point. It didn't have a big enough market. It wasn't what the market needed, wanted, or could afford. Bottom line: it wouldn't sell.

To be honest, I learned the importance of answering the question "Will it sell?" even earlier on in my career. During the seven years I spent designing stuffed animals and characters and selling them on street corners and at state fairs, county fairs, crafts fairs, and wherever I could set up a table, I found out very quickly that if a product didn't sell, I didn't eat. So I would always test the market before bringing out anything new. I'd make a small number of the new product and wait to see how quickly people started looking at it, asking questions about it, and buying it. I could tell within a few days if it was going to sell and how well it would sell.

Later, when I set up shop as an independent product developer, I didn't want to spend a lot of money, time, and effort developing an idea only to be told no. To get potential licensees to say yes, I needed to know that my idea would sell before I presented it to them. Actually, I decided I needed to know whether my idea would sell before *I* went to the trouble of developing it.

That's when I realized that I needed to design *for* the market, rather than design something and then test the market. At the same time, I decided I wanted to be able to sell potential licensees my ideas without having to build fancy prototypes and get expensive patents. What I came up with are a few simple strategies for quickly and cost-effectively proving that an idea will sell and can be brought to market easily and profitably. I've had a lot of success using these strategies, and so have many of my students. You can too.

I touched on the first and most important strategy already in Chapters 4 through 6, which is to design *for* the market. When you design for the market, you set yourself up for success, because, for one, you can be sure that a market for ideas like yours exists. Testing your idea is still important, however.

Evaluate the Marketability of Your Idea

As you create, flesh out, and refine the design of your idea, it is easy to get caught up in the creativity and the "me" of it. Yes, it is your idea, after all—a product of your intellect and imagination, *your* intellectual property. But if you want your idea to see the light of day, if you want to see it selling in the marketplace, you need to continuously evaluate the marketability of your idea throughout the design process—because at the end of the day, you'll need to be able to answer yes to the question, "Will it sell?"

That door-opening question is easier to answer than you might think. It's just a matter of finding and evaluating the answers to these questions:

- Does your idea sizzle?
- Who is going to buy your product?
- Why are they going to buy it?
- Where are they going to buy it?
- How much will they be willing to pay for it?

Bear with me as I repeat myself a bit in order to drive this point home. If you've been doing your homework as you work to find and refine your idea, you should already have much of this information already. You should have found out how your idea stacks up against comparable products as well as where comparable products are sold, how they're packaged and displayed, who buys them, and how much they're selling for. You should know which features and benefits your idea offers that comparable products do not. You should have assessed the low and high ends of your product category and everything in between, and you should know where your idea fits into that market. You should know all this because you've studied the market, talked with industry experts, consulted your mentor, and researched the Internet as well as other resources such as trade magazines, trade shows, and trade associations.

But before you take the next big steps of prototyping, patenting, and presenting your idea to potential licensees, it's *always* a good idea to step back and evaluate, or reevaluate, the marketability of your idea. For one thing, during the process of finding and fine-tuning your idea, you'll most likely discover flaws and/or opportunities for improving your idea. For another, markets change quickly and are affected by external factors such as the economy and emerging technologies. What's good today is not necessarily good tomorrow. So unless you come up with a slam dunk—an idea you can develop and license quickly and easily, like my Michael Jordan Wall Ball—you'll probably need to do more homework and reevaluate the marketability of your idea as you go. Timing matters.

In a perfect world, you would test market your idea by doing a small production run, giving it to a group of consumers, collecting test data, evaluating it, and tweaking your design accordingly. Then you would use this data to help convince a potential licensee to produce your idea and distribute it nationwide or worldwide. Test marketing reduces risk and is about as good a proof as you can get that an idea will sell. But test marketing is expensive and time-consuming, and therefore simply not practical for the vast majority of independent product developers.

Just asking the opinions of people you know doesn't work either. As I've said before, the only opinion that really matters is your potential licensee's.

The good news is that there are other ways of testing the market. Here is an example of one quick and simple way to test an idea, or at least get feedback. When I was working on developing my guitar pick company, I convinced the owner of a local convenience store to put up a small display of the picks. The display included a short survey asking customers what they thought of the products, whether they would buy these products, and which of the designs they liked best. From the returned surveys I was able to determine whether the idea would sell and which designs were the favorites. Of course, not all stores will allow you to do this. It was possible in this case because it was a small retailer in my neighborhood and I knew the store owner. I also gave the store a cash incentive for every completed survey it returned to me. This was my way of conducting a focus group. It was helpful because it targeted potential customers, not just my family and friends. If you

conduct your own version of a focus group, make sure that the participants are people who would actually consider buying your product. In
other words, if your idea improves upon a kitchen tool, make sure to
conduct a focus group with people who are home cooks. The data you
collect will be more worthwhile that way.

Another way of testing your idea is by showing it to industry
experts. You will need to create a one-page sell sheet to do so. (Sell
sheets are discussed at length in Chapter 12.) You could also show
your idea to potential retailers to get their opinion, as well as venture
capitalists and/or angel investors (who are bound to be brutally honest
with you). How do they react? Does your idea pique their interest? Of
course, before you show your idea to anyone, you will want to have
filed a provisional patent application, which I explain how to do in
Chapter 11.

Test-Market Your Idea by Crowdfunding It

Crowdfunding is a new avenue for test-marketing ideas. It has a powerful benefit beyond raising capital that's not often discussed: successful
campaigns demonstrate proof of demand. Companies want to know
that consumers will want your product idea. Even more crucially, they
want to know whether consumers are going to be willing to reach into
their pockets to pay for it. There's no better way of confirming that
yes, they are, than running a successful crowdfunding campaign. The
proof is indisputable! And highly compelling.

One of my students, Eskil Nordhaug, successfully used crowdfunding as a way of test-marketing his idea. Eskil is the creator of the
StayblCam, a compact portable video stabilizer for smartphones and
action cameras like GoPro. Eskil observed that a lot of the videos on
YouTube and America's Funniest Home Videos are so shaky that it's
hard to tell what's going on. He thought, "There has got to be a way
for people to make better videos."

Eskil thought his idea was cool, but he didn't know if other people
would agree. He wondered if his idea was really something that was
needed and something people would pay for. In other words, he felt

like he needed to get market validation before moving forward. He didn't find anything that solved this problem in the market, so he started dabbling with product design in his garage. In the spring of 2014, after spending months drumming up interest in his product by sending prototypes to influential bloggers, Eskil launched a campaign on Kickstarter. Four weeks later, he had raised $123,000—exceeding his goal of $35,000 by 350 percent. His campaign made one thing abundantly clear: his idea was one people wanted and were willing to pay for.

But Eskil told me that in the back of his head all along he had been thinking about ultimately licensing the idea. Orders from his Kickstarter campaign started rolling in from around the world, but he was more intrigued by the interest he started receiving from potential licensees. Shortly after his Kickstarter campaign ended, international distributors from Brazil to the Middle East began contacting him— including one of the largest distributors of camera and tech products in Japan.

Eskil knew that he couldn't scale up fast enough to meet demand and make sure the StayblCam was perceived as the original of its kind in the eyes of consumers, similar to how GoPro is thought of as *the* action camera, even though there are others. He smartly recognized that partnering with a powerful licensee that had established world-wide distribution channels and shelf space was the best way to get his product out fast.

Because Eskil had proved that consumers wanted his product, he was in an advantageous position when it came to negotiating royalty rates with potential licensees.

However, his story is not to say you can simply throw your idea up on Kickstarter and sit back as orders roll in. Running a successful crowdfunding campaign is a lot of work; it's more akin to a presale than anything else. It requires ample funds and a sizable network. A tiny fraction of the people who come across your campaign will actually donate to it. So you must truly build up a sizable audience weeks and months before your campaign begins. Enlist powerful influencers like bloggers and podcast hosts to help you get the word out. Be active on social media. More likely than not, you will also need to hire

PR support and pay to have killer graphic design work done. In order for your campaign to be persuasive, it needs to look good. At the end of the day, crowdfunding is an excellent way of test marketing your idea, and it may be the right choice for you. Always remember to label your idea as "patent pending" whenever you promote it. If you don't put the public on notice, you won't be able to collect a monetary reward in the event that someone infringes.

As a last resort (because this option is the most time-consuming and expensive), you could gauge interest in your idea by doing a small production run and selling the product on a commerce site such as eBay or Etsy or with a Google ad or Facebook ad linked to your own website. This will give you an idea of whether and how well the idea will sell. A good time to consider doing a small production run is in the event that potential licensees are failing to grasp the value of your idea. If they reject your idea because they aren't sure there's a market for it, you could prove to them that there really *is* a market with sales data. If you do a small run (and it should be small), you will need to carefully keep track of your sales, because that's the evidence you're going to use to convince potential licensees. Please, don't rush out and purchase a ton of product. Also know that in order for the sales data you collect to be relevant and useful, you will need to price the product you sell at the price you believe your potential licensee would sell it for—not what you actually paid for it. (Because you're ordering a smaller amount, manufacturing costs will be higher than they would for your potential licensee.) In other words, don't plan on using your test run to make a profit. This is also a strategy worth considering if you have already ordered product. Again, make sure you have established perceived ownership—like filing a provisional patent application and getting a URL—over your idea before sharing it with the world.

No one has a crystal ball that can tell him or her with absolute certainty that an idea will sell. Not even Apple, Coca-Cola, General Motors, and other big corporations that spend millions of dollars on market research and test marketing truly know if something will sell. Besides, people are very fickle. Their tastes change very quickly. So the best you can do is take a close look at what's working and not working in the marketplace and adjust your course accordingly so you develop an idea that has a good chance of selling.

Most of the time, you can gather all the information you need to answer the question "Will it sell?" using the same methods you used to find your marketable idea and prove its marketability, as discussed in Chapters 4 through 6. It's also a good idea to learn more about the potential buyers of your product. Trade associations and market research firms are good sources of information on consumer buying habits. You can also do an Internet search for information on consumer spending in a specific product category, industry, or demographic (e.g., "teens"). The more you know about the market, the better able you'll be to design a product with the features, benefits, and price point that will sell there. Later, you can also use this information to help convince potential licensees to say yes to your idea.

Just make sure to evaluate your idea objectively using real-world information—based on what you know to be true, not on what you assume or wish to be true. Some product developers have a hard time with this. They get attached to an idea and refuse to adapt it for the market, no matter how clear and compelling the need to do so might be. Or worse, they move forward even when it becomes apparent that there is no viable market for their idea. Don't waste your time, money, and talent on go-nowhere ideas. Innovate for the market. Evaluate your idea to verify, qualify, and quantify your potential slice of the pie. Be analytical, not emotional. If your evaluation reveals that your idea will not sell or will not sell well enough to make it worthwhile to a licensee, either let it go or find a way to make it marketable.

8

Is It Doable?

WHEN companies are even remotely interested in your idea, the two questions they'll ask you first are: "How do we do this?" and "How much is it going to cost?" At the end of the day, no matter how great an idea is, if it can't be manufactured or if it's too difficult or expensive to manufacture, it's not going to get made—at least not by a licensee.

The answers to these questions are very important to your licensee. If producing your idea requires purchasing new manufacturing equipment, that's risky. Manufacturing costs affect retail price points. If your idea will retail for more than its competitors, a company is unlikely to want to license it. It's that simple.

Companies are only interested in licensing ideas they can:

- Slip into their existing production lines quickly and easily, with little or no modification to their manufacturing processes
- Distribute using existing or closely related distribution channels
- Produce at a cost and sell at a price that is profitable

It makes absolutely no sense to find this out *after* you've designed a product, prototyped it, filed a provisional patent application, and presented it to potential licensees! Your time and resources are valuable, too. You'll save yourself a lot of time, trouble, and heartache and you'll be much more successful in licensing your ideas if you answer these two deal-breaking questions.

Yet another one of the benefits of sticking to inventing small improvements to existing ideas is that those innovations are much more likely to be able to be manufactured at a reasonable price point. I estimate that upwards of 90 percent of the ideas I see from my students—whom I also instruct to focus on making small improvements—are clearly doable. So much of the following advice is really the most relevant for those ideas that fall into the 10 percent. What I'm saying is: most simple ideas don't require *that* much investigation. Don't get me wrong. Developing an understanding of manufacturing processes is always smart because knowledge is power. But you shouldn't let yourself get tripped up by it.

This is a good time to mention that if you've done your homework and studied the market to find and design your idea, making note of comparable products and the different materials and technologies used to manufacture them, you've mostly likely set yourself up for success when it comes to manufacturing. In other words, if you've designed your idea using the same materials and processes, your idea is probably doable as well as affordable.

I'm going to spend the rest of this chapter teaching you how to learn about manufacturing. But first, I want to let you in on a secret. Remember how I'm all about testing my ideas as quickly as possible? After all these years in the industry, I know my time is precious. I don't want to waste it. So sometimes I show potential licensees a sell sheet before I know whether or not my idea is doable. That's because I want to know if there's any interest in my idea *as soon as possible*. Why would I spend time on an idea that no one is interested in? This sounds gutsy, but it's really a reflection of the fact that licensing is a numbers game. I'm not attached to my ideas; I know I'll have more of them. What's most important to me is that someone wants them. Not everyone is comfortable with this approach, and that's fine. Again—this is an approach that works with simple ideas. If you want to license a big idea, a game-changing idea, you will definitely need to know how your idea will be made and for how much.

I learned about the importance of manufacturing firsthand when I worked at Worlds of Wonder. We had a team of people from different areas of the company—engineering, marketing, sales—who evaluated ideas from the outside. We had fantastic ideas come in all the time. But no matter how much we loved an idea, if it was going to cost too much to make or if we couldn't do it with our existing production and distribution capabilities, the idea got kicked to the curb.

Since then, I've looked at a lot of patents and accompanying prototypes and technical drawings, and I'm convinced that one of the main reasons so many patented innovations fail to ever see the light of day is because the inventor never even thought about these two crucial questions, much less considered them during the design process. I've seen some really whacky ideas that were clearly conjured up without thought as to how it would be manufactured and at what cost. If a company would have to spend hundreds of thousands of dollars on equipment upgrades, expensive materials, or new technologies to manufacture your idea, it is highly unlikely it is going to be interested in manufacturing it—if it can even be made at all.

It's always worth remembering that companies are risk averse. That's why you need to know about manufacturing. You could decide to leave it up to the potential licensees to figure out, but I would never recommend that, because they won't. If you can lessen the work your licensee has to do to license your idea, your idea is that much closer to being licensed. If a licensee shows interest in your idea but comes back to you and says it's going to be expensive to make, and you're able to respond with some preliminary figures? That's gold. You've made it that much easier for the licensee to work with you.

Is It Doable and Affordable?

To be clear, you won't need to answer these two questions too thoroughly in most situations. If the technologies and facilities needed to make your product exist *today*, it's easier to license your idea to a manufacturer. A potential licensee will want to do the least amount of extra work and have the least amount of added expenditures to bring your idea to market. If they have to purchase new equipment, modify production processes, source and test new material, train production personnel, engineer new parts, or adapt their manufacturing, packaging, and distribution systems in any other way, companies are going to be much less likely to consider licensing your idea. But I've written this chapter in the event that you do have a big idea, and you need to educate yourself about manufacturing.

The reality is that some big ideas do get licensed. If an idea has huge market potential but will be somewhat complicated and expensive to manufacture, a potential licensee may decide it's worth the added trouble and cost. But it will be up to you to provide companies with enough information to truly grasp the market potential of your idea and to gauge their ability and willingness to bring it to market. If your idea is highly technical or calls for materials or production methods that are new or unusual for your product category, you'll need to do more extensive research to determine how to manufacture it and how much it will cost. You'll also need to provide more hard evidence to prove to a potential licensee that it's doable and affordable.

To prove to a potential licensee that your idea is doable, you must know how your product will be manufactured and how much it will cost to manufacture it. You don't need to become a manufacturing expert. You just need a basic understanding of the materials, processes, and associated costs involved in manufacturing and packaging your product. That information is easy enough to find.

How to Determine Manufacturing Methods and Costs

When I was on the evaluation team at Worlds of Wonder, I saw a lot of ideas. Many of them had a wow factor, but only a handful got licensed. One of the main reasons so many great ideas failed to make it to market was because they were too expensive to manufacture. The engineers would estimate the cost to produce the product, and no matter how much everyone loved the idea, if it didn't hit a particular price point, it didn't get made.

The first place to turn for information about how to manufacture your idea and what it will cost is someone who has successfully licensed an idea in the same product category or who has firsthand knowledge of the manufacturing process for a similar product. This might be your mentor or another expert you've met through a trade show, trade organization, or trade magazine.

YouTube is an excellent source of manufacturing information. These days, one of the first things I do when I'm researching manufacturing processes is search for "how to manufacture . . ." on YouTube. I watch as many videos as I need to in order to understand how certain products are made.

Another way to find out if your idea is doable and affordable is to talk with a *contract manufacturer* that produces similar products. Contract manufacturers exist in every industry, and many of them manufacture products not only for big corporations (maybe potential licensees for your idea) but also for smaller companies and entrepreneurs. Some also manufacture and distribute their own products.

You can find contract manufacturers through a trade association. Trade associations exist to provide information and put people in contact with one another. I recommend contacting a trade association in your industry or product category and asking for the names and contact information of three or four vendors in your area of interest. For example, if you wanted to talk to manufacturers of guitar picks, you might contact the National Association of Music Merchants (NAMM) for referrals. If you wanted to find manufacturers to talk to about affixing a fold-label to medication packaging, you might contact the Packaging Machinery Manufacturers Institute (PMMI). If you wanted to learn who manufactures bottle caps and sells that equipment, the PMMI could tell you. From the association's perspective, giving out a list of vendors may help generate business for its members. Everyone wins.

Once you've got a lead, call the manufacturer and ask for someone in sales. I would say something like, "I'm Stephen Key with Stephen Key Design. I'm working on a special project for a client, and I'd like to send over some drawings and get a price quote."

The sales rep is going to fall all over him- or herself trying to help you and supply you with what you need. Just make sure to send over a *nondisclosure agreement* (NDA), and make sure you've already filed a provisional patent application on your idea. You'll learn more about drawings, prototypes, NDAs, and patents in Chapters 9 to 11.

If I send over a drawing, I make sure to include "Patent Pending" on the drawing so the recipient knows intellectual property protection has been filed. I always specify a few different quantities so I can get a per-unit manufacturing price as well as any volume discounts. For example, I might ask for a price quote on 10,000, 100,000, and 1,000,000 units. The sales rep will go to work for you and come back with a price quote and other information to help you because he or she wants to get an order! It's brilliant.

Occasionally, I will call contract manufacturers and ask to speak to engineers. If I ask a few basic manufacturing questions and don't ask them to divulge any trade secrets, they're usually very helpful. Sometimes I can't get them to shut up, because they're so happy to have someone interested in what they're doing.

If the sales rep or the engineer tells you that the company can't manufacture your product, ask him or her why. If you understand the manufacturing process, you can redesign or reengineer the idea if necessary. You can also ask if the rep or engineer knows of a company that *could* produce your idea. Then contact that company to find out how it can be manufactured and at what cost.

Another great resource for finding out how something is manufactured is television programs like the Science Channel's "How It's Made," websites such as http://www.howstuffworks.com, and the free online encyclopedia HSIM (http://howstuffismade.org).

There's a new strategy for getting manufacturing price quotes that I want to talk about as well: Alibaba. Alibaba is China's biggest online commerce company. It made waves in 2014 when it had the largest IPO ever. Every contract manufacturer in Asia and around the world is on Alibaba. In other words, you can find a manufacturer who can quote you for anything that you want to make—in English. The website is relatively easy to use, and protection mechanisms have been put into place that didn't use to exist. (For example, you can sort by prequalified manufacturers, which are labeled "Gold.") Someone will get back to you immediately, too. I think Alibaba is only going to grow in significance.

It's not a perfect system, but if you navigate it properly, you can get some meaningful information. I recommend getting quotes for large quantities, like 10,000 units, as well as getting multiple quotes. However, you need to be smart about it and to have thought about intellectual property rights. For example, I would never send my exact idea to anyone overseas. That's too risky. But let's say your idea mixes and matches: can you divide it into two different parts and get quotes on those two different aspects of your idea? If I were still running Hot Picks and wanted to get a price quote on guitar picks that had Mickey Mouse's images on them, I would send a contract manufacturer a photo drawing of a pick with a different image on it—like a dog. You do not want to let anyone know what your exact idea is.

Far too many inventors and independent product developers overlook this step. They design with no knowledge of and no regard to manufacturing. I think that's one of the major reasons most patents aren't worth anything. The idea simply cannot be made. Even some industrial design firms are guilty of overdesigning—developing a product that is too expensive to manufacture. I know this for a fact, because part of my job at Worlds of Wonder was to take those ideas from inventors and industrial designers and then pull my hair out attempting to redesign them for the manufacturing line.

Don't make that mistake! Don't get caught off guard when a potential licensee asks, "How can we make this?" and "How much will it cost me?" You must find out before you present your idea and before you take your idea through the whole design process. Doing so will show potential licensees that you are a professional, that you think things through and know how to develop an idea that benefits them. Your professionalism will go a long way toward getting a company to say yes.

Design for Production and Profit

Only after researching the methods and costs of manufacturing your idea can you determine with any certainty whether your idea is doable. Sometimes the research you do will blow your idea right out of the water, making it crystal clear that there is no viable and affordable way to bring it to market. Many times, however, it's possible to head back to the drawing board and research, rethink, and rework your idea to come up with ways to make it possible and profitable for companies to manufacture it.

I've had several ideas that did not get licensed because they were too difficult or expensive to manufacture. It's always disappointing. But I was able to make that determination by talking with a few contract manufacturers before I had invested a lot of time and money. On the other hand, I've also been able to lower the cost of producing a number of ideas by reworking them. For example, I reworked my rotating label to reduce the manufacturing cost by more than 50 percent. It was out of production for years, but now it's back.

An inventRight student of mine wanted to do something special with toilet paper. Unfortunately, she did all her design work as well as filed a patent before taking our course and before calling a contract manufacturer to determine whether her idea could be made. It couldn't, but they told her what they *were* capable of. That information enabled her to rethink and rework her idea, file some provisional patent applications to protect it, and go back to the same company with her redesigned-for-manufacturing idea. Unfortunately, her original patent had no value.

There will be times when you'll have to just give up on an idea. But that doesn't mean you should give up easily. In this game, passion and persistence pay off. So, have faith in your ideas, but be flexible. Do your homework and be analytical. Design for marketability, manufacturability, and profitability . . . but also follow your heart and trust your gut. If you do that and focus on simple ideas—at least in the beginning—you will be successful in bringing your ideas to market.

9

To Prototype or Not to Prototype

IF YOU'RE following the traditional path of inventing or designing a new product, this is how it goes:

You're working on an idea you're excited about and anxious to get to market. You don't have all the answers yet and you haven't run it by any potential licensees yet, but you're afraid someone is going to steal your idea, so you file for a patent. Just like that, you're $10,000 in the hole, and you don't even know whether your product can be made. Then you build a prototype, or have one engineered and built, only to discover that you didn't do everything right; your product can't be made or doesn't work the way you had envisioned. Now you're a couple thousand dollars more in the hole, but you still have nothing to show potential licensees. So you iron out the kinks, build and test another prototype, and file for another patent. Now you're $20,000 or more in the hole for this idea, and you don't even know if anyone wants to license the thing, much less whether and how you might change it so someone *would* want it. Painful to think about, isn't it?

I cannot tell you how many people have $20,000 patent plaques hanging on their walls but no products in the market. And I guarantee their wives and husbands are giving those plaques the evil eye, thinking, *How could you have spent so much money on a stupid idea?* Not only have I seen this painful scenario play out with countless others, I've also lived it. That's why, early in my career, I said, "Forget the prototype, forget the patent!" and found other ways to prove and protect my ideas so I could avoid needless prototypes and patents.

Shortly after I left Worlds of Wonder, I formed a partnership with Russell Hicks, who had done the illustrations for Teddy Ruxpin. I would come up with an idea, and Russell would draw it out. I'd write up a benefit statement, and we'd create a sell sheet. Sometimes, we'd make an inexpensive mock-up of the idea, photograph it, and incorporate the photo into the sell sheet. Then we would call companies, and if we got a nibble, we would fax them our idea. If they said yes, we'd move forward with the design. If all we got were nos, we'd either go back to the drawing board or let it go, based on what we learned from our research and analysis, which, by the way, included feedback from companies that had rejected us. We didn't worry about fancy prototypes, and we definitely didn't worry about patents.

I've done pretty much the same thing since. I have never spent more than $100 to make a prototype, and I've licensed ideas without any prototype whatsoever. To be sure, I've been able to do this in large part because I like simple ideas whose value I can easily demonstrate to companies without a complicated and pricey prototype.

Even if your idea is complex, I think it's really important not to spend too much time and money on it until and unless a potential licensee says yes to your idea. In my mind, that is the ultimate goal: to develop a product that someone wants to bring to market *without* spending a lot of your own money. So rather than building an expensive prototype that looks and works like a finished product, I suggest you do what I do: find another effective but inexpensive way to show the benefits of your idea. What I usually do is create a simple and inexpensive model, what I call a "fake" prototype, of my idea. After filing a provisional patent application to protect my idea, I trot my fake prototype out to potential licensees to gauge their interest in my idea. I don't even send them the prototype itself; instead, I photograph it and include the photo on my sell sheet or I make a video of someone using it. I figure that if I can show companies how they can make money on my idea, they will pay me to license it—and if they want or need a fancy prototype, sometimes they'll pay for that, too.

Another important thing to remember is that when I submit my sell sheet to companies, I'm not only fishing for a licensing deal, I'm also looking for feedback. I'm starting to build a relationship with the company. I want the company's representatives to tell me what they like and dislike about my idea, what works and doesn't work for them, how I can make my idea more doable, marketable, and profitable for them and, ultimately, for me. That way, I can tweak and perfect my design before going the whole nine yards with the design, prototype, and patent.

There is nothing wrong with a nice prototype. I *love* building prototypes. I love seeing, touching, and playing with them. But sometimes you don't need one, at least not a full-on prototype. Sometimes a drawing or a faux prototype is enough to get a company interested in your idea. Certainly, for more complicated ideas, especially if they employ materials or technologies that are new or outside the norm for your product, you'll need a prototype to convince people of the concept, to prove that it works, or both. Even then, you may not need an expensively engineered and manufactured prototype that is an *exact* clone of your idea. And sometimes, when it comes to simple ideas, a killer benefit statement and a kick-ass sell sheet are all you need to seal a deal.

We'll talk about sell sheets, benefit statements, and patents later in the book. For now, let's focus on prototypes.

Types of Prototypes

You almost always need to show potential licensees some kind of physical or visual representation of your idea. You'll probably also need to create a prototype for your own use, as well. When the time is right, one benefit of making a prototype is that it often helps you to discover ways to improve your idea and refine your design. So it's really not a question of whether to prototype or not to prototype. It's a question of *how* to prototype.

There are three types of prototypes:

- "Works-like" prototype
- "Looks-like" prototype
- "Works-like/looks-like" prototype

Works-Like Prototype

A works-like prototype demonstrates how your idea works—mechanically, electronically, chemically, or whatever other working part, process, or technology applies. It is essentially a "proof of concept." It doesn't need to look anything like the finished unit; it can be extremely crude looking, even ugly. It may not even need to include all the "working" elements of your design; the prototype may only need to demonstrate whatever "working" element of your design is a new technology, unusual for this type of product, or otherwise in question.

The best way to show a works-like prototype to a company is to videotape someone using it, because you don't want to send an ugly prototype to a potential licensee. You just want to prove the concept. And you don't have to make a high-dollar production of it. My students use their iPhones to make their videos and then put them up on YouTube, using the feature that enables them to restrict who can view the video. Sell sheets will be discussed in depth later on.

One of my students, Tom Christensen, made a simple video to demonstrate his idea, the Disclub: a flying disc that a regular person can throw the length of two football fields. Tom made a crude prototype and filmed two people playing with it. In the video, you can't see how rough the prototype is; all you see is that the Disclub does what Tom claimed it could do. Had he sent only his sell sheet and his works-like prototype to potential licensees, it would not have shown the sizzle of his idea. It wouldn't have shown the magic of hurling a disc more than 700 feet! When the members of the sales department at the company saw the video, they told the president they had to have the Disclub. Tom's video proved his concept and got his idea licensed.

Looks-Like Prototype

A looks-like prototype may be either a visual image or a physical representation of your idea. Its purpose, regardless of which method you choose, is to provide you with the most effective, and cost-effective, way to show potential licensees what your product will look like. *Visual* means you can see but not touch the object. The visual image may be one-dimensional (flat: paper, photograph, digital image) or three-dimensional (e.g., a computer model). *Physical* means a three-dimensional object made out of paper, clay, wood, metal, or another material—something you can actually hold in your hand and evaluate. But a physical prototype doesn't always need to show all sides of your product; for example, the front of the object can look like the real deal, while the backside can be totally flat and blank. You don't always have to show potential licensees the physical model itself. Often, you can simply take a photograph of it.

For many ideas, a looks-like prototype need not be very refined. Sometimes a simple drawing or a makeshift mock-up will suffice. A looks-like prototype is really just a sexy drawing or 3-D rendering of what the idea could look like on the store shelf. Services like Elance and Fiverr have made it extremely affordable and easy to hire a freelance graphic designer, so there's really no reason not to. One of my students created a computer-generated 3-D image of her idea that looked so real that one of the companies she showed it to wanted to order her product right then! It cost her around $100.

There are times when a refined looks-like prototype of your idea will go a long way with potential licensees. Just make sure that a refined prototype is really to your advantage and that you can afford the time and money to create it. The window of opportunity for new ideas can close very quickly, and you should always look for the least expensive way to effectively "show" your idea.

Works-Like/Looks-Like Prototype

A works-like/looks-like prototype is a functional physical model of what the finished product will both work and look like. Depending on the complexity of the idea, it can range from a rough model demonstrating some or all of the design elements, to a close model of most or all of the design elements, to an exact model incorporating all of the design elements.

Many independent product developers assume they need to create a prototype that is a very close or exact model of what their idea will work like and look like. That is typically the most complicated and expensive type of prototype to create, and it is usually unnecessary and may even be unwise. Your idea is likely to change several times during your initial design process as well as during the product development process, once you've secured a licensee. So before you go this route, make sure you really need a works-like/looks-like prototype to work out the design and to license it to a company. (Remember, you're selling benefits—not features.)

If you do need to demonstrate both how your idea will work and how it will look, try to find the easiest, most inexpensive way to accomplish that. If possible, model only those elements that really need to be demonstrated. Sometimes, rather than building a works-like/looks-like prototype, it is as effective and easier, faster, and less expensive to create a crude-looking works-like prototype *and* an inexpensive looks-like prototype. That's what I usually do: create a crude prototype that works like it should and a sexy drawing or computer-generated 3-D rendering. Using these two simple prototypes in conjunction gives a one-two punch that proves the idea!

That said, I have licensed ideas without any prototype at all—with only a benefit statement and a sell sheet. I licensed one idea with *only* a benefit statement. It was a product called Sweet Darts, and the benefit statement was, "A plastic dart with a suction cup and the message, 'I'm stuck on you.'"

Remember these two things above all else: you are always selling benefits, and your idea will change. You will make improvements, and potential licensees may request improvements. Before you spend all that money on a prototype, you need to make sure that the benefit of your idea is strong enough to warrant that kind of investment.

So my advice is, don't get too caught up in making the perfect prototype. The reality is, most companies don't need or expect you to give them a fancy looks-like/works-like prototype. They understand the cost, processes, resources, and time that go into creating those kinds of prototypes. Do only what you absolutely need to do to show off the benefits of your idea, using the easiest and least expensive ways of creating an effective prototype. Then when a company is interested, it can work with you to refine your idea and your prototype. That way, it may pay for all or part of the final product development, prototyping, and testing costs.

Inexpensive Ways to Prototype

There are a number of inexpensive ways to create a looks-like prototype. Here are some of the most affordable and effective options for creating good-looking prototypes.

"Cannibalized" Mock-Up

This is one of my favorite ways to prototype. You simply find existing items that mimic different elements of your design, take them apart, and glue or fasten them together to create a mock-up of your idea. My prototype of the Michael Jordan Wall Ball is a perfect example of this. I took a poster of Michael Jordan holding a basketball at about his waist level, glued it to a sheet of cardboard, and cut out the outline of Michael Jordan's image, minus the ball, in roughly the shape of a backboard. I bought an indoor basketball game that Ohio Art already had on the market, removed its backboard, and glued my Michael Jordan backboard to it. This prototype made with cannibalized parts cost about $10 and took about 15 minutes to make. Another way to create a cannibalized prototype is to use clay or spray paint to change the shape, texture, color, or form of an existing product you bought at the store.

Constructed or Sculpted Model

Industrial designers often construct or sculpt models that are shaped like but are not necessarily the same texture or finish as the end product. One of the materials they use to sculpt models is foam core. Foam core is an easy material to scrape away at, and it can be easier to work with than clay. It's fairly expensive, but if your idea is small and can be effectively demonstrated using foam core, it might be a good option for you.

Clay and wood are other materials that can be used to form looks-like models of certain products. Some models are constructed, rather than formed or sculpted, using a variety of materials: wood, metal, rubber, cloth, and so on. This typically requires cutting the materials and then gluing, welding, stapling, nailing, sewing, or otherwise fastening them together.

You don't always have to form or sculpt your prototype from scratch, though. Often, you can change the shape or form of an existing product by adding clay and then spray painting it.

Paper or Cardboard Mock-Up

I use paper and cardboard all the time to make prototypes that illustrate my idea and cost next to nothing to make. You can print or paint paper to look like plastic, wood, metal, glass, stone, and other materials. You can cut and paste it into just about any shape and configuration imaginable: just think of 3-D puzzles and origami, though that might require practice or you might need to hire an artist to do it. Paper comes in all kinds of colors and can be changed to any color you want. You can glue photographs, lettering, images, cloth, and other materials to it. You can even create mock packaging for your products with paper or cardboard. I love it! Paper is such a versatile and inexpensive medium for creating prototypes.

Of course, the prototype itself might look kind of funky up close. But here's the trick: just take a photograph of the paper or cardboard prototype. Pictures can be deceiving; they can look like the real deal. Digital photographs can also be altered using graphics software like Photoshop to make them even more realistic by adding texture or other elements.

A good example of a funky mock-up that did the trick was for my Pocket Pops idea. The concept was a Swiss army knife with lollipops instead of blades and tools. I made the prototype out of paper and lollipops I bought from the store; then I took a photograph of it. In the photo, the prototype both looked and worked like the real deal.

The Spinformation label was one of my most successful ideas, and I created all the samples for it at the local Kinko's, using color copies, an X-Acto knife, and glue. A year later, it was being demonstrated on TV by Alex Trebek and being sold in Walmart. The employees at Kinko's were amazed to see a product on TV that they had watched being built in their store.

Silicone Mold

I've known people to spend tens of thousands of dollars on an injection mold to create a plastic or metal prototype of their idea. Next to paying for a costly patent on an unproven idea, this is the single most costly mistake independent product developer make. The manufacturer should pay for the injection mold, not you, and 99 percent of the time, whichever company ends up licensing your idea is going to want to make changes to it before it creates the injection mold.

But if you really think you need the perfect prototype and only a mold will do, you don't need to lay out $10,000 to $20,000 for a plastic or metal injection mold. If your idea is small, you often can make a silicone mold on your kitchen table for under $100 worth of materials. Describing how to make a silicone-mold prototype with words alone is akin to teaching a preschooler how to tie his shoes without showing him. You need to watch someone else doing it to really understand how simple it is. I recommend using Google and YouTube to search for tutorials. You can usually make several prototypes using the same silicone mold. Sometimes, you can make as many as 50 to 100 prototypes using the same mold. And they look like a professionally made prototype!

Plastic Vacuum Forming

Using a vacuum former to create a thin plastic form of your product is another alternative to injection molding. Many of the clear plastic shells used in packaging—for example, the tray stacked with cookies and placed inside the bag—are made with thermoplastic vacuum forming.

This is how the process works: First, a positive is made out of clay, wood, or some other material. The positive is placed in the vacuum form machine, a flat sheet of thin plastic is laid over the positive, and the machine is turned on. The vacuum former sucks the air downward while it heats up the plastic, causing the plastic to melt over and take the shape of the positive. Once the plastic cools, the positive is removed and the plastic shell is in the shape of your product.

If you are going this route, look for a vacuum or thermoforming company in your area. A small company is your best bet; mom-and-pop and one-person operations tend to be the most accommodating.

3-D Printing/Rapid Prototyping

Many companies and individuals use this method of prototyping, which consists of a part first being designed and dimensioned on a computer. The file is then uploaded to a machine that literally prints a three-dimensional object using liquid plastics that are applied in layers before hardening. There are several rapid-prototyping technologies. Some machines lay down a string of ABS plastic that melts to itself, gradually building up your prototype layer by layer. Another rapid-prototyping technology looks like something out of the movie *Terminator*, with your prototype literally rising up out of a vat of liquid and being hardened at a crosshairs by lasers.

For this type of prototype, you'll need someone to design your prototype on a computer using a computer-aided-design (CAD) program as well as a service provider with a rapid-prototyping machine. If you can't find someone locally, you can mail your CAD file and a return address to a rapid-prototyping service provider, who will return your prototype in the mail.

Rapid prototyping and 3-D printing have been around since the 1980s, but have become superaffordable only in recent years. Small units often can be printed for less than $100, and this technology can be used to make prototypes in many different materials and colors. Although the 3-D printing/rapid prototyping can be done quite affordably, having someone design the prototype on a computer may not be so easy. With that in mind, make sure this is the best method of prototyping for you. If it is, get several quotes on for your CAD drawings and use Elance or Fiverr to help you find the right hire.

Since this book was first published, 3-D printers have become even more affordable—so much so that some units now retail for as low as $1,000. Some entrepreneurs and small businesses have begun purchasing them to prototype their ideas on their own. Major retailers including Staples, Home Depot, and UPS are rolling out 3-D printing services in select stores. We're still a few years out from their mainstream adoption, though, because technology is still so rapidly improving. In my mind, a grand is still far, far too much to spend prototyping your idea. As far as personal use goes, this is a method to keep your eye on for the time being.

Virtual Model

Virtual models are by far the most popular prototyping technique my students use. They range from a black-and-white pencil drawing on paper, to a full-color digital rendering created using a graphics application such as Adobe Illustrator, to a fully animated, three-dimensional computerized model. Most graphics software and CAD programs are expensive. To use them effectively also requires some artistic skill as well as training and a lot of practice. So unless you already have those skills and the right software, it is usually wise to find someone who does have that expertise to create your virtual model for you. It won't cost you more than $50 to $100.

But What If They Ask for a Prototype?

It's important to understand that just because potential licensees ask you for something, it doesn't mean you have to give it to them. Let me explain. At some point—perhaps even early on—a company may ask you for a prototype of your idea. Before you rush off to mail one—or, more likely, freak out that you haven't had one made yet—take the time to qualify the request. You do not have to respond immediately. Is this potential licensee truly interested in your idea? How can you be sure?

At a minimum, you should have a dialogue with the company going before thinking about sending it a prototype. Have you talked to anyone about your idea? Even if you've spent 10 to 15 minutes on the phone with an employee discussing your sell sheet, that's worlds away from having had no discussion at all. For one, it's just not wise to send prototypes to a lot of companies. As I've mentioned, prototypes can get expensive. There's also no guarantee that the prototype will be returned to you in decent shape, or at all. It may not even be used correctly. You need to be sure that the company is truly interested before moving forward. You don't want to send something that isn't going to be taken seriously. Ultimately, you want to make sure that no one's time is being wasted, nor your money.

And of course, one of the other benefits of having a dialogue about your sell sheet before mailing a prototype is that you might discover that you need to change and/or polish your prototype in some way. The moral? Always take the time to qualify a request for a prototype.

If you really need a fancy do-all/show-all prototype and you can afford to spend the time and money to create one or to have one made for you, go for it. But 9 times out of 10, you don't need to go to that length. You can usually find an easier, faster, cheaper way to prototype your idea and get it in front of potential licensees via a dynamite sell sheet—especially if you focus on simple ideas with easy-to-demonstrate benefits *and* features.

The message I'm trying to impart is that prototypes have value, but most inventors aren't getting the most out of them, or even anything! They obsess over and spend their hard-earned money creating a perfect prototype, instead of focusing on how creating a prototype can help them refine and improve their idea. For example, one of the benefits of building a prototype is that it forces you to think about potential variations of your idea. Having thought about potential variations will lead you to file much stronger intellectual property (IP). So, if you think about it that way, building a prototype is one way of strengthening your IP. Having a prototype is also handy in the event that you're not sure your attorney truly understands your idea. Does he or she get it? Some people need to hold or look at a prototype to grasp what an idea is really all about. You could also use building a prototype to help you learn about different manufacturing techniques and processes. As I've said before, having an understanding of manufacturing is important, because potential licensees are going to ask you, "How do we make this?"

But at the end of the day, you can't go through the trouble of prototyping every idea that you have if you want to be successful at licensing. You need to be discerning. You need to hack your way to a prototype that is, above all, functional for your needs.

Whatever kind of prototype you end up with, make sure to incorporate it into your sell sheet. Often, a sell sheet is the only "prototype" a company needs to see to get interested in licensing your idea.

PART FOUR

Protect Your Idea

You've come up with a great idea and worked hard to perfect it. Now you want to put your stamp of ownership on it to ensure that someone, or some company, doesn't steal your idea out from under you.

But is rushing from the drawing board to the patent office really in your best interest? *No.*

And does a patent really guarantee that you own your idea? *No.*

Is there anything else you can do—and anything you should not do—to protect your idea? *Absolutely, yes!*

10

The Smart Way to Safeguard
Your Idea

Now, it's important for me to start this conversation about protecting your invention by saying this. If you live outside the United States, you *must* check on the patent, provisional patent, and intellectual property laws in your country.

When President Obama signed the America Invents Act (AIA) into law on September 16, 2011, the United States joined most of the rest of the world in becoming a "first-to-file" country. What that means is that entitlement to a patent is awarded based on the date of the application, regardless of the date of the actual invention. The new system became effective March 2013, so it's relatively new.

Does this mean that you must rush to file a full-fledged patent application? Not necessarily. In many countries in addition to the United States (Australia, Japan, the United Kingdom, and China, for example) "provisional" patent applications, which will be discussed in greater detail later in this chapter, allow an inventor to obtain a priority date and a patent pending number that is valid for one year. A final or complete nonprovisional application must then be filed before the 12-month anniversary of the provisional patent application or the original date will be lost.

Furthermore, in most countries a mutual nondisclosure agreement (NDA) signed by both the inventor and the person with whom the inventor wishes to show or discuss his idea can protect the confidentiality of an invention prior to submitting either a provisional patent application or regular nonprovisional patent application. This is a must in "first-to-file" countries.

The bottom line is this. For my international audience, know that you too can file a PPA as well as a nonprovisional patent in the United States (in addition to other countries). After you file a PPA in the United States, you can always decide to file a nonprovisional patent in your own country after you've shopped around the idea for one year. However, don't simply take my word for it: please research the individual intellectual property protection laws in your country! The rest of this chapter is based on my experience in the United States.

The first thing most entrepreneurs and inventors do when they come up with a new product or process or technology is run out and file for a patent. They're so scared someone is going to steal their idea that they want to put their stamp of ownership on it before they show it to a soul. That's understandable. The risk of someone infringing upon your intellectual property rights is real. It happens. Rarely, but it does happen. However, I've recently come to the conclusion that when it comes to IP, what truly matters is establishing *perceived ownership*. I used to think that when I received a patent, I "owned" my innovation. I don't believe that anymore. I learned (the hard way) that the only way ownership is truly established is in court. Who wants to go to court to defend his or her IP? I did, and it's not an experience I ever intend to repeat. If you're in this game to truly live the licensing lifestyle, it's just not worth it. What is more important is to establish the appearance that your innovation is yours to dissuade other companies from trying to lift it from you and persuade them to instead decide that paying you is just a better and smarter route for them.

However, what is much more likely to happen than a company ripping you off is that while you're waiting for a patent to issue, the window of opportunity for your idea closes. Remember: the number one rule of this game is *first to market wins*. So if you don't get your idea to market quickly, someone else probably will. Another entrepreneur or a big company could bring a comparable idea to market and gobble up the lion's share of the pie, leaving you with the crumbs.

Meanwhile, you will have invested $10,000 to $20,000 and waited three or four years for your patent. Anyone who says you can get a patent more quickly or inexpensively than that is out to lunch. Between all the office actions and going back and forth with the patent office, that is what it typically takes: tens of thousands of dollars and a lot of time.

The idea you end up with is always different from the idea you started with. Your idea will go through a lot of changes during its development. So if you file a patent early on, the next thing you know you will have to file *another* patent to cover a design change. As you go along, you'll make more changes and have to file more patents. Maybe you will find a potential licensee that likes one aspect of your idea but not another, so you will make more changes and file more patents. This old-school method of design-and-patent, design-and-patent, design-and-patent can get very expensive very quickly and drag on for years.

There is another, smarter way to protect your intellectual property *while* getting your idea to market. It's called a *provisional patent application* (PPA). Yes, some ideas still need to be patented. But you have more control and flexibility over whether and when to file a patent—as well as who pays for it—than patent attorneys and old-school inventors would have you think.

A Primer on Patenting

Understanding intellectual property rights and how the process works *before* you call a patent attorney and *before* you show your idea to any companies will save you a lot of time, money, and heartache down the road. My advice is to learn as much as possible about patents, copyrights, and trademarks, especially if you want to make a career out of creating and licensing ideas.

I am not a legal expert, and even if I were, it would take an entire book to cover everything you need to know about patents. (Conveniently, I recently published a book on this topic entitled *Sell Your Ideas with or without a Patent*.) So, in this chapter I'm going to go over the basics and share some of my and my students' experiences. But I encourage you to seek out other sources of information on patents as well. The U.S. Patent and Trademark Office (http://www.uspto.gov)

is an excellent place to start, as are patent offices in other countries. I also recommend David Pressman's books *Patent It Yourself* and *Patent Pending in 24 Hours.*

What Is a Patent?

A patent is a legal property right granted to the person or entity that designs, invents, or cultivates a new (novel) and original (nonobvious) product, process, technology, or service of monetary value. A patent grants the patent holder the exclusive right to make, sell, or use the idea for a specified period of time, during which only the patent holder can authorize (*license*) the manufacture, sale, or use of the idea by another party (*licensee*) or sell outright (*assign*) the idea to another person or entity.

Patents are issued by a federal governing body and are enforceable only in that country. In the United States, patents are issued by the U.S. Patent and Trademark Office (USPTO). Check with your local government agency for details in your specific country.

What Is Patentable?

The USPTO grants three types of patents:

1. Design patents
2. Plant patents
3. Utility patents

Here are some general guidelines on what can be patented:

- A new and original species of plant (*plant patent*) that can be reproduced sexually (with seeds) or asexually (without seeds).
- A reproducible change in the decorative appearance, configuration, ornamental design, or shape of a utilitarian item (*design patent*). For example, a change in the appearance (not the functionality) of a bottle, chair, eyeglass frame, necklace, computer icon, or type font.

- A new method of doing business or a new manufacturing process (*utility patent*).
- A useful apparatus, machine, manufactured item, or composition of matter (*utility patent*). The ideas of most entrepreneurs, independent product developers, and small businesses fall under this category.
- Computer programs and mathematical algorithms used in computer programs (*utility patent*). (You cannot patent an abstract mathematical algorithm, only those used in computer software.)

Some ideas require both a utility patent and a design patent. In fact, some ideas may require two or more utility patents, two or more design patents, or both.

How Long Is a Patent Valid?

Design patents protect property rights for a period of 14 years from the date the patent is *granted*, while a plant patent protects property rights for a period of 20 years from the date the patent is *filed*. A utility patent, the most common type of patent, provides property rights for a period of 20 years from the date the patent application is filed. Unlike design and plant patents, however, a utility patent currently requires the patent holder to pay a maintenance fee of $800 at three and a half years, $1,800 at seven and a half years, and $3,700 at eleven and a half years. If you have licensed your patent to a firm that has more than 500 employees, these fees double. Failure to pay a maintenance fee results in the termination of the patent.

How Much Does a Patent Cost?

A utility patent costs about $10,000, including attorney fees, though I have known that figure to vary in both directions. A design patent costs less. But keep in mind that most inventions require more than one patent, and a price tag of $10,000 to $20,000 for a single invention is not at all unusual.

How Long Does It Take for a Patent to Be Issued?

Each patent application is reviewed by a patent examiner, a process that takes at least 24 months, sometimes more. Rarely is a patent granted immediately upon this single examination. Typically, the examiner comes back to the patent applicant with questions and requests for additional information, drawings, documentation, or other clarification. These requests are called "office actions." In fact, the patent examination process usually consists of two or more rounds of submitting "replies" and then waiting for a response.

After all of that, which can easily take three years, the examiner may reject some of the claims in the patent or reject the patent application outright. In fact, it's overwhelmingly likely, at least in my experience: the claims of every single one of my patents have been rejected at first. I think it's a conspiracy . . . but that's just life at the USPTO. This is also why hiring a patent attorney with an agreeable temperament is a must. You are going to have to go back and forth again with the examiner—a delicate and lengthy process that I found to be quite frustrating. (Thankfully, my attorneys knew how to keep their cool and had great people skills.) You then have the option of filing a request for reconsideration or an appeal, which prolongs the process even further. So you can see how the patent process can easily take three to four years and still not result in a patent being issued.

What Is a Provisional Patent Application?

A provisional patent application (PPA) is a new device that the USPTO began offering in 1995. It is a straightforward application that uses text and drawings to specify how to make and use an idea. PPAs apply only to ideas that fall under the utility patent category. A provisional patent is in force for a period of 12 months, after which you can either file a regular nonprovisional patent application or let it expire. You can file a PPA without submitting formal drawings, but I recommend that you do because they strengthen your perceived ownership.

The Power of PPAs

To be successful in the ideas business, you must show a lot of ideas to a lot of companies. Sending one idea to one company or a couple ideas to a few companies is not enough. A PPA gives you a fast, easy, and affordable way to protect any idea you come up with so you can get your idea in front of as many potential licensees as possible. The whole purpose of a PPA is to test the waters—to get feedback from potential licensees, to test and refine your design, and to make sure your idea is doable and desirable to potential licensees—before you go to the time, trouble, and expense of getting a regular nonprovisional patent.

There are some real advantages to filing a PPA:

- The filing fee is only $65 if you make less than $150,000 a year; if not, it is $130.
- The application is simple enough that you can do it yourself, without an attorney.
- It does not require the formal documentation that a regular non-provisional patent application requires. You can submit simple drawings and even photographs of rough mock-ups.
- It provides the same legal protection as a regular patent application.
- It is in force for a period of 12 months—plenty of time to do your design work and to find potential licensees.
- You can include a "Patent Pending" notice on documents, drawings, sell sheets, and prototypes you present to potential licensees.
- As long as the patent is pending, no potential competitor can access your patent application to rip off your idea. In fact, the USPTO won't even read your provisional patent application until and unless you either file a regular patent application or someone disputes your rights to the idea.
- You can file more than one PPA as you work out the design, paying the application fee for each PPA. Once the design is finalized, you would then consolidate the PPAs into a single nonprovisional patent application.

- It establishes an official patent filing date for your idea. Should you decide to go for a nonprovisional patent, the filing date of your PPA becomes the filing date of your regular patent, thereby extending the duration of your patent from 20 years to 21 years.

Most attorneys will not recommend a PPA. They want to get you for a full patent application. After all, they stand to make more money by pursuing a full patent application. Most argue that they will spend as much time writing a PPA as they would a regular patent application.

In my experience, PPAs are the most powerful tool anyone can use to protect and license an idea. They safeguard your intellectual property rights, enabling you to focus on refining your design and finding a licensee. Once you have a PPA in hand, you can and should start calling potential licensees right away, first to get their feedback and then, after you've incorporated that feedback into your design, to secure a license.

But filing a PPA should *not* be your first step! Wait until your idea is ready to present to potential licensees. Do your homework first: prove your idea will sell and can be manufactured. Then file your PPA and start calling companies immediately. If you file for a PPA before doing your homework, you've started the clock on your year's worth of protection before you were ready to use it, and if your research provides you with negative feedback that discourages you from continuing, you'll also have wasted your application fee.

Inventor's Logbook: Still a Must-Have

Before you even think about initiating a PPA—in fact, from the moment you first come up with your idea—you should start an "inventor's logbook" and religiously keep it updated. An accurate and detailed logbook is your first line of defense in protecting your idea.

Although the AIA changed U.S. patent law from a "first-to-invent" system to a "first-to-file" system, there is still some gray area. For example, the new law offers a "grace period" of one year after you disclose your idea to a second party during which you can still file for and obtain a patent. What kind of disclosure counts? That's unclear—and is why I'm of the opinion that maintaining an inventor's logbook is still a really good idea. Document your idea from the moment you conceive of it, through each of its design changes, and all the way to its final look, licensing, and manufacture. For this purpose, I strongly recommend that you maintain an inventor's logbook for each of your ideas. It's simply a good habit to begin doing.

Begin by documenting the date you came up with the idea and a detailed description of the idea, including any sketches or mock-ups of the idea. Record and date every consecutive step you take thereafter, in chronological order. Include any variations or changes to the idea; detailed notes on any testing and prototypes; additional drawings, computer-aided-design renderings, technical specifications, computations, and so on; notes from conversations with industry experts and potential licensees; meetings with patent attorneys; and so on. Cite as many details as possible. Include the full names of any participants in your project and clearly specify their roles. Make sure to also retain your receipts for purchases of any materials used to make prototypes, samples, and sell sheets.

To be legally viable, the logbook must adhere to the following:

- The journal must be bound so that any removed pages can be detected (a notebook with prenumbered pages is ideal). Never use a loose-leaf binder.
- No lines or pages can be skipped.
- Each entry must be dated and written in ink (not pencil).
- Each entry must be signed and dated by a third party, signifying the person understands the contents of that entry. This person can be anyone other than an immediate family member who is capable of reading and understanding what you've written in your logbook.

The purpose of a logbook is to prove that you created the idea and made improvements to it at specific times. This chronological record of your idea is vital to proving that the idea is 100 percent yours.

If you have not been documenting your idea thus far, backtrack as far as you can remember with accuracy. Include when you got the idea, when you began working on it, what you have done to date, and any specifics you can recall.

When the ownership of an idea is in dispute, the one with the most detailed and precise records is the most likely to win. If you maintain a well-documented inventor's logbook and file a PPA, you are well on your way to establishing perceived ownership.

HOW MARGO LICENSED HER IDEA WITHOUT A PATENT

Margo came up with a way to label beverage and food items in the refrigerator. One of the things I love about her product is that it is a simple idea: basically, rubber bands that come in an assortment of colors upon which you can write your name, a date, or whatever other information you want to use to label the contents. Margo filed a PPA before she started presenting it to manufacturers. She also consulted with a licensing attorney, who told her no company would touch her idea if she didn't own any intellectual property (which, I later advised her, is not the case). Further, the licensing attorney told Margo that the company she had in mind—which sold in 80 percent of the ideal market for Margo's product—would never pay her royalties on foreign sales, even if her U.S. patent did eventually issue.

Margo called the company anyway. In fact, she called all the major companies in her market, but after speaking with the dominant player, she knew it was a good fit for her idea. She liked how the company operated and how it handled other products. She also felt encouraged by how receptive it was to open innovation and to her sell sheet.

Well, the company did license Margo's idea. What is more, even though she had PPAs only in the United States, she also received royalties on sales in territories in which she had no patent protection. Further, as part of her licensing contract, the company agreed to continuing paying her royalties even if her patents were never issued!

continued

Margo understood that first to market wins. She protected her idea with a provisional patent application. She studied the market, identified the best licensee for her idea, and went for it. She didn't wait three or four years for a patent to issue, and she didn't go to the extreme expense of filing foreign patents. As Margo learned, the company that licensed her idea didn't expect her to file patents in those territories, and it had every intention of paying her royalties on all sales, because as the CEO said, "It's your idea."

Of course, not all licensees are as flexible and generous as the company that licensed Margo's idea, but many are, because they, too, realize the value of first to market. More and more of our inventRight students are licensing their ideas with only a PPA.

How to Get a Patent

For some product categories and industries, you may not ever need to file a regular nonprovisional patent application. In the toy, novelty gift, and fashion industries, for example, product life cycles are so short that most companies don't require a patent in order to license your idea. The direct-response television industry (DRTV) is another example of an industry that doesn't necessarily require IP. I still recommend filing a PPA, though.

For big ideas, it is best to have some type of intellectual property protection filed. For really big ideas, you will need to file multiple patents, to build a "wall of protection," as my attorney, John Ferrell, has always told me. This "wall of protection" sends a message to potential intruders that you will protect your intellectual property rights. After all, patents are perceived ownership, and anything can be argued in a court of law. Building a wall of protection around your intellectual property helps keep you out of court by discouraging people from being dishonest.

When it is prudent for you to file a nonprovisional patent application, you can sometimes negotiate with your licensee to pay all or part of the costs associated with filing the patent(s). If you negotiate for the company to pay patent fees on an idea it has licensed from you, you (and your attorneys) still control all filing and office actions.

Whether an idea is big or small, filing and defending a patent takes a lot of time, money, and expertise. I would not even consider filing a nonprovisional patent application myself, and I strongly advise you to retain the services of a patent attorney if and when you need to file a patent for your idea.

Choose the Right Attorney

Not all patent attorneys are created equal. I have 15 patents and have filed dozens of overseas patents, and I have worked with many attorneys over the 35 years I've been licensing my ideas. In my experience, the best way to find an attorney is to get a referral from someone else.

Ask for a referral from someone who has patented an invention, preferably in your product category. If your idea is highly technical or complicated, you should hire a patent attorney with expertise in that industry. I cannot emphasize enough how important this is. Knowing patent law is not enough. The attorney also needs to have a working knowledge of the correct terminology and peculiarities of the product category in question so that he or she will understand the design details and the specifics of each patent claim. Hiring an attorney with expertise in the right industry is far more important than hiring one in your neighborhood. The firm I use is a two-hour drive away, and we use e-mail, phone, and express mail services to communicate. In the almost 20 years we've been working together, I've met with them only half a dozen times. Also, make sure the attorney is registered with the USPTO.

I recommend searching for a patent attorney that has prior litigation experience, which will be invaluable should you end up deciding to go to court. It's a good idea to ask the attorney about his or her success rate. How much experience does the attorney have writing patents that have actually been issued? Hire someone who truly understands how to navigate the lengthy journey ahead of you. And on that note, I also think it's a good idea to ask the attorney to let you read some of the patents he or she has written that have been issued. Do you understand what they are saying? If you don't, that is a problem—because if you can't understand them, it's unlikely that a judge, jury, or potential licensee will either. A patent only has value when its claims are written clearly and concisely.

A good patent attorney will have common sense as well as people skills. You want an attorney who understands what your goal is: to profit from your innovation. Questioning you about the merit of your idea is not your attorney's job, but it's a great sign that your attorney is looking out for you. For example, if your patent attorney points out that your idea may be difficult to patent due to the prior art that exists, you know you've found a winner.

How to Write a Patent That Has Value

Before calling a patent or licensing attorney, you need to do your homework. Learn as much as you can about the patent application process and about intellectual property protection. Make sure you also know how your idea will be manufactured, and document those manufacturing processes.

In order to successfully navigate this process and write strong IP, you need to know what has already been patented when it comes to your innovation. You also need to be aware of "prior art"—all of the information that has been made available to the public, in any form, that is relevant to your claim of originality. It isn't possible for you (nor patent examiners, nor an independent firm you could hire) to find every single piece of prior art, so don't trip yourself up trying to. The point is that you need to know what is out there in order to carve out what is unique about your innovation, and therefore why you deserve to "own" it. When you search through old patents and prior art, your goal is to determine where the holes are—holes you can take advantage of and ownership over. You may even be able to patent features of your innovation that you hadn't considered after reviewing prior art. On the other hand, you may discover that the field of your innovation is crowded and that others have claimed several important features of your product. In that case, you will have to go back to the drawing board.

You can search through prior art using Google Patents or the USPTO's website. It is important that you read through the claims section of each patent carefully. You can hire an independent search firm to do this, or you could instruct your patent attorney to hire one for you. But, as always, I think learning how to do this is very valuable. The more you personally know yourself, the more you will be able to guide your patent attorney. Searching for prior art takes practice, and I wouldn't say it's thrilling, but before you know it, you will be a pro. I like to be able to tell my attorney myself what the claims in my patent application need to say. I make a list, and I annotate the differences between my ideas and other similar ideas out there. I don't want attorneys to be creative; I want to be the one in control, always. After all, I'm my idea's biggest advocate. Don't be alarmed when you find prior art that covers your innovation; trust me, you will. Focus instead on how you are going to work around the prior art. (This is a big part of the reason why I don't believe anyone ever owns anything—all prior art can be worked around one way or another, it just depends on how difficult it is to do.)

Before contacting an attorney, you should make sure your inventor's logbook is up-to-date and complete. Create any additional documentation and drawings you may need to fully describe your idea. I recommend that you hire a professional via Elance or Fiverr to do your drawings, because it's affordable and the final product will be fantastic. Make sure to show your attorney your sell sheet, so he or she understands the benefit of your idea, as well as a prototype (if you have one).

Remember: your attorney is only as good as the information you provide to him or her.

Meet with the Attorney and Get a Quote Before Retaining

Most patent attorneys are willing to meet with you briefly for free or for a small fixed fee. During that initial meeting, ask the attorney to give you a rundown of what he or she will do, and ask what it will cost. Make sure that you understand how the attorney bills. Get the price quote in writing. Make sure the quote includes *office actions*, because the attorney will most likely need to go back and forth with the USPTO to get your patent issued, the cost of which can add up quickly.

Keep in mind that you will be working with the attorney repeatedly, and you will be charged for every phone call, e-mail, and hour spent on your patent application. So be prepared for the actual cost to exceed the quoted price.

If, after the initial meeting, you feel uncomfortable with the patent attorney, or he or she seems reluctant to represent you, shop around for another one. It's going to be a long and challenging process, and you want to be working with someone you are confident understands your idea and is on your side.

Be an Active Participant in the Process

When you hire an attorney, you should start out by strategizing with him or her about how best to protect your idea. If you have a highly marketable or highly technical idea, a single patent will not be enough protection; the claims will not be broad enough. I have more than 15 patents on my Spinformation label, because I realized I needed to build a wall of intellectual property around my idea to discourage someone from designing around it. A good patent attorney can help you expand the scope of your patent to a certain degree, but you will need to do the homework. Research and brainstorm other ways your idea could be manufactured, as well as every conceivable way the design could be changed and improved upon: different materials, sizes, shapes, configurations, functionality, and other features. Think of other product categories for which your product may be applicable and how you might modify the product's design for that market. Ultimately, again, you need to be the expert on your idea, and you will need to figure out all the ways a competitor may try to get around you as well as provide that information to your attorney. That way, your attorney can include all those possible design and manufacturing variations in your patent applications.

Fight the Good Fight

The first patent I applied for came back from the examiner's office after about 14 months with every single claim rejected. I was crushed. My attorneys weren't fazed at all. They knew this was part of the process, and they knew how to respond. However, I knew my technology better than anyone, and it was up to me to provide my attorneys with the information they needed to prepare the response to that office action.

Essentially, it was a matter of rewriting the patent to get all the terminology just right and then defending it to the examiner. Language—it all came down to language. After the first office actions, I was granted 6 of the 25 claims I'd asked for. After the final go-around, I ended up with 16 of those 25 claims.

Of course, this took time and money, and it was emotionally draining. That's why it's important to hire experienced patent attorneys and to provide them with the information they need to go to battle for you.

HOW I OUTSMARTED A BIG CORPORATION AND PROTECTED MY BIG IDEA

I came up with the idea of a rotating label in the mid-1990s after reading an article in the newspaper about how there was never enough information on product labels. As always, I worked out the design, talked to a few industry experts, built a few crude prototypes using over-the-counter medications I had purchased at Walmart, created a benefit statement and a sell sheet, and started talking to companies. When a packaging exec at a company that provided labels for many of the major players in the packaged goods industries asked, "Do you have a patent on this?" I knew I was on to something big. So I worked with my attorneys to file a couple of patents on my rotating-label idea, which gave 75 percent more space for information than any other label on the market.

Then a friend of mine gave one of my samples to her father, who ended up giving it to one of his golfing buddies, who happened to be the president and CEO of Procter & Gamble. Next thing I knew, I got a call from P&G saying the company wanted me to come out to its headquarters in Cincinnati and present my idea to its tech group. *Wow!* I thought, *I've hit the jackpot!* My wife wasn't so sure. Janice has

continued

an extensive background in packaging and product development; she had worked at Clorox, and she had actually been offered a job by P&G, the largest packaged goods company in the world. She was worried P&G wouldn't play fair. But I convinced her to go with me. I needed someone on my team, and this was her world. Figuring manufacturing issues would come up in the meeting, I also invited a representative from a company called Krones, one of the largest manufacturers of processing and labeling equipment in the world, to be part of my team too. I had already established a relationship with Krones while I was working on the idea.

So the three of us flew to Cincinnati, and I was so exited! Our P&G contact person took us to lunch in the company cafeteria. Afterward, walking across the campus of P&G with the sun on my face, I felt like I had finally arrived. As we walked, I thanked our contact person for lunch. He said, "Steve, remember, there is no such thing as a free lunch." I'll never forget the "I told you so" look on my wife's face when he said that.

We went to a huge meeting room and sat across a huge table from about 20 P&G employees—from marketing, engineering, product development, and legal. I did my part of the presentation. Janice gave her presentation of all the benefits. The guy from Krones got up and explained how easily the labels could be manufactured.

Then the gentleman who had taken us to lunch slid a piece of paper with some numbers written on it across the table to me and said, "Mr. Key, we're not going to pay you one penny for this idea." The numbers were patent numbers.

Now, when I first came up with the idea, my attorneys had a prior-art search done by a firm in Washington, D.C., that specializes in patent searches. It was such a Forest Gump idea, so simple, that my attorney was sure someone had thought of it before. So he was surprised, and I was pleased, when the search revealed that there was no prior art for a rotating label.

continued

As it turns out, the legal department at P&G found two 40-year-old patents for rotating labels that the Washington firm had missed. They weren't similar to mine—they were *exactly like mine*. My attorneys confirmed what P&G said. "You'll never get a patent for this. No one's ever going to pay you a penny for it." By that point I had already spent a lot of money on two patents, more money to fly to P&G, and even more money for patent summaries confirming that, yep, not one, but two other people had already invented this idea. I felt pretty foolish. (My attorneys did as well.)

For the next couple of weeks, I was stunned. I went on vacation with my family. But I kept thinking about the label. Something was wrong. If this was such a great idea, if P&G was interested and its attorneys spent all that time trying to avoid paying me for my idea, why weren't the labels on the store shelves? Why hadn't there been any rotating labels on any products ever? It just didn't make sense to me.

So when I got home, I started examining those two 40-year-old patents. I read them over and over and over again. Then it dawned on me! I realized something that those 20 P&G experts didn't see and that my attorneys, one of the premier patent law firms in Silicon Valley, didn't see: not one claim in either of those patents said *how* to do it—not one!

After I realized there were no claims on how to manufacture a rotating label, I toured labeling facilities throughout the country, observing and asking questions about how fixed labels were applied to containers. Once I understood how labels that didn't rotate were applied to containers, I figured out how to reengineer the labeling process so that labels that rotated could be applied to containers. I couldn't patent my rotating-label idea, but I sure as heck could patent how to make it. And that's exactly what I did!

Today, I have more than 15 patents on the manufacturing processes used to apply my rotating labels to containers. More than 400 million Spinformation labels have sold to date.

continued

The message here is this: You need to be in control of the situation. You need to understand every aspect of the design, including how to manufacture it. You need to do your homework and make the necessary adjustments, either to the design, the patent, or both, to get your idea to market. If it can't be done, it can't be done. Let it go. Move on to another idea. But don't stop until you've turned over every leaf. Don't give up without a fight.

Procter & Gamble didn't license my rotating label, but that's OK. Many other companies have, and I'm finding additional applications for my Spinformation technology all the time. At the end of the day, P&G gave me the keys to the kingdom by forcing me to take a closer look at my idea. As a result, I figured out how to manufacture—and therefore patent—my rotating label. Although it was a stressful experience at the time, I realized the P&G employees were just doing their job. They weren't trying to steal my idea; they just weren't willing to pay me for an idea that they believed had already been patented.

I've been doing this for almost 30 years, and I've presented thousands of ideas to hundreds of different companies. In my experience, most companies are not out to steal ideas. Most are willing to work with you if they're interested in your idea. It's your job to do your homework so that your design is, indeed, *novel* and so that you know how to build a protective wall around your intellectual property.

Another thing to keep in mind is that most of the ideas in my licensing portfolio are simple. I licensed the vast majority using a benefit statement, a sell sheet, and a PPA. Most of the ideas I have patented were paid for by the licensee; I had my attorney file the patent, and the licensee paid for the patent in lieu of an advance.

I actually like that the USPTO is slow to issue patents, and I love PPAs, because they give you time to test the waters, to see whether your idea has legs, whether a company is going to want to pay you for your idea. When a company is interested in your idea, 9 times out of 10 it's not concerned about the patent. A "patent pending" provides the perception of ownership, which is usually enough to satisfy most companies, and it provides a sufficient warning to competitors to back off. Ultimately, what companies really care about is getting great ideas to market fast.

11

Control Every Step of the Process

AFTER YEARS in the idea business, during which I've developed hundreds of ideas and licensed more than 20 of them, I've learned a few valuable lessons, some, admittedly, the hard way. Hands down, the most important thing I've learned is that I'm the one who has to be at the control panel every step of the way—from the moment I conceive of an idea until it's brought to market and beyond. Whether I win or lose at this game depends on whether I do the right things in the right way at the right time. That includes asking the right questions of and saying the right things to the right people—and only those people.

So many entrepreneurs, inventors, and independent product developers seem to want to generate an idea and then turn it over to someone else to do all the work for them. Over and again, I've seen otherwise intelligent "idea people" repeat the same dumb pattern: They come up with an idea that gets their creative juices flowing. They work on the design and build prototypes in virtual solitude and often in a vacuum, without doing market research, without talking to industry experts, and without getting feedback from potential licensees. At most, they run the idea past family and friends, who typically have no expertise in developing, manufacturing, and marketing anything, much less that particular product or process. Once they're happy with their design, they file for a patent.

They wait two, three, or four years for their patent to issue, a period during which they're paying a patent attorney a small fortune to repeatedly revise their patent claims. Then they rely on inventors' services, idea buyer and seller networks, marketing consultants, public relations firms, invention submission companies, invention contests, and the like to sell their ideas for them. But there are no takers. No one buys their idea. No one brings it to market. Or worse, someone else brings a similar idea to market, which is always a risk when you broadcast an idea all over the Internet and publicize it before securing a licensee.

The primary reason so many ideas die on the vine is because their designers didn't stay at the control panel. They either neglected to do their homework and legwork, or they left it to someone else. They didn't consult with the right people at the right time, or they shared their idea with the wrong people at the wrong time.

To protect your idea and to get it to market quickly—which is essential, given that the number one rule of this game is *first to market wins*—you have to control your own destiny. No one is going to be as passionate about your idea as you are. No one is going to work as hard on your idea as you will. No one knows more about your idea or has as much invested in it as you do. So why in the world would you turn over control of your idea to someone else?

That's a question I can answer with one word: fear. Fear of the unknown. Fear of failure. People are so afraid of the unknown and so afraid of failing at things in which they have limited or no expertise—which typically are marketing, manufacturing, licensing, and patenting—that they relinquish control of these critical steps in the process. It doesn't make sense, it doesn't work, and *it doesn't have to be that way.*

You can learn how to design for the market. You can find out whether and how to manufacture or otherwise implement your idea. You can be selective about who you work with and ensure that they're working for, and not against you. You can protect your ideas and profit from them. You can control the entire process of developing and licensing your ideas. How? By following the simple strategies outlined in this book.

Now let's talk about two important facets of protecting your ideas. The first is a necessity for every idea and the second runs counter to what many experts preach and many entrepreneurs practice.

A Necessary Precaution When Sharing Your Idea

When you come up with an idea you're passionate about, it is only natural to want to know what the people closest to you think about it. And of course, you want them to love it! It is also wise to consult with industry experts and a mentor, if you're fortunate enough to have access to either. Just make sure to show your idea only to people you can trust and share design details with an exclusive circle—your patent attorney, colleagues you hold in strict confidence, and potential licensees.

It is also critical to have anyone who looks at your idea sign a nondisclosure agreement (NDA) first. When people or companies sign your NDA, they're promising to keep your idea and every detail about it a secret.

My feelings about NDAs have changed over the years. I used to think that as long as I had protected my idea with a provisional patent application (PPA) or a nonprovisional patent, I didn't need to bother with an NDA. Now, after witnessing how others have benefitted from using NDAs as well as using them myself, I think an NDA is a good idea whenever you show your idea to anyone other than your immediate family and most trusted friends. Before showing your idea to anyone you consult with during the product development and licensing process (e.g., when researching how to manufacture your idea), you should have the person sign an NDA.

However, I do not recommend asking a potential licensee to sign your NDA right off the bat. A company's reason for not wanting to sign your NDA is usually the same as another company's reason for wanting one: to avoid the risk of being sued in the event they already have a similar product in development or may develop a similar product in the future. This is of particular concern to large companies that develop many different products and that look at hundreds or thousands of outside ideas every year. In that case, it is virtually impossible to ensure that none of those other ideas and products will involve information that you feel is "confidential" to your idea but that, in fact, is known by someone else. I sometimes hear inventors complain about companies that refuse to sign their NDAs; in their eyes, that's a clear sign the company isn't inventor-friendly. I strongly disagree. If you ask a company to sign your NDA before it is even interested in your idea, I think that could easily be perceived as a red flag—to the company! How could a company that is taking open innovation seriously possibly keep track of all of the individual NDAs it is signing?

A better time to ask a potential licensee to sign your NDA is after the company's representatives have seen your sell sheet, have expressed interest in your idea, and are asking you for more information. At that point, it's a reasonable request. When you ask an employee if you may e-mail him or her your sell sheet and the response is to ask you to sign the company's NDA, it's up to you to read the document closely and determine whether or not you are comfortable signing it.

The aforementioned reasons are why it's important to include a provision in the contract that limits the scope of the NDA to information that is known to be confidential.

A good NDA will contain these key provisions:

1. The parties agree not to disclose each other's confidential information to others.
2. The parties agree not to use each other's confidential information without compensating the other party.
3. The parties agree to return all documents, information, and prototypes supplied by the other in the event that no agreement is reached with regard to the idea.
4. The parties agree that information that is already known to the receiving party or that is known and used by others is not deemed confidential.

Almost all NDAs that a potential licensee will provide you with will include these four provisions. An NDA that you provide should include them as well. Your attorney can draw up an NDA for you to have people sign before showing them your idea, or your attorney can advise you about what to include in your NDA.

If a person or company refuses to sign an NDA, point out that your NDA includes a provision that limits the scope of the contract (see key provision 4). If anyone other than a potential licensee refuses to sign an NDA, simply do not show or discuss your idea with that person. If a potential licensee refuses to sign an NDA or provides an NDA that doesn't give you enough protection, you have two choices: (1) walk away, which could reduce your chances of licensing your idea, or (2) offer to modify the NDA in a way that gives the company the flexibility it needs and gives you the protection you need.

It's a good rule of thumb to never assume that a company has your best interests in mind when it comes to an NDA, or really any legal document. I've seen some NDAs that are bizarrely unfair. If you ever come across an NDA you're not sure about, do not hesitate to have an attorney look it over. In a lot of ways, licensing comes down to cultivating trust. How confident are you about working with a specific company or person? Use your judgment. Hopefully the research you did online earlier has taught you something. It's also worth noting that what is standard practice in one industry is not necessarily standard practice in another.

When to Toot or Silence Your Horn

There is a common misconception running rampant in this era of open innovation that the best way to get your idea to market is to tell the whole world all about it. It's the Information Age version of *If you build it, they will come*, and it goes something like this: *If you build it and get word out on the Internet, Twitter, TV, and the radio and in every publication you can, some company or investor will come and buy your idea*. It doesn't work that way. Not only is this an inefficient and ineffective strategy for licensing your idea, it also puts your idea at risk of being copied or worked around.

For one thing, very few, if any, companies and investors go searching the Internet and Twitter for ideas to license or fund. Nor do they routinely (if ever) scout social media or any other media for ideas to bring to market. Nor do they frequent (if they visit at all) inventor and product developer forums in search of the next big idea, which in reality is usually a simple idea with big market potential.

These services and media channels may serve a good purpose, but it is not to bring a licensee to your door, despite innumerable claims to the contrary. Sure, if you've already been issued a patent on your idea and listed it with a few respectable "inventions/ideas for sale" listing services, it might get noticed by a product scout who happens to be looking for something along the lines of your idea. It might even result in a licensing deal. But it's a long shot—an extremely long shot. And it should never be your first or only shot, because your odds of a hit are extremely poor. Infinitesimal.

It is far more effective to go out there and *find* a licensee for your idea. Doing your homework to identify and qualify potential licensees and calling those companies to get their feedback and gauge their interest in your idea gives you a much better shot at licensing your idea. It is a much easier and faster way to get your idea to market. It is also a lot safer.

Some entrepreneurs and independent product developers think, *If enough people can see my idea, surely someone with money will come forward and invest in it. If I can just get some exposure, surely a company will see it and want to license it or pay me a lot of money to buy the patent outright.* In my experience, that's backward thinking. You should publicize your idea *after* you've licensed it, not before. Until and unless you do license your product and a company is actually bringing it to market, you should *protect* your idea and *not* show it to everybody and his uncle.

Exposing your idea to the wrong people can have dire consequences. It can enable someone or some company to design around your patent and beat you to market with a similar idea. And if you don't use an NDA and don't have a patent or patent pending on your idea, sharing it with anyone—much less, indiscriminately to everyone—is just plain foolish. Also, in other countries outside the United States you can lose your right to patent your invention.

There is also risk in exposing your idea too soon. A product or process can be touted as "new" for a relatively short period of time, and the media only covers new stuff once or twice. So you don't want to toot your horn until your idea is on the market or at least ready for the market. Otherwise, not only could you blow your only opportunity to publicize your idea, you could also give competitors the opportunity to beat you to market with a similar idea.

When the time is right—*after* you've protected *and* licensed your idea—by all means, go toot your horn. Let the world know your idea is out there in the market. Announce it on your website, on your social media pages, and use whatever media channels are available to you. Most licensees will welcome your promotional efforts. Just make sure to coordinate your promotional efforts with theirs.

For example, I was able to get Accudial, one of my Spinformation licensees, on the television show "The Doctors." During the segment, the Accudial representative talked about the benefits of my rotating label. That helped Accudial sell more product and helped me find other licensees. In fact, I use a video clip from that TV segment on my website, because it functions as a testimonial of the benefits of my idea, which in turn helps promote it to other potential licensees.

But remember: one of the great things about licensing your ideas is that you can leave the marketing and publicity to your licensees. The licensees will do all of that for you, so you can simply kick up your heels, collect your royalty checks, and move on to your next great idea, if you choose.

So, in summary: To successfully bring an idea to market, you must control every step of the process from developing your idea to protecting and licensing it. Throughout the process, you must also control who knows about your idea, what they know about it, how you tell them about it, and when. So make sure to protect your idea with a PPA and an NDA before showing it to anybody.

And remember: as nice and helpful as kudos and feedback from your inner circle and industry experts might be, the only opinion that really matters is that of the company licensing your idea. So focus on finding and wowing potential licensees—while controlling the process and protecting your idea—using the tools and techniques provided in this book.

PART FIVE

Prepare to Pitch Your Idea

You've come up with a simple idea that has big market potential. You've confirmed it can be manufactured using existing technologies and processes. You've created a drawing, mock-up, or some other kind of visual representation of your idea. And you've filed a provisional patent application (PPA) to protect it. Now it's time to find a licensee that will bring your idea to market.

But before you start calling companies, there are a few simple things you can do to give yourself a huge advantage in licensing your idea.

12

Create Sales Tools That Sell Benefits

THE BIGGEST myth about licensing is that you need to prototype and patent your idea in order to submit it to a potential licensee. While that might be the case with some big ideas, it is definitely not the case with most ideas. As I've said before, you don't need an expensive prototype that looks like and works like a finished product to get a potential licensee to say yes to a simple idea. An inexpensive visual representation of your idea will do just fine (see Chapter 9). You also don't need to spend $10,000 to $20,000 and wait three to four years for a patent to issue. You can protect your idea immediately by filing a $65 to $130 provisional patent application (PPA). You don't need to show and sell every feature and every element of your design. All you need to do is effectively demonstrate the *benefits* of your idea.

When a company understands what is uniquely beneficial about your idea, it can quickly assess whether it will be profitable for it to bring to market. That is all companies care about: whether they can make money on your idea. They don't care if it's the most mind-blowing innovation since the discovery of electricity. If they can't see the benefits of your idea and how they can profit from it, they will not be interested. It's as simple as that.

The three most powerful tools you can use to show and sell the benefits of your idea are:

- A one-line benefit statement
- A one-page sell sheet
- A video sell sheet

What's beautiful about these three benefit-selling tools is that you can create them yourself—quickly, easily, and inexpensively.

Create a Door-Opening Benefit Statement

I can't count how many times I've stood and listened to entrepreneurs or product developers ramble on for 15 to 30 minutes or longer after asking them to tell me about their idea. In these instances, it didn't matter how long they talked or how in-depth their description was: most of the time, I've walked away not knowing how the product would benefit the end user.

No company is going to spend 15 to 30 minutes listening to you pitch your idea or even 10 to 20 minutes reading a long e-mail. In fact, if you can't articulate to companies how your idea is going to benefit their customers (and by extension, the company) in two minutes or less, you are unlikely to get even five minutes of their time, much less their interest in your idea. They want to know from the get-go, "What's in it for me?" So it is vitally important for you to know precisely what the benefits of your idea are and to be able to articulate them in a clear and concise way.

Here's what I do and what I teach my students to do:

1. Make a list of the benefits your idea offers that similar products do not. Try to come up with at least three. Describe each benefit in one or two sentences.
2. Rank the value of each benefit on a numeric scale—with the benefit that has the highest value being number one.
3. Create a one-line benefit statement for the number one benefit of your idea.

Your one-line benefit statement is the most powerful tool in your arsenal. Done right, it stops people dead in their tracks. Take this one-line benefit statement for the iPod: "1,000 songs in your pocket." Who wouldn't want to buy that?

Believe it or not, I have licensed an idea using only a benefit statement. Granted, the idea was simple and could be easily manufactured, so all it took for the company to grasp the idea and see how it would benefit them was that one powerful sentence.

The purpose of a benefit statement, however, is about getting your foot in the door, not about getting a licensing agreement. It's a great way of getting a company to open the door so you can step in and wow them with your idea.

Benefit Statements That Opened Doors

Here are some benefit statements that have helped my students and me license our ideas:

> *This basketball game adds exciting graphics to the backboard and gives you a better return on your money by better utilizing your Michael Jordan license.*
>
> —STEPHEN KEY, LICENSED TO OHIO ART

The Michael Jordan Wall Ball was on the market for more than 10 years, and it sold more than one million units its first year.

> *My label innovation adds 75% more space to a label.*
>
> —STEPHEN KEY, LICENSED TO CCL LABEL, THE LARGEST PRESSURE-SENSITIVE LABEL MANUFACTURER IN THE WORLD; TO ACCUDIAL PHARMACEUTICALS (FOR CHILDREN'S LIQUID MEDICATION); TO ABC BEVERAGE (FOR DISNEY'S *HANNAH MONTANA* AND *CARS*); AND TO COCA-COLA MEXICO

My Spinformation rotating labels have sold more than 400 million units worldwide and have been used on such products as Rexall Sundown Herbals, Nescafé coffee, Lawry's spices, and Jim Beam DeKuyper Pucker.

> *Throw a disc two football fields.*
>
> —TOM CHRISTENSEN, LICENSED TO SPORTCRAFT

The Sportcraft brand has become synonymous with family fun. More than 13 million customers a year choose Sportcraft products—and they're able to buy Tom's Disclub.

Don't let stress control your life. Get Relaxium and escape from anxiety!

—Timea Ciliberti, licensed to Nature Trade Direct, as seen on direct-response TV ads

The most versatile organization system available.

—Dario Antonioni/Orange22, licensed to Cocoon

Dario's GRID-IT! technology is used on more than 1,500 products—everything from backpacks to handbags, luggage, MacBook covers, and more.

Your guitar will not come apart when the strings are taken off, and it will sound and sustain like never before!

—Dwight Deveraux/TonePros

Some of the world's top guitarists and the world's best guitar companies currently use TonePros Patent Issued System II Components.

You can still pile and stay organized. Keep your papers neat and organized with PileSmart desktop organizer tray.

—Linda Pollock, licensed to Pendaflex

These are sold in every major office supply store in America.

Skins doors in less than 10 minutes.

—Tim Gerhards, licensed his Skin Zipper tool, an air-hammer-driven door-skinning tool, to Steck Innovative Autobody Tools and Equipment

Clear a clogged drain in less than 30 seconds without harmful chemicals.

—Gene Luoma, licensed to Cobra Products

His Zip-It Clean tool for unclogging drains is sold in every major retailer in the United States and Canada, including Walmart, Home Depot, Lowe's, Walgreens, and more.

Tips for Writing a Killer Benefit Statement

Though writing a benefit statement may seem simple, it can be quite challenging. I have to admit that my wife often helps me with mine. According to Janice, I tend to "throw everything in but the kitchen sink," and then she has to whittle it down and sharpen it into a short, concise, power-packed one-liner.

Since I can't lend you Janice, here are some tips for creating door-opening benefit statements for all of your ideas:

- **Identify and focus on the one big benefit of your idea.** In most cases, the biggest benefit will be to the end user (the consumer), but in some cases it will be to the manufacturer. One way to articulate this big benefit is to first state a problem and then state your solution.
- **Keep it short.** It should be no more than one line and no more than about 25 words.
- **Be concise.** Don't clutter the benefit statement with unnecessary details. Stick to a brief description of your product and its one big benefit. Think of the taglines in TV commercials and in magazine ads that in one short and powerful line tell you what the product is about and make you want to go buy or see it.
- **Be specific.** State precisely how your idea provides that one big benefit. Don't just say it's the best thing since sliced bread; specify what makes it so great. For example, a generic statement such as, "This game is so fun, kids of all ages will want it!" does not tell the company what kind of game it is, how it's different, and why kids will want it. In fact, a generic statement like that not only fails to articulate the benefit of your idea, it also gives companies reason to suspect that your idea has no real value. "The first interactive video game for preschoolers that entertains, teaches, and tickles little funny bones" tells a potential licensee exactly what type of game it is, how it's unique, and why kids (and parents) will want it.
- **Use easy-to-understand language.** Avoid jargon, cutesy catch phrases, and big words that might confuse or annoy the reader or listener. The objective is to communicate the key benefit of your idea, not to show off your vocabulary or entertain.

- **Try out a few.** Come up with four or five different benefit statements. Then pitch them to your family, friends, or mentor. Have someone read them to you so you can hear how each sounds. Then pick the one that most clearly, concisely, and compellingly articulates the benefit of your idea.

When I first started calling companies about my rotating label, I simply said, "I can add 75 percent more space to your label." When they asked, "How do you do that?" I responded with, "Can I send you a free sample?"

The goal of your one-line benefit statement is to grab a potential licensees' attention right off the bat and get them thinking, "I want to know more." Before open innovation was as popular as it is today, I used to state my one-sentence benefit statement over the phone when I called potential licensees to get in. These days, I advise my students to avoid selling over the phone at all costs. It's hard to do, and frankly, there's simply no need to. Instead, your goal is to get permission from an employee to send him or her your sell sheet (which should prominently feature your benefit statement). Techniques for getting in will be discussed at length in Chapter 16.

Create a Deal-Generating Sell Sheet

A sell sheet is a one-page advertisement for your idea that shows off its benefits in a flash, sort of like a mini-billboard. When you're driving along the freeway at 60 miles per hour and see a billboard, you know exactly what it's selling. In a similar fashion, your sell sheet should tell potential licensees exactly what you're selling in 60 seconds flat. Another benefit of the format of sell sheets is that they are familiar to the people inside the companies you will approach to license your idea. Companies use sell sheets to introduce new items to wholesale and retail markets (their customers) all the time. If you have a great benefit statement and an effective sell sheet, you don't need to be a sales pro. Your sell sheet will do most of the talking for you!

A sell sheet uses words and images to tell potential licensees exactly what your idea is about and why their customers will want it. Creating one is much less expensive and time-consuming than creating a works-like and looks-like prototype, and it is the most effective sales tool you can use to submit your idea to companies.

You must create a sell sheet *before* calling potential licensees. When you call a potential licensee to get in, you are going to get to the point quickly, and the point is to ask him or her, "Can I send you my sell sheet?" As I've said before, the great thing about sell sheets is that they do the selling for you. So, you need to put yours to work as quickly as possible.

The goal of a sell sheet is not to show potential licensees everything about your idea. It is to sell them on the benefits of your idea so they'll call you back. When you first approach a company, you want to give only enough information to pique the recipient's interest—and you want to make sure *not* to give the company any reason to say no. Usually, when companies are interested in an idea, they like most things about it but dislike or are confused about something. If that happens right off the bat—say, if your sell sheet or benefit statement includes a design detail about your idea that's problematic for the company—the company might say no to you without giving it a closer look. But if the company's employees get hooked on the major benefit of your idea and discover that one negative later in the game, after they've gotten to know you and your idea better, companies are usually more willing to work with you to resolve the issue.

The Makings of a Kick-Ass Sell Sheet

I limit my sell sheets to one page, just a regular sheet of paper. I also limit the amount of information and images on the page. Potential licensees need to understand your idea and the benefits of your idea quickly. If your sell sheet is longer than one page, chances are it will get tossed in the trash. If it's too cluttered, it may not articulate the major benefits of your idea clearly or quickly enough.

Every sell sheet should include these critical components:

- Your one-line benefit statement
- A visual representation of your idea

- An embedded link to your video sell sheet
- Your contact information: your name or business name as well as your e-mail address and business phone number
- A few additional benefits of your idea—as concise and compelling as your big benefit statement
- Evidence of your intellectual property protection, in small type in the lower corner: "Patent Pending" or the patent number, if issued; never list an application number

Your one-line benefit statement used to be the most important component of your sell sheet. It should still be in large and bold type, as well as prominently displayed, usually at the top or along the bottom of the page so that readers' eyes are immediately drawn to it. The visual representation of your idea should be the other prominent element on your sell sheet. There are many different ways to "show" the benefits of an idea on a sell sheet, and you'll need to decide which type of image works best for you and your idea. For some ideas, a single line drawing, illustration, computer-generated 3-D image, or a photograph of a mock-up of your idea is all you need. For other ideas, you may need to create a storyboard: a series of two or more images that tell a story in pictures, like a cartoon strip. Whatever type of image you decide to use, just make sure that it depicts the big benefit of your idea.

Remember, you don't need to spend a lot of money building a looks-like/works-like prototype that is an exact working replica of your finished product. In Chapter 9 we discussed several inexpensive but effective ways to model your idea or to create a visual representation of your idea. Just make sure that the visual of your idea looks good and clearly shows the benefit of your idea.

Creating Your Video Sell Sheet

The third component of your one-page sell sheet is your video sell sheet. My students are increasingly filming videos that showcase the benefit of their ideas and including an embedded link to them in their sell sheets, which makes a lot of sense. People love to watch videos.

They resonate with us. There is so much you can convey in a very short video. Video is compelling! Although I am calling your video a "sell sheet" (because it is a kind of sell sheet), I want to be clear that filming a video is never a replacement for your physical one-page sell sheet. It's an important supplementary tool. People still need to have something static they can absorb without having to press play.

You may be thinking, "But I don't know how to make a video!" Don't worry—you'll be amazed by how easy it is to do. First of all, the goal of your video is very simple: it should concisely present a problem and how your product is a solution. It should be very short—between 30 seconds and two minutes, max. It can and should be filmed using your smartphone. Don't bother including any music, because it's distracting. And again, you absolutely do not need a perfect prototype to film an effective video. There are ways of editing and filming your video so that your message gets across without a perfect prototype.

TIPS FOR CREATING YOUR VIDEO SELL SHEET

- Practice makes perfect. If you're not camera-ready, and most people aren't, film yourself until you are. Figure out what your best angle is so you look the way you want. Not everyone wants to be on camera. If you think someone else would do a better job of appearing on camera, hire someone else to help you. You still need to be the one in charge of directing your video, though. Voice-over can also be effective. I've seen great videos that use voice-over only, or even just lines of text on the screen. You need to assess how best to showcase *your* idea.
- Stage your video appropriately. If your product idea is a kitchen innovation, film your video in the kitchen. If you have an idea for a children's toy, film children using it.
- Always shoot horizontally. If you're filming an action shot, use a stabilizer. Make use of your phone's "lock exposure" option, because you don't want the focus to keep coming in and out. Taking shots from different angles will make your video more interesting.

continued

- Do not introduce yourself or talk about yourself. There's no time for your backstory, where you live, how long you've been inventing, etc. Not to be harsh, but, potential licensees don't care. They only care about what your idea is going to do for them. An exception to this rule of thumb is if there's something about your idea's backstory that you think could be used as a PR angle or is newsworthy. One of my students, Richard Monson-Haefel, submitted his young daughter's ideas for tween products to potential licensees. They wouldn't respond to him until he made it clear that the ideas were his daughter's. They loved that angle, and he started getting in every time.
- Focus less of your video on the problem and more on how your idea is the solution. The problem portion could be as short as 10 seconds. The last frame of your video should be your contact information, including your phone number and e-mail. Let it linger on the screen for a bit.
- Watch the videos on Allstar Products Group's website. Allstar makes what are essentially mini-commercials for its products. Your video definitely does not need to be as professionally made, but it should follow the same format. (If you envision your product being sold via DRTV, having a video is a must.) Your video will be much better if you have watched some examples.

The goal of your video sell sheet is the same as your one-page sell sheet: to pique recipients' interest. After watching it, a potential licensee should want to ask you more questions. Like a regular sell sheet, your video doesn't provide all the facts, like how your idea will be manufactured—it is, as always, all about the benefits.

When you're done filming your video, test it out on your friends and family. Watch their faces. Do they look puzzled? Or do they instantly grasp the benefit of your idea? Ask them if they do. They should, because that's the entire point of your video: to elicit an immediate emotional response.

When you embed a link to your video on your sell sheet, make sure that it is highlighted—you don't want someone to accidentally skip over it and not watch your video. You can password protect your video on YouTube to prevent the public at large from viewing it. If you include a link to a video in your sell sheet, you can track how many times it has been viewed on YouTube via Video Manager. If you click on the number of times watched, YouTube will give you an expanded view of the data, including number of times viewed, minutes viewed, and location viewed from.

Don't get too caught up creating a sleek-looking video. It's just a tool—a really great way of showing off the benefit of your idea. And unlike prototypes, videos can't be broken, lost, or improperly used. Not all product ideas necessitate creating a video, but I think most of them do.

How to Create Your Sell Sheet

These days, I think the best way to create a professional-looking sell sheet is to hire a graphic designer via Elance or Fiverr. It's so affordable (as little as $10), and the results are top notch. I've seen graphic designers transform a sketch on a napkin into a 3-D design that looks so realistic you want to order the product right then and there. In fact, unless you are a graphic designer yourself, I strongly recommend it. However, to get the sell sheet you want, you will have to be the art director. Look at how products that are similar to your idea are marketed and packaged. Are there certain colors that are used frequently? What about certain words? When you find marketing materials you like, send them to your graphic designer in addition to the other materials you have provided him or her, like your one-sentence benefit statement. Prior to hiring anyone, check out the other sell sheets the designer has created to ensure that you're working with the right person for the job.

However, if you want to do it yourself, you can use graphic art software such as Adobe Photoshop or Adobe Illustrator, which is expensive, or less expensive software such as Corel PaintShop Photo Pro. But you can also create a good-looking sell sheet using Microsoft Word or a similar program. A free alternative piece of software you can use to design your sell sheet is Inkscape. It's fairly easy to learn and will give you more flexibility than Microsoft Word. You can find it at http://inkscape.org. It's available for both Mac and Windows platforms. Creating a sell sheet on your computer gives you a lot of design flexibility. After you've created a visual representation of your idea, you just import it to your sell sheet, where you can resize it or move it to different parts of the page to see what looks best. For the words, you can use different fonts, sizes, and colors as well as bold and italics.

If your idea is highly technical, you might want or even need to include a technical illustration on your sell sheet. However, in my experience, it is better to keep it simple, and a rendering of the finished product is usually best. The purpose of the sell sheet is to show the benefits of your idea, not to show every feature of your idea and how it works.

Submitting Your Sell Sheet to Potential Licensees

Never send a sell sheet to a company without first getting permission from the company. Otherwise, it will be considered junk mail. How much junk mail do you open? Call the company first, introduce yourself as a product developer, tell the employee you have an idea you would like to submit to the company, and ask if you can e-mail your sell sheet over. If the employee says yes, e-mail your sell sheet immediately.

When you e-mail your sell sheet to the employee you talked to on the phone, briefly state who you are, make sure to include the fact that you just spoke to someone on the phone who gave you permission to send it over, and thank the company for reviewing your product.

Most of my students send their sell sheets to potential licensees electronically, as an e-mail attachment. If you take this route, make sure to use a document format that the company can open, read, and print but cannot change in any way.

The only two types of electronic files I recommend for sell sheets are web pages and PDF files. In my opinion, creating a web page is more difficult than a PDF, but if you want to do it, the easiest way is to subscribe to a service such as Squarespace. You can more easily build your sell sheet using its online tools. Squarespace costs about

$8 per month, a fee that includes your domain name. There are also free services available. Google "build a website" to find them. From that point, you can start sending people links to your web page. The benefit of having a web page is that you can tell someone to check it out while you're talking to that person on the phone.

PDF files are electronic files that can be opened, viewed, and printed using Adobe Reader—a free program that is usually provided on new computers. It can also be downloaded for free from the Adobe website (get.adobe.com/reader). You cannot create a PDF file with Adobe Reader. To create a PDF file, you need a PDF writer. Adobe sells PDF writing software (called Acrobat), which is kind of pricey. You can also download free and inexpensive PDF writers from the Internet. One free PDF writer I've used is CutePDF (http://www.cutepdf.com); it is easy to use and the instructions are easy to follow. Also, if you are using Microsoft Word 2007 or later you can save your document as a PDF. Alternately, if you are using a Macintosh, you can easily turn any document into a PDF: simply go to the Print function of that program, select "PDF," and click "Save As PDF... ." This function is now built into the Mac's operating system, so you don't need any additional software to create a PDF.

Why spend a small fortune and several years of your life trying to license your idea the conventional way—with a fancy prototype and expensive patent—when there is a faster, cheaper, and simpler way to bring your idea to market? Remember: getting a potential licensee to say yes is all about selling the company on the benefits of your idea. And the best sales tools for selling benefits are your one-line benefit statement, your one-page sell sheet, and your video infomercial. I have licensed more than 20 of my ideas using only a benefit statement, a sell sheet, an inexpensive prototype, and a PPA. Most of my inventRight students have licensed their ideas the same way. You can too.

13

Get in the Game Without Quitting Your Job

CONTRARY TO popular belief, you can play with the big guys—and be taken seriously—without having to go through the time and cost of starting a full-on business. With my 10-step strategy for creating and licensing ideas, you can do this as a hobby or as a very part-time second job, or you can slowly build it up to a full-time profession that allows plenty of time for your family, friends, and other interests. You can even live the licensing dream on a shoestring by creating a business image and by outsourcing some of your work to young professionals and students.

Fit the Dream into Your Life

I am the quintessential dreamer. The creative type. A kid at heart. In my early twenties, I decided I wanted to make a profession out of creating and licensing my ideas, which I have been fortunate enough and have worked hard enough to do. So I understand, I really understand, how tempting it can be to throw caution to the wind and just go for it. But that would be a bad idea, a very bad idea.

I cannot say this often and strongly enough: do not quit your day job. Do not mortgage your house to the hilt, go into debt, and use up your kids' college education funds and your retirement funds. Do not let creating and licensing your ideas consume your resources—or you. The whole point of the licensing lifestyle is to have the time, resources, energy, and presence of mind to enjoy your life and your family, *not* to diminish or neglect either. It's all about making your life better, and that means creating a healthy balance between work and play, between work and family, and between work and rest.

It has taken me a while to learn some of these lessons, and I want you to avoid the mistakes I made! There was a time when all I talked about, all I thought about, all I did with my family had something to do with my ideas. I remember seeing a glazed-over look in their eyes. I have changed. I have learned to make my family a priority in every way: in providing for their material needs, in giving them my time and attention, and in listening to and supporting their dreams. In turn, they do the same for me.

Connecting with other creative people who have similar interests is another thing I have done that I recommend you do as well. Find a group of entrepreneurs or inventors to meet and talk with regularly. Laugh with them. Cry with them. Share with them. Having a supportive outlet like that will give your family a little break from all your ideas and enthusiasm. Being passionate about your idea is a good thing, but not if it's your only thing and the only thing your family hears about.

I will always remember the passionate inventor I met years ago whose wife divorced him because he got so caught up chasing his dream. He had spent $250,000 on prototypes and patents, which may well have been money either that he and his wife couldn't afford to spend or that she didn't want him to spend in that way.

The sad thing is, he didn't *have* to do it that way. If he had followed my approach to licensing ideas, he might have licensed his idea by now—at a fraction of the cost and time he's already invested. And more important, he might have saved his marriage.

Janice and I celebrated our 26th wedding anniversary in 2014. Had I been foolish enough to put our financial security at risk and to put my dream before our life together, she would have left me years ago. I found a better way to do this, and we're all the better for it. I've also helped many other people use these same tools and techniques to live their dreams without turning their lives upside-down.

How Two Drummers Banged Out a Winning Idea in Record Time

Two of my inventRight students have taken it one step further. Jeff and Mark not only have full-time jobs, they are also part-time musicians (drummers). They have been friends for 30 years, but they live 80 miles apart in Southern California, where commuting 10 miles can take 60 minutes in rush-hour traffic. They are both married and have children. So they don't have much time to meet face-to-face. But they had an idea for a new take on an old percussion instrument—maracas, or rumba shakers.

Jeff and Mark developed a new take on this sleeping dinosaur, which their benefit statement describes better than I can: "A new shaker innovation that provides multiple sound qualities, precision control, and the ability to create complex rhythmic patterns in one compact instrument." Using the methods they learned at inventRight, the friends developed their idea over the phone while commuting to and from work (using hands-free mobile phones, of course), sometimes at lunchtime, and on the weekend. They developed an inexpensive prototype, filed a provisional patent application (PPA), created a sell sheet, and recorded a video that they put on YouTube with password protection.

They called potential licensees the same way they developed the product: on their hands-free cell phones driving to and from work and at lunchtime. Four months and $800 later, they had a licensing deal with Latin Percussion, the largest percussion instrument manufacturer in the music industry.

Jeff and Mark have a new motto: "Invent yourself out of a day job one idea at a time." They're well on their way. You can be, too, by taking it one idea—and one step—at a time.

Now let's look at a couple of ways to bring you closer to living the licensing dream.

Create a Professional Image

When you're pitching ideas to potential licensees, it is imperative that you present yourself and your idea in a professional manner. Everything you present to a company—from your business card to your benefit statement and sell sheet—must be pitch-perfect. These are the tools that will get you in the door and get a company interested in your idea, and they need to pop!

Companies want to know they're dealing with a legitimate business, with a professional who knows how to develop an idea for the market. A potential licensee is far more likely to take you and your idea seriously if you present yourself as the entrepreneur or owner of a design firm rather than as a weekend inventor who comes up with kooky ideas for a hobby or as a regular guy or gal who happened to come up with an idea (the implication being that it's your one and only idea).

That does not mean you have to go out and lease and furnish an office, hire an assistant, and get a fancy brochure made. Nor do you have to hire an attorney and form a corporation. What you do need to do is name your business. If you use your full name in the title of your business, most states do not require you to register your business. You don't need to decide how to structure your business before you begin submitting your ideas, but you do not want to sign a licensing contract in your own name. Once your ideas start getting closer to being licensed, you can speak with the Small Business Association (SBA) in the United States and Canada, the Federation of Small Businesses in the United Kingdom, or an attorney to figure out the best way to structure your business. In the beginning and for the purposes of contacting and pitching your idea to potential licensees, the only thing you need to have is the *appearance* of a legitimate business.

You can cultivate an air of legitimacy with business cards, letterhead, a dedicated phone line, and a dedicated business address. Your business phone can be a mobile phone, and your business address can be a post office box. The point is, presenting yourself as a legitimate business conveys to potential licensees that you are a professional who understands the business of developing and licensing ideas. That's important.

Outsource Without Breaking the Bank

Few entrepreneurs and independent product developers have the skills to do everything themselves. Truth be told, few want to. Most either can't or don't want to come up with and develop marketable ideas *and* design good-looking business cards and letterhead, *and* write good benefit statements and cover letters, *and* build good prototypes, *and* create effective sell sheets, *and* do all the other tasks involved in developing and licensing ideas. And you probably can't, either.

Even if you can and want to do all those things, doing everything yourself is probably not the best use of your time and abilities. To succeed at this game, like catching a fish, you need to have a lot of lines in the water at all times. You need to be constantly coming up with new ideas and casting them out to potential licensees. Outsourcing the tasks you don't do well or don't enjoy, or that simply take too much of your time, enables you to focus on finding and developing ideas.

Now, you could hire a top-notch professional copywriter or an advertising firm to come up with a benefit statement and content for your sell sheet. While you're at it, you could also hire a professional graphic artist to design your sell sheet, business cards, and business stationery; a web designer for your website; an industrial engineer or model maker for your prototype; and a commercial photographer to take a picture of your prototype. The more experienced the professional, the more you can expect to pay for their services. So if you were to hire everything out to top-notch pros, it could quickly add up to thousands of dollars. I do not recommend this approach.

A more cost-effective and time-efficient option is to take my approach: do as much as you *want* to do and *can* do well yourself. Then outsource everything else to independent contractors who are able to provide good service and willing to give you a better price than design firms or more experienced professionals. In the past, I have frequently hired freelancers to help me with my sell sheets. You can also hire independent contractors (e.g., industrial engineers) to create prototypes, specifically if you need a technical drawing, a 3-D rendering created with computer-aided-design (CAD) software, or a clay model. Sometimes, you may need to hire an expert with technical knowledge (as well as, ideally, manufacturing insight) to help you execute your project, like a mechanical engineer, software engineer, or electrical engineer. It's one thing to build a single prototype; it's another to really understand how your idea is going to be implemented on a manufacturing line.

As I've gotten older, I've realized that I want to focus more on creating and developing ideas and less on doing all the other stuff I need to sell my ideas. So I've built a team of talented people to help me create prototypes and sell sheets, protect my intellectual property, maintain my website, and provide other assistance. I'm selective about who I work with and am very hands-on. I make sure we're all on the same page and that it's a win-win business partnership.

What's important is that you find the right people to do whatever tasks you need or want to outsource—whether that's creating a logo for your business card, a technical drawing of your idea, or your sell sheet—so that you can bring your ideas to market as quickly, effectively, and economically as possible. In my opinion, the right person for the job is someone who is competent, professional, trustworthy, and affordable.

Where to Find Help

Sites like Elance and Fiverr have made it extremely easy to find—as well as affordable to hire—people with skills in CAD, copywriting, graphic design, illustration, industrial design, model making, photography, prototyping, and other services. When I hired a freelance graphic designer to create a logo for my company many years ago, he charged me $1,000—a small fortune! Today, I could hire someone to design that same logo for a mere $50. Recently, I hired a freelancer from India to update my entire website for a grand. 3-D graphics used to be so costly that using them was out of the question—now they are accessible too.

Here are the types of people to whom you can outsource those tasks you don't want to do or can't do yourself:

- 3-D animator
- 3-D modeling expert
- CAD engineer
- Electrical engineer
- Graphic artist
- Illustrator

- Industrial designer
- Machinist
- Mechanical engineer
- Model maker
- Prototype specialist

Here are a few places to locate skilled talent to do the work you need help with:

- Local companies providing the services you need—for example, advertising and marketing agency, industrial engineering firm, commercial photography, and so on
- Local independent contractors—for example, graphic artists, industrial engineers, and illustrators
- Community colleges, universities, design schools, and trade schools in your area

However, my students have overwhelmingly begun to rely on websites that allow them to post a description of what they need done and review the different bids that come in, like Elance and Fiverr. On sites like these, you could find an affordable freelancer who lives on the other side of the country, or even in Canada, India, or South America—the possibilities are endless.

How to Outsource Your Work

First, do your homework. There are more than a few sites these days that connect freelancers with work that needs to get done. Read the fine print closely. What are the site's policies in regard to payment and nondisclosure issues? Does the person you hire have the right to post what she creates for you on her own website? Spend some time familiarizing yourself with how each site works to make sure you're hiring the best person for the job.

Before you provide a potential vendor with any details, drawings, or mock-ups of your idea, have him sign a work-for-hire agreement (WFH). It should include language about your being the sole (100 percent) owner of the idea. This prevents the person you've hired from claiming to be a co-owner in the event that he or she makes any changes to your idea or product. The WFH should also include a confidentiality statement that specifies the person cannot ever reveal anything about your idea to anyone or use your idea in any way without your explicit written permission.

Before hiring people, you should always get some evidence that they have the ability to do the work you need done. Just because someone has a computer and CAD software or a Photoshop program doesn't mean he or she knows how to use them properly and is a good designer. Most important, what's their track record like? How long have they been on the site? What is their rating? How much money have they collected? Have any of their clients hired them more than once? If they have repeat business, that's a great sign. Designers that actively use these sites are invested in them, and their work is likely to be good.

Once you post a description of the job you need done and how much you're willing to pay, you'll start receiving bids. Here are a few things to keep in mind when that happens.

- Don't necessarily pick the lowest bid. I interview potential free-lancers through Skype, because I want to be able to look the person I'm hiring in the eye. In my experience, it's the best way to start building a one-on-one relationship. Always get price quotes up front, too, and from at least three different sources for every project. Prices can vary dramatically, and a high price is not always (or even usually) an indication of quality. My students are able to get great work done at a reasonable and even low cost. In my experience, the freelancers who get back to me quickly over e-mail tend to turn their work around faster as well.
- Make sure to be very specific about the job you need done. A lot of confusion can arise unless you are very clear about what you're looking for. Provide the freelancer with an ample amount of information, including examples of the job that you need performed. When I hire a freelancer to design a sell sheet, I make sure to provide him or her with the marketing copy I want to be used, a photograph, and even examples of other similar products.

Essentially, provide them with everything they need. Frankly, I don't think it's possible to provide a freelancer you hire with too much information. Err on the side of caution rather than assuming that he will understand your needs.

- Ask up front: How long is this going to take? You will need to communicate with your service providers and manage the process closely. Be accessible in the event they have questions or concerns, and check in frequently. For more complex jobs and jobs that have a tight deadline, don't rely on a single due date. Instead, create a series of check-in points. This will enable you to catch and correct problems before things get too far, or find another source if you discover you've hired the wrong person for the job. Most freelancers will provide a rough sketch or design before they finalize it, but you should ask about the person's process so you understand what to expect. Also, make sure you know what form the final product is being delivered in. If you need to make changes later, will you be able to?

- And finally, don't pay in full up front. I learned this lesson the hard way when a freelancer whom I paid up front failed to finish the work I assigned him. This is why creating an explicit series of milestones is so important. Look over the final product closely before delivering a final payment.

There are so many options for outsourcing your sell sheets, prototypes, and other projects. I love that you can outsource your work all over the world as well as to talented professionals who need the money and the experience. You can outsource your whole team, and if you choose carefully, you can get the professional help you need at an affordable price. That way, you can better manage your time, your costs, and the whole product development and licensing process.

PART SIX

Submit Your Idea to Potential Licensees

You've followed all the right steps to bring your idea to life: created a unique idea and designed it for the market, proved it can be manufactured and will sell, protected your intellectual property, and created a benefit statement, a sell sheet, and a professional business image. Now it's time to pitch your idea to potential licensees.

This is when many product developers choke. Why? Because they don't know where to go, whom to talk with, and what to say. They're intimidated by the mere thought of knocking on the doors of big companies.

But it doesn't have to be that way. There are simple ways to get your idea into the right hands and get you one big step closer to having a company say yes to your idea.

14

Kick Fear to the Curb

IF YOU'RE like most people, the biggest obstacle standing between you and getting your idea to market is fear. That is understandable, especially if you're new to the licensing game. The truth is, everyone has fear. In fact, every successful entrepreneur and independent product developer I know, myself included, has had multiple fears. But here's the other truth: fear is surmountable. Because in the vast majority of cases, fear is just "**f**alse **e**vidence **a**ppearing **r**eal."

I've found that the best way to dispel fear is with preparation and persistence. Studying the game, getting ready for the game, and practicing the game not only will give you more confidence, but also will greatly improve your batting average. The more you know and the more experience you get under your belt, the less fear you'll have and the more success you'll have. Remember: this is a numbers game. No one, not even the most brilliant and prolific creative minds on the planet, hits a winner every time or even every tenth time. To be successful and enjoy the fruits of the licensing lifestyle, you need to generate lots of ideas. So you need to get smart, get rid of your fear, and get many ideas in front of many companies.

Now let's take a look at the most common fears that prevent people from even trying to rent out their ideas and what you can do to kick each one of them to the curb.

Fear of Getting Ripped Off

One of the biggest fears people have about licensing is that a big company, or an employee within a company, is going to steal their idea. Although it is largely unfounded, this is truly a paralyzing fear for some people. Every once in a while you'll hear a story from a David claiming that a Goliath has lifted his idea. But usually that's all it is: a *story*, with little or no truth to it. In those rare instances when a company does stake claim to an idea that is similar to someone else's idea, it usually turns out to be a misunderstanding or mistake that is resolved to the mutual satisfaction of both parties. It is not in the best interests of any company to pilfer ideas. Both the odds and costs of getting caught are high. It's not worth it, and it's not necessary.

One reason it's unwise for companies to steal ideas is because the Internet has provided the little guy with a platform for his voice. If something were to go wrong in your dealings with a licensee or would-be licensee, you could go online and use blogs, forums, and social media networks to post complaints and warnings, telling the whole wide world about it. So trying to steal an idea would be a public relations nightmare for a company.

But if you suspect a company *is* trying to work around your idea, make sure you have all the facts straight and think it through carefully before you start blowing whistles. Be careful not to make false statements or to say anything that might slander the company or anyone associated with it. You don't want anyone to file a libel suit against you. You also don't want to cry wolf or make a fuss too many times, because then other companies won't want to work with you.

No company wants to go to court over a patent infringement or other intellectual property dispute. Litigation is expensive and time-consuming. No matter how deep big companies' pockets might be, they don't want to spend time and money trying to prove an idea is theirs and not someone else's. They need their resources for all the other things involved in running their business.

Some patent attorneys would like you to think that big companies are in the habit of mowing over the little guys. These attorneys want you to be fearful because they want your business. They want you to be so scared of getting ripped off that you'll pay them to file patents for you. You should never get a patent out of fear. First of all, as discussed earlier, you can protect your idea with a $65 to $130 provisional patent application (PPA) for up to 12 months, a period you should spend showing your idea to manufacturers to get feedback and secure a licensing deal. Second—and I can't state this often or strongly enough—companies are *not* out to steal your ideas. It happens so rarely that you are a hundred times more likely to have your identity stolen (1 in 200) than you are to have one of your ideas stolen.

This is what happens more often: two people end up working on the same or a similar idea at the same time. So an independent product developer could approach a manufacturer with an idea that is close to an idea the company's R&D team is already working on. When that happens, it can actually pose a bigger risk to the company than to you. For example, when I submitted my Michael Jordan indoor basketball backboard idea to Ohio Art, I also submitted a few other ideas. Here is an excerpt from the letter I received from my contact at Ohio Art:

> *Dear Stephen:*
>
> *As per our telephone conversation, I am returning all of the items that you sent to me for review with the exception of the Michael Jordan Poster Basketball game.*
>
> *I will not be reviewing any of the other items with our Design Staff due to the fact that we have been very actively working in this area in the past, and I fear that they could be influenced by something you presented, and I certainly do not want that to happen. As a matter of fact, we may be marketing some of these items in the future and you must understand that we have been working in this area and would have no obligation in the event that we do market some products of this type.*

Another reason it is unwise for companies to steal an idea is because they need open innovation to compete in today's fast-changing global marketplace. Most companies understand the value of the multiplying effect: of having people outside their walls working for them. It's like having an R&D team of thousands of people without the overhead.

If a company were to start taking ideas without paying for them, the news would spread and no designers in their right mind would submit ideas to them.

One of the best ways of protecting yourself is also very simple: look into the companies and people you're thinking about working with. Before you begin submitting your idea to potential licensees, Google them. These days, it's highly unusual for a company not to have a presence on the Internet. What are people saying? Is the company friendly to inventors? Search specifically for "lawsuits" and "complaints." Doing a little background research might be extremely useful.

I'll be frank. I think the fear of getting ripped off is overblown. I've submitted thousands of ideas over the years, and only once has a company used my idea without licensing it. (I'll tell you more about that in Chapter 18.) Even then, it was more a matter of miscommunication and confusion than deliberate theft—and this is coming from a person who had to go to federal court to settle the ordeal. If you've used one of the intellectual property protection tools provided by the U.S. Patent and Trademark Office (USPTO) or your appropriate government body, and done your homework to find the right companies to approach with your idea, you'll be fine.

Fear of Cold-Calling

Everyone feels at least some apprehension about calling someone they don't know, and for some people, it is downright terrifying. The first thing you can do to help dispel that fear is to realize you're not really cold-calling; you're presenting your idea—an idea that, if you've done your homework, you know has value to the company. In fact, I've begun referring to the process as "getting in" rather than cold-calling, because that's really what it is. For one, if you follow my advice, you're not going to be doing any selling over the phone. If you've nailed your one-line benefit statement and your one-page sell sheet, your idea will sell itself. And second, calling isn't the only way of getting in. It's more a matter of finding the right company and getting your foot in the door.

However, what is imperative is that you communicate with an actual human being before you submit your sell sheet. The most straightforward way of doing that is to call the company and actually speak to someone who has the authority to review ideas. If you just send an e-mail to someone you don't know—or worse, to "The Vice President of Product Development" or to "R&D," or the worst of all, "To Whom It May Concern"—you will never get the response you want. Almost every day, I hear from a student or client who is afraid to make phone calls. They'll say things like, "I've sent hundreds of e-mails, but no one responds," and "I've been sending drawings, but I haven't heard back from anyone." What a surprise! To a busy executive, an unsolicited submission from a stranger is just more junk mail.

So, the majority of the time, if you want to submit your ideas to potential licensees, you are going to have to bite the bullet and call them directly. I know what you're thinking and what you've been told. I've heard every objection to cold-calling in the book: *People who work at big companies are too busy to talk with little guys like me. It's impossible to get past the gatekeepers to the real decision makers. Everybody prefers e-mail these days.* Yada, yada, yada.

Here's the reality: These guys need you! They are looking for ideas. There are project managers everywhere who are so busy putting out fires that if you come along with a great idea that's going to make the company money and make them look like a hero, they're going to love you. If they get a bonus or a promotion because of your idea, they might even start coming to you for ideas.

So before you make those calls, make sure that you are in the right frame of mind. Believe in yourself and in your idea. Know the benefits the company will derive from your idea. Practice your one-line benefit statement over and over again. Be yourself, and let your passion for your idea shine through. Your confidence and enthusiasm will jump right through the phone, making the person you're talking to want to know more about your idea.

Another thing that may help relieve your anxiety about getting in is to remember that the purpose of that first call is not to sell your idea. It's to introduce yourself, discover what the company's procedure for reviewing outside ideas is, and to ask whether the company would like to know more. So the call should be brief: get on, ask permission to e-mail your sell sheet, and get off. When you get permission, you'll quickly follow up your conversation by e-mailing your sell sheet over.

Here's another fear-squelching tip: When you're first starting out in this game, don't call your top choices of potential licensees first. Call the lesser choices and long shots so you get some practice. My first call is usually a little rough, the second is better, and by the third and fourth, I've found my voice and lost my fear.

Practicing your spiel will go a long way toward alleviating your fear.

Fear of Fumbling

Potential licensees want to determine very quickly whether your idea is a potential fit for their company. So, if they're interested in your idea, they're likely to ask questions and need additional information. It is the fear of not knowing all the right answers, of misspeaking or making a mistake, and of coming across like a bumbling idiot that stops many entrepreneurs and independent product developers dead in their tracks.

The first step to overcoming this fear is realizing this: you're never going to have all the answers. No one does, and no one expects you to. If I don't have an answer, I don't lie or pretend I do. Instead, I say, "I have to get back to you on that." Then I reach out to my network for the answers.

Actually, that's the second step. The first step is to do your homework and your legwork before you make these calls, by:

- Studying the marketplace
- Talking to someone who has done it before
- Knowing how your idea stacks up against similar products in terms of features, benefit, and sales price
- Finding out whether and how your idea will be produced (or implemented, if it is a process or service) and at what cost
- Having a basic understanding of patents, and filing a provisional patent application (PPA) or another type of intellectual property protection

- Researching each potential licensee to get a good understanding of its products and customers
- Knowing the big benefit and all the other benefits of your idea
- Having your one-line benefit statement and your sell sheet ready to go

If you know all of this information, you will be as informed and prepared as possible for the manufacturer's questions and queries.

Everything in this book will help prepare you for all of your dealings with potential licensees. That preparation will help allay the fear of not being able to answer an important question or to provide important information when asked. If you do fumble when pitching your idea to a potential licensee, as everyone does once in a while, be able to laugh at yourself and keep going, perhaps making sure to first review your notes more carefully next time.

But sooner or later, someone is going to ask something you can't provide on the spot. Don't panic! It's OK not to have all the answers, and it's better to be honest about that and get back to the company with the right answer than it is to fake it or give faulty information. If a company representative ever asks for something you're unsure of, always give yourself a day or two to gather the information, your thoughts, and your confidence before getting back to the person. When this happens to me (and it still does, after many years in this industry), I either call back or e-mail the answers in 24 to 36 hours. That's enough time to pull myself together and come back swinging, but not so much time that the company starts to lose interest or question my professionalism. In truth, it's actually better to get as much as you can in writing. Maintaining an extensive paper trail is another way of protecting yourself. I conduct most of my business over the phone, as many entrepreneurs do, but I always make a point of recapping what was discussed in a follow-up e-mail. You should do the same.

On that note, you should file all your research notes, drawings, receipts, sell sheets, and other materials in the same place. Retain a copy of every e-mail and letter you send and receive from each potential licensee, and keep a written record of every meeting (as well as every phone call) you have with each company, making sure to date each entry and briefly note the outcome. A good paper trail will give you the backup you need to both present and protect your idea—killing two fears with one stone: the fear of messing up *and* the fear of getting ripped off. If you ever do find yourself in court—which I hope never happens, and it rarely does—all this documentation will come in handy. The one and only time I had to defend my idea in federal court (see Chapter 18), I had to provide evidence of certain events and timelines.

Fear of Rejection

Rejection is always hard to swallow. No one likes it. But I really think that the fear of being rejected can be worse than actually being rejected—especially when the fear of being told no inhibits you from giving companies the opportunity to say yes to your idea.

One way to reduce fear is to face it. And let's face it: rejection is inevitable in this game. You're going to get a lot of nos before you get a yes.

So here's how I look at it: the more nos I get, the closer I am to that yes. I've come to actually appreciate the nos. Sometimes being rejected motivates me even more. It makes me practice more, prepare better, and give it my best shot. I also always try to find out why the company rejected my idea so I can determine whether I need to and can possibly improve my presentation or my idea, or both. Ultimately, that feedback is very useful. It either improves my chances of eventually getting a yes or brings me closer to the realization that I need to let the idea go and move on to something else.

With these first calls, that's what's most important: the feedback you get from potential licensees. If your idea or your presentation isn't ready or up to snuff, you need to know. This isn't about getting a pat on the back for coming up with a brilliant idea; it's about licensing your idea and getting it to market so you can get paid and go find other ideas. When someone tells you no, put your ego and anger aside, and don't try to argue the point. Ask why your idea isn't a good fit for the company, and really listen to the answers. Many times, a company has rejected my idea but then given me the keys to the castle by telling me why! I was then able to improve my product and resubmit it either to that company or to someone else. Sometimes the guy who rejects my idea will even direct me to another company. At the end of the day, the only way you lose is if you never try. Because once you begin submitting your ideas, you will start forming relationships with contacts at different companies. If a company rejects one of your ideas, who cares? Submitting your next idea to that company just became that much easier. As companies begin to know and trust you, you will get better and better feedback from them.

Every successful entrepreneur on the planet will tell you that rejection is just part of the process. I'm willing to bet most will tell you that it is a critical part. Mistakes are opportunities to learn and grow. As Soichiro Honda, the late Japanese engineer and founder of Honda Motor Company said, "Success is 99 percent failure."

Don't let fear of rejection keep you from presenting your ideas, and don't take rejection personally. Get that feedback, and keep moving forward.

Fear of Failure

This is the big kahuna of the fears that inhibit product developers. This is the fear that you're going to spend a lot of time and money for nothing, that no one will want your idea, and that it will never see the light of day.

I'm not going to kid you: you will fail. This is a numbers game; to be successful, you need to constantly be coming up with new ideas. Some will get licensed; others will not. There is no way to guarantee an idea will get licensed. But there is a way to guarantee failure, which is to quit. It would be a crying shame to quit without giving an idea your best shot.

That's what this book is all about: giving you the information and tools to give yourself the best shot at licensing your ideas—*without* breaking your spirit or your bank account. That's why I developed this faster, easier, and cheaper way of bringing your ideas to market.

I am living proof that you do not have to spend a lot of money and time to successfully license your ideas. My students are living proof that you don't have to let fear force you to spend a small fortune and years of your life on prototypes and patents. You can find and develop marketable ideas and get them licensed by kicking your fear to the curb and following my road map to bring an idea to market.

HOW A FEARFUL ROOKIE KNOCKED IT OUT OF THE PARK!

To describe Linda Pollock as shy is an understatement. She is so "painfully shy," she says, "that it hurts." Often, the mere thought of going to a networking event terrorized her to the point that it made her physically sick, giving her an excuse not to go. When she did muster the courage to attend a conference or workshop, she would try to make herself invisible and would leave as soon as the event ended to avoid talking with anyone. Needless to say, this was not conducive to building a network.

It was at such an event in Santa Rosa, California, that I met Linda. I happened to be a speaker at that event, and Linda took every word I said to heart. She also purchased the inventRight course, *10 Steps to Bring Your Idea to Market*, and she's taken some of our webinars. You see, her desire to succeed as an inventor was greater than her fear of talking to strangers and failing.

Linda had so many great ideas that she could not decide which one to work on first. I suggested she focus on the one she was most passionate about. Linda is a professional organizer, and she had developed a great idea for a desk organizer. Then she did all the fear-busting, confidence-boosting things I recommend to everyone. She researched potential licensees, created a benefit statement and a sell sheet for her idea, wrote out a getting-in script, and practiced it, practiced it, and practiced it.

Never mind that it then took her three days to "get up the nerve" to make the calls. Never mind that she "fell on [her] face the first time, and the second time, and the third time." Never mind that by the fourth

continued

and fifth calls, she says she was "still spitting out words so fast that I was surprised anyone understood me." What's important is that she made those calls, she articulated her idea and its benefits, the company representatives she spoke to did understand, and she got in the door of many companies.

Then an interesting thing happened: companies started calling Linda. They asked her questions about her product and her profession. She took that opportunity to ask them questions, too. That's how Linda learned from the experts, licensed her PileSmart idea, and became an expert herself. One company was so impressed with Linda's knowledge that it asked to see more of her ideas *and* hired her to do a presentation of its product line. That's how Linda found her voice.

With some knowledge, a few tools, and several successes under her belt, Linda Pollock is no longer afraid of being a fool or failing. When she goes to events, she talks with everybody and is among the last to leave. Picking up the phone and making calls is a breeze. Now, she can open any door and walk right in. Linda, thank you for being my first student.

Over the last decade, I have helped thousands of people like Linda kick their fear to the curb and get their ideas into companies. In my experience, I have found that the best offense against fear is information and preparation—and the best defense against fear is information and persistence.

My entire approach to bringing ideas to market is based upon acquiring the information, tools, strategies, and *confidence* you need to get into this game and win it. So kick fear to the curb, get started today, and take it one step at a time.

15

Find the Right Doors to Knock On

M ANY PEOPLE set their minds on licensing their idea to a particular company and don't bother to look any further. Then when
that company says no, they decide to abandon their idea. That is a
huge mistake! And it's one I'm intimately familiar with, because I did
the same thing a couple of times early in my career.

The first time I made that goof was with a simple but novel idea:
to combine toys with books. For example, I included a box of crayons
with a coloring book. I glued the coloring book to a sheet of cardboard
that extended about six inches beyond the right edge of the coloring
book. Then I glued a plastic tray filled with crayons or colored markers
on the cardboard next to the coloring book. My daughter Madeleine
loved this idea, and I used a photograph of her playing with it on my
sell sheet. Other variations included plastic animals that were tied to
the story in the book and game pieces for a book of games.

I submitted several variations of my toy-with-book ideas to a company; it said no to every one of them. I did not ask them why, nor did
I call any other companies. I just tucked my tail between my legs and
put my idea in the reject file.

Today, you can go into any toy store, department store, drug store,
or grocery store and find books packaged with toys. I came up with
the idea a long time ago, and I can't remember now how much later
it was that I saw a book-and-toy product in a store for the first time.
What I do know, and what's important for you to know, is that I threw
a really good idea away by pitching it to only one company and not

even asking for feedback. If I had asked the company why it wasn't interested, chances are I would have realized that my instincts had been right. My idea *was* marketable; it just wasn't right for that company. And that would have given me the confidence I needed to find another company to license it.

It only takes a five-minute phone call to find out why a company rejected your idea. Sometimes the idea is close to what the company needs, but not quite. Sometimes it has nothing to do with the merit of your idea. The timing is just off. The company you contacted may have too many similar items in its product line at that time—but it may be the perfect time for another company.

I didn't realize that back when I came up with and prematurely abandoned my book-and-toy idea. Now that I do know better, I cannot stress enough the importance of finding as many potential licensees for your idea as possible and of learning as much as you can from them. Just like you need to come up with many ideas to win this game, you need to knock on the doors of many companies.

How to Find Potential Licensees

When you first came up with an idea, I advised you to study the marketplace to find out who might buy the product, where they might buy it, and which companies might produce it. You examined similar products and made notes. Then you designed your idea with those consumers, stores, manufacturers, and notes in mind. The manufacturers you identified, then, are your potential licensees! A lot of people think that these companies are their competitors. In reality, they are your potential licensees.

Once you are ready to submit your idea to companies, I want you to go back and look at the marketplace again, this time to make a more complete list of all the companies that manufacture products similar to yours. Start by reviewing your notes from your earlier market research. Before you begin to create your formal list of potential licensees, think about where you envision your product being sold. Do you see it being sold in brick-and-mortar stores? Online? In catalogs?

On television? It's important that you don't limit your potential distribution channels. Don't make the mistake of limiting yourself by geography, either. Inventors often think of only the brick-and-mortar retailers that are familiar to them. Different retailers exist in different parts of the country! Search the Internet and visit the websites of trade associations to find all the major and minor players in a given product category. Searching Wikipedia can be helpful as well. I've noticed that entries on industries frequently include a list of retailers. As you go about creating your list, check out each company's website and online catalog to ensure that your idea fits in with its product lines.

A common mistake inventors make is not casting a wide enough net when it comes to creating their list of potential licensees. These days, I push my students to create a list of 30 companies to call. Yes, 30. At its core, licensing is what? A numbers game. The more potential licensees you come up with, the greater your chances of success are. It's that simple.

Zero in on Your Best Bets

After you've identified all the key players in your product category, you'll need to determine which are most likely to be interested in your idea. Back when you were researching whether and how your idea could be manufactured (Chapter 8), you should have uncovered much of the information you'll need now to determine which companies to submit your idea to. But you'll probably still have to do a little more homework.

This should go without saying, but I'm going to say it anyway because I'm constantly amazed by how many people fail to do this: do yourself a favor, and only approach companies that have the ability to bring your idea to market. Remember how important it is to know whether your idea will sell and how your idea will be manufactured? It makes me a little crazy when someone calls or sends me an e-mail saying something like, "I tried to pitch my bicycle idea to Radio Shack, and it wouldn't even hear me out. What do I have to do to get in the door?" Well, to begin with, go to another door: to a company that actually makes and sells bikes!

Sometimes people just don't do enough research. They'll find the big players in their general product category but won't look into the range of products they produce within that category. Just because a company produces snack foods doesn't mean it has the ability to produce the frozen snack food idea you've come up with. For example, if it makes only dry goods—say, cookies, crackers, chips—it probably doesn't even have the capacity to do frozen snacks. So of course it's not going to be interested in your idea. If a company is making an orange, don't show it an apple. Introducing a whole new product line that requires new manufacturing, distribution, and marketing processes is very expensive and very risky, and companies rarely go that route based on a single idea they've licensed from someone outside the company. For example, when I was selling guitar picks in the music business, I thought about diversifying our product line by making stuff for drummers. Even though the drumstick aisle was right there—just 10 feet away from where we were selling picks in music stores—it proved to be too difficult. There were different buyers, we would have had to work with different distributors, and so on. It was more like starting over, which was ultimately too risky.

On the other hand, don't make the mistake of getting too narrow, either. For example, if you have an idea for a new kind of ice cube tray, you should hunt for companies that are making kitchen accessories out of plastic, as well as companies that make ice cube trays. In other words, include on your list companies whose product lines complement yours, if the products they are manufacturing are made of the same material as yours. If you are wondering whether the company is a good fit for your product idea, find out. My attitude is that within reason, you should call everyone. Why not? It won't take you that much time. You've already done the work; it's not that much harder to call one more company. I'd rather you call companies that end up turning you down than pass up an opportunity.

Another thing to remember when deciding which companies to call is that size matters. The biggest companies, the ones that own most of the shelf space, tend to innovate slowly and from within. Although many large corporations have begun to embrace open innovation, that doesn't necessarily mean they're licensing ideas from independent product developers. More often, it means that they're looking for ideas from and communicating more extensively with their network of affiliate producers. That doesn't mean big players don't license ideas from us little guys. Some do, and more are looking outside their walls for fresh ideas all the time. But as a rule of thumb, the biggest doors are the hardest ones to open. That's because scaling up is especially time-consuming and expensive for big companies. They're more reluctant to take on risk. When I tried to license an idea to Coca-Cola, it had dozens of manufacturing facilities in the United States. Can you imagine implementing a change at dozens of facilities? That's an enormous and inherently risky undertaking. You should also know that working with big companies takes much longer. You will have to be patient!

To put it simply, smaller companies have embraced open innovation because they need it more. They are actively looking for opportunities to set themselves apart. That's why they are more likely to license ideas. However, on the flip side, companies that are too small often don't have the resources to make and market your idea.

Midsize companies are the most desirable because they have the resources, the need, and the desire to bring new ideas to market. Most midsize companies don't have large in-house R&D departments, so licensing ideas is a more economically feasible way for them to innovate for the market. They're often hungry for ideas that will help them grab a bigger chunk of market share—to go from being the number three to the number two or even the number one player in the market. They are more motivated to take chances.

I have a great example of why aiming high isn't always the answer. One of my students, Dario, observed that he had to buy different protective cases for all of his electronic gadgets. He wondered why no one had designed a one-size-fits-all solution. So he came up with an innovation he named GRID-IT!—a "unique weave of rubberized elastic bands made specifically to hold personal objects firmly in place." Immediately he realized that GRID-IT! had enormous implications, that it could be useful in everything from cars to airplane seats. He started contacting the leading makers of electronics and electronic accessories, but none of them were interested. In fact, they flat out told him they didn't get his idea. They couldn't see beyond the fact that it was "just a web of elastic bands." He eventually found a partner in a relatively small company called Cocoon. Cocoon understood the benefit of his idea and licensed the idea from him. Soon, the innovation exploded in popularity. A Cocoon backpack that had panels of GRID-IT! inside it became one of the Apple retail store's best sellers. Global distribution came next. Today, the innovation is featured on no fewer than 1,500 products. The big guys passed on a fantastic idea. Instead, it took an innovative company that was gunning for market share to become his licensee.

I've licensed ideas to companies of all shapes and sizes. So, I think it's a good idea to identify and get to know all the players in a product category and to not rule out anybody based on size alone. At this point, the only companies you should cross off your list of potential licensees are the ones that do not sell products similar to yours. But know that—most of the time—midsize companies are your best bet.

When it's time to start pitching a new idea to manufacturers, I always make a list of all my potential licensees and the city in which each is located (the corporate office or headquarters). You should too. Sometimes, I make two lists: an A list of my top choices, the companies I think are the best fit for my idea, and a B list of my secondary choices.

Find the Right People to Contact

Many people think they should pitch their ideas to a potential licensee's product development or R&D department. In some companies that have open-innovation programs, the product development team members may look at ideas from the outside, but they wouldn't be my first choice to contact with an idea. Their job is to create new products, and they may not be receptive to someone calling them with a new idea they should have thought of. It makes them look bad. An exception is big companies. When you pitch an idea to a big company, the R&D team will have to vet it before it ever lands before marketing or sales.

Contrary to the belief of many inventor types, you should not pitch your idea to someone in engineering or manufacturing, either. Their job is to figure out how to make something *after* marketing and product development have decided they're interested in bringing a new product to market.

Neither do you want to talk with purchasing people. Their job is to cut costs and to buy the materials used to manufacture the company's products. They are usually not involved with licensing ideas, other than perhaps to advise management on the availability and cost of materials required to manufacture an idea.

You want to pitch your idea to someone who will understand how your idea will benefit the company. You want to get it in front of someone who is going to get excited about your product and say, "This is a great idea! How do we license, manufacture, market, and sell it?" Most of the time, that "right person" is in marketing or sales: a brand manager or director, a marketing manager or director, a sales manager or director, or a product manager.

The very best people to pitch your idea to are product managers in the marketing department. Their job is to take an idea from concept to market, and unlike the guys in R&D, they don't care where a good idea comes from. They are also among the hardest people to get a hold of. So if you can't get through to a product manager, your next best bet is someone in sales. Sales reps like to talk and never want to miss a sales lead, so they always answer their phones. If a sales rep or product manager really likes your idea, he or she will pitch it to the marketing manager or marketing director. Then the marketing manager will become your superman. The marketing manager will take ownership of your idea and take it to the vice president or president. So do everything you can think of to get to people in marketing or sales. They are the ones best able to champion your idea and bring it to market.

Sometimes, when you call a company about an idea, you'll be transferred to the legal department, which is OK but not ideal. In that case, you may be asked to submit your idea to the legal department, and if it passes the legal reps' muster, they'll pass it along to marketing or product development. But if you can bypass legal and go directly to someone in marketing or sales, that is the better route to go.

The ideal method is to call a company, introduce yourself as a product developer, explain that you have a product idea you would like to submit to the company, and ask if the company looks at outside ideas.

If it does, you should ask about the process and to speak to someone who is familiar with it. If there is no such person, ask to speak to a product manager or someone else in marketing or sales. If the operator seems confused by your request, that's also a good time to ask to speak to someone in sales or marketing. But these days, many of the companies my students are contacting understand how to manage their calls. Because online submissions are growing more and more popular, a lot of my students aren't calling much to get in whatsoever.

You usually want a director or manager—not a president or vice president. High-level executives of big corporations don't look at new ideas; they pass them along to someone farther down the totem pole. At small companies, it may be OK to approach the president or a vice president with your idea, but if there is a lower-level marketing or sales manager, try that person first.

In the past, I strongly advised against initiating contact via e-mail, but times have changed. Many people prefer to use e-mail as well as check their e-mail more regularly than their voice mail. Approach using e-mail the same way you would a phone call. Introduce yourself, explain that you have a product idea you think is a great fit for the company, inquire about how the company goes about reviewing outside ideas, and ask to e-mail your sell sheet. Keep it very brief—a few sentences should do the trick. Please remember that you should never send your sell sheet without having gotten permission first.

If you are searching for an accurate e-mail address, LinkedIn is a great resource. Similarly, if you're having trouble getting in to a potential licensee, asking to speak to a product manager, brand manager, sales manager, or some other management-level person in marketing or sales by name is a strategy you could use. However, I recommend starting by calling the phone number of the corporate office. That's the first place where you're most likely to find the right person to pitch your idea.

Sometimes the company's toll-free number will be printed on its products or on the products' packaging. When you're studying the marketplace, it's a good idea to always look for and make note of this phone number—which is usually for customer service. Just call that number and ask customer service for the phone number of the corporate office. You can also track down a company's phone number by searching the Internet using the company's or product name and the word *headquarters* or *corporate* as keywords. Still another way to find a phone number is to go to the company's official website, where a phone number is often given on a "Contact," "Corporate," or "About" page. Sometimes, you'll visit a company's website and hit pay dirt! For example, I went to Black & Decker's site and clicked on the "Contact Us" page. Bingo! It not only lists the address and a toll-free number for the corporate office, it also has links to the website of each of the company's brands—organized by product category, no less. Each brand website also has a contact page listing an address and a toll-free number. Not only that, but the corporate website has a "Submit an Idea" page that includes links for submitting ideas!

But I'm getting ahead of myself here. For now, your mission is first to find the right companies to call and then to get a phone number, any phone number, for each company on your list. Call the number, and follow along until you speak to a human. You may need to be persistent, but it is not difficult. As for what to say when you make a connection, I'll cover that in the next chapter.

16

The Call That Gets You in the Door

I THINK ONE of the main reasons so many entrepreneurs go to the time, expense, and trouble of making fancy prototypes and getting patents is because they've bought into the myth that "if you build it, they will come." They think the only way to get a company to say yes is to put on a big show. They think the only way to play with the big boys is to deliver a finished, patented product to their doorstep. It just isn't so.

Prototypes and patents don't open doors, and they don't sell ideas. Preparation and persistence open doors. And benefits kick them wide open.

All the critical steps outlined so far in this book—studying the market, designing for the market, proving your idea, protecting your idea—will help prepare you for the next big step: bringing your idea to market. Now I'm going to show you how simple it really is to get in to potential licensees. When I first began inventing, I used to fax my sell sheets over. Needless to say, that's no longer an effective strategy! Since this book was first published, my techniques for getting in have changed substantially. Increasingly, my students are using e-mail to get in (and sometimes even social media). As open innovation has grown more popular, so have online submission forms. Regardless of the method you use, what's important is that you don't give up until you make contact with an actual human being that you can talk to about your idea.

Why Calling Is Still One of the Best Ways to Open Doors

Like I mentioned earlier, I stopped referring to this process as cold-calling because it's more accurately described as getting in. "Cold-calling" implies that you're attempting to sell something over the phone. You're not. You're going to let your sell sheet do the selling for you. Selling over the phone is just too hard. Why get tangled up trying to sell your idea over the phone when your sell sheet does such a better job? In the past, when companies were less familiar with open innovation, you had to explain the benefit of your idea during that initial call—you needed to pique people's interest to get their permission. That's no longer necessary.

I'm going to go into detail about other methods of getting in later, but for now, know that I think making a phone call is still one of the most effective strategies available to you. When I can, I prefer using the phone because it's efficient. I can have an actual conversation right there on the line, and answer questions if need be. I know that my confidence in and passion for my ideas come through better when I use my voice rather than text. The good news is, the way I teach my students to do it, it's going to be a very easy phone call for you to make. Virtually painless, in fact!

However, I'm not saying that calling always gets you to the right person quickly and easily, or even that it always gets you in the front door. Sometimes you have to go through other doors, and often you have to make several calls before you get your idea to the right person. But calling is a lot easier than you might think when you follow my simple approach to contacting potential licensees.

The Right Way to Call

Most often, you will have to call a company's general number and go through one or more gatekeepers to find the right person to review your idea. Then you may have to make several more calls before that person actually answers the phone or takes your call. No wonder calling is so nerve-racking and frustrating to so many people!

You can make calling a lot easier and more effective by following these simple strategies.

Prepare a Script and Practice, Practice, Practice

Whenever it's time to start pitching an idea to potential licensees, I always write out what I'm going to say on an index card. I practice reading the script out loud over and over again, and then I practice it with my wife or one of my kids until it feels and sounds right.

When you call to get in, you're going to keep your script short, sweet, and to the point. My students tell me that less is actually more; it doesn't take much for the person on the other line to understand why they're calling and how to help them.

Start by introducing yourself, explain that you are a product developer who has an idea you would like to submit to the company, and ask if the company accepts outside submissions from product developers. This is what I say.

> *Hi, my name is Stephen Key. I'm a product developer with Stephen Key Design. I have a great new product I would like to submit to your company. Who could I speak with about that?*

If the operator says something like, "I don't know who handles that," or "I'll transfer you to purchasing (or some other inappropriate department)," I'll say something like, "Maybe I could speak to someone in marketing or sales," or "Is there someone in marketing who deals with (that product category)?"

Sometimes, an operator will tell me the name and title of the person to whom he or she is about to transfer the call: "Certainly. I'll connect you with Sheila Sanders. She's the director of marketing." If that happens, quickly jot down this information. If you have time, ask the operator for the person's extension or direct line. That way, you can bypass the operator the next time you call. If the operator says only, "Certainly. I'll transfer you now," try to ask for the name, title, and extension of the person to whom the operator is forwarding your call. If you're prepared to ask, you may be able to get this information before the operator gets off the line.

If all the stars are aligned and the operator gives you the name of the person he or she's transferring you to and that person answers the phone, start off by greeting him or her by name. Keep it simple and recite virtually the same thing. Then offer to send additional information:

> *Hello, Ms. Sanders. My name is Stephen Key. I'm a product developer with Stephen Key Design. I would like to start submitting my ideas to your company. Can I send you additional information?*

When you make that first call, you have several goals. Your first goal is to understand how the company reviews submissions from outside product developers. Is there a certain person you should talk to? Does the company prefer to receive submissions via its online form? You need to find out. Your second goal is to get permission from the person you're talking with to e-mail him or her your sell sheet, and then to get off the phone as quickly as possible after that. You just want to send him some more information! That's a very simple request.

At some point during your conversation, you may feel tempted to start pitching your idea, but you should resist. Amateurs pitch their ideas over the phone. One of the issues with pitching your idea on the phone is that it fails to create that paper trail I mentioned earlier. Remember, creating a paper trail is for your protection. When you insist on submitting your idea electronically rather than talking about it on the phone, that action in and of itself tells the company that you know what you are doing.

Write a script that covers all of these possible scenarios, and then practice it by role-playing with a family member or friend. Once you've nailed your script, start calling companies.

Call the Last Company on Your List First

With getting in, as with most things, practice makes perfect. The first calls you make will probably feel awkward, and you'll probably fumble a few. But eventually, you'll have more experience and be more familiar with this process than the people you are talking to on the other line. A good idea is to use the one or two companies that are least likely to license your idea or that you're the least excited about licensing your idea to as trial runs. Then work your way up your list so that the fifth or tenth call you make is to the company you most want to license your idea.

Even after you have some getting-in experience under your belt, you may find that the first couple of calls of the day go less smoothly than those you make once you've warmed up a bit. After years of calling, I still sometimes fumble my first calls of the day. So again, I start off my morning by making the least important calls, and if I trip up, I try to recover as quickly and gracefully as possible. I've also learned to just laugh at myself. Once in a while I'll bumble a call so badly that I'll chuckle and say, "Hey, can I start over?" No one has ever said no.

Never Call Yourself an Inventor

The word *inventor* has negative connotations for many people. They immediately envision a hermit with thick glasses, wild hair, and a pocket protector stuffed with pens who tinkers with weird stuff in his shed or basement and never talks to his neighbors. To marketing and salespeople—the folks you want to talk with—the word *inventor* often means someone who is out of touch with the market and builds complex prototypes and files patents on stuff nobody wants.

So never introduce yourself as an inventor. Instead, say that you are a "product developer" or give the name of your "design" company:

> *Hi, my name is Stephen Key. I'm a product developer,* or *Hi, I'm Stephen Key with Stephen Key Design.*

The words "product developer" and "design" both imply that I'm developing products for the market, not for my own curiosity. These terms convey legitimacy, and they are words marketing, sales, and R&D people commonly use themselves.

Stay Focused on the Call

When you're calling potential licensees, you want to be in a quiet place and focused solely on making calls, not doing or thinking about anything else. If you're on the phone and something, someone, or some thought distracts you, you're more likely to blow your spiel: to speak too fast, ramble, not offer to send additional information, or make some other goof. If potential licensees hear your radio, television, coworkers, family, or some other background noise, like people talking in a café, it could signal to them that you're not very professional, and then they may not give your idea the consideration it deserves. Along that same vein, make sure to have set up your voice mail before you start making calls and to always make calls from your dedicated phone number. You want to make it as easy as possible for people to call you back.

Call at the Right Time

People ask me, "When is the best time to call?" The answer is that it's always a good time to call! Some of our students have even gotten in to companies by calling during the holidays—a time most people might assume is a bad one. A much bigger threat than not calling at the "right" time is not calling at all. If you're having trouble reaching someone, try calling 10 minutes before the office workday begins, 10 minutes after lunch, or 10 minutes before the workday ends, when managers are more likely to answer their own phones.

I once mentioned to my wife that I could get through to anyone within any company. At the time, Janice was the VP of marketing at E. & J. Gallo Winery, and she said, "There is no way you could get to me." She knew her gatekeepers, the operator and her secretary, would screen all her calls. But I knew that my wife, like other people who are climbing the corporate ladder and trying to get ahead, would always be at her desk before the gatekeepers arrived and after they had gone home. And she would pick up the phone at those times, just in case it was her boss or another higher-up in the company. Guess what? I got through!

Of course, in today's age of caller ID, the people you're trying to reach may just ignore a phone number they don't recognize and let your call go to voice mail—no matter when or how many times you call. In that case, you'll have no choice but to leave a message, so make sure you leave the *right* one, such as the example I provide in the next section.

Speaking of caller ID: make sure to unblock your phone and make a habit of answering incoming calls whenever possible. The person you've been trying to reach may call from a different number than the one you called, and you don't want to miss a call from a potential licensee.

Leave the Right Message

When I'm calling someone to pitch my idea, I try not to leave a voice message. I just keep calling back until I make contact, and I look for other ways to get in the door. But after you call four or five times without success, leaving a voice mail isn't a bad idea.

Leave a message that goes something like this:

> *Hi! This is Stephen Key; I'm a product developer. I'm calling because I have a product idea I would like to submit to your company. How can I submit my idea to you? You can reach me at 1-800-701-7993. If I don't hear back from you, I'll keep trying.*

That last line tends to do the trick. It tells them that I am persistent and will keep trying.

Call Several Companies

The more companies you have looking at your idea, the more likely you are to get a hit. I always submit my ideas to many companies at the same time. If I had showed my ideas to one company at a time, there is no way I would have been as successful as I have been. Licensing is a numbers game; to succeed, you have to submit a lot of ideas to a lot of companies. An exception to this rule is the direct-response television industry (DRTV). This industry is small, and companies will get back to you very quickly. So if you are planning to submit your idea to a DRTV company, submit to just one company at a time.

Companies do not expect you to submit your idea exclusively to them. Very rarely are two companies interested in an idea at the same time, and if they are, that's a good problem to have! Not only does it give you the option of choosing the best licensee for your idea, it also gives you leverage to cut a great licensing deal.

Don't Hesitate to Call More than One Person Within a Company

If you are trying and trying to get through to a particular person, but are unable to, try calling someone else in the company. If you can't get through to someone in marketing, try another department: sales, brand management, product development, R&D. If one person says he or she is not interested in seeing your idea, try someone else. Just because a product manager doesn't want to see your idea doesn't mean someone in sales won't. Likewise, while marketing and sales tend to be more receptive to outside ideas than product development and R&D are, that may not be the case at the company you're trying to get into. Your idea may be exactly what companies are looking for, but the only way they'll know that is if you call and tell them. The best way for you to get your idea licensed is to cast a wide net, pitching it to as many receptive ears as possible.

By knocking on several doors within a company, I've been able to get at least one of them to open and to get someone to look at my ideas. You can too!

Be Persistent

Some companies are huge, and you may run into a few obstacles, like having to call numerous times before you get through to someone who actually takes your call. Other companies won't know how to handle your call because they don't have "official" open-innovation programs or because they get few, if any, calls from independent prod-uct developers. Most people don't realize they can license their ideas to companies, and so most companies get few, if any, calls from people like you and me.

Regardless of a company's program, or lack thereof, for reviewing outside ideas, one of the most common obstacles to get past are the gatekeepers: the operator who answers the company's main number, an assistant who directs all calls for a particular department, or an assistant to the person you're trying to reach. An operator may be unaware the company even looks at outside ideas for products, and assistants may be unfamiliar with the company's open-innovation policies or may simply be overly focused on running interference for their boss. That is why it is a good idea to get the name and the direct line of the person you want to reach, which increases the odds that that person, rather than a gatekeeper, will answer the call.

Once you get the name of a product manager, or any other name, keep calling until you connect with that person. These people are busy; it could take several calls—a dozen calls!—before you get the person you want on the line. Keep calling until you get to actually talk with the person you're trying to reach. Don't take it personally, and be persistent.

Every once in a while you will call a company and a gatekeeper will tell you the company does not take outside submissions. Just because the gatekeeper says so doesn't make it so. For some companies, calls from product developers wanting to submit their ideas may be few and far between. The operator may simply be unaware that the company has an open-innovation policy. The secretary may just be overprotective, trying to do his or her job. Your job is to get around the gatekeepers to someone who is involved with marketing, selling, or developing new products. Those are the only people who can really say whether your idea is a possible fit for their company.

One of our inventRight graduates called one day to tell me about how he had called a company, delivered his "fast pitch" to the operator, and was told the company did not take outside submissions. But he followed my advice. He was persistent. He called back about an hour later and asked if he could speak to someone in sales. That's all he said: "Can I speak to someone in sales?" When the sales rep came on the line, he introduced himself and asked if he could send him some additional information. "Sure," the sales rep said. "Send me more info on that. It sounds interesting!"

Sometimes you need to be creative to get around roadblocks. And you always need to be persistent.

Speak with Confidence and Enthusiasm

I have found that how you speak is almost as important as what you say. If you have a positive attitude and are passionate about your idea, that will come through in your voice. Likewise, if you're feeling down or insecure, that will come through over the phone, too. After all, the person on the other end of the phone can't see you or read your body language; he or she can only listen to the tone of your voice and your words. If you don't seem confident and enthusiastic about your idea, how can you expect someone else to be?

So first of all, believe in your idea. Because you've done your homework, you can be confident that you've innovated for the market, your product can be manufactured, and it will sell. Practicing your pitch will also help you gain confidence and get more comfortable with calling to get in. Then do whatever else helps you put yourself in a positive and professional frame of mind. If that means making calls in your pajamas, do that. If it means putting on business clothes and going to your private office, do that. If you feel more energized and clearheaded when you stand, then stand up when you're talking with someone. And smile. That's what I do: when I call a potential licensee, I'm feeling good, I'm dressed, I'm standing up, I'm excited about my idea, and I'm smiling. All that confidence and enthusiasm carries right through the telephone line to that other person.

Keep It Short and Focused on Benefits

The purpose of your first call is to get your foot in the door. That's it. The person you're calling—out of the blue, as far as he's concerned—doesn't want to hear a detailed description of your idea. He doesn't want to know how it works and how it's manufactured. He doesn't want to hear some sales spiel. And he sure as heck doesn't want to hear that it's the hottest, most innovative, most perfect product for his company ever. He wouldn't even absorb all of that, given that people remember only about 7 percent of what they hear. But he isn't going to give you time to say all of that, anyway. You're going to have a minute or two to say the only things he wants to know: *Who are you? Why are you calling me? What's in it for me?*

On those rare occasions when the person tries to get you to talk about your idea at length during that first call, don't do it. Instead, tell her that the literature you're sending will explain the benefits of your idea, and then politely end the call.

Take Notes

Keep a detailed record of all your calls. This log can be on paper or on the computer, but it should include the person's name, the company's name, the date of the call, and a note summarizing the call itself. It is very important that you keep track of everyone you've pitched your idea to, what you said to that person, and the person's response. Later on, when you start following up, these notes will be very valuable to you.

How to Make the Most Out of Online Submission Forms

Website submission forms are becoming more and more popular. When a company wants you to use its submission site, you don't have to make a call to get in at all. How easy is that? The way I see it, there are two main reasons why companies are using online submission forms. The first is that the company is receiving so many submissions that it needs a better way of keeping track of them all, which makes sense. The second reason is that the company is not actually very serious about licensing ideas, and its online submissions form is being used as a screening mechanism more than anything else. Let me explain.

If a company wants you to submit your idea via its form, you should. It always helps to follow the procedure a company has in place, which is why the goal of your first call is to figure out what that is. When it comes to online submission forms, what you really need to be aware of is the fine print. Read it carefully. What exactly are you agreeing to when you submit your idea? Some online submission forms include language that is so unfair to the inventor and wrong, it is ridiculous. For example, my students have showed me forms that essentially commit inventors to giving up their rights to their ideas! Who in their right mind would agree to that? Assume that whatever you sign is binding.

When it comes to online submission forms, what you *don't* want to do is submit your idea into a black hole. So when you fill out the form, this is what I would type out in the comments section.

"Hi, my name is Stephen Key. I'm a product developer with Stephen Key Design. I'm wondering if someone is actually reading these forms. If so, could you please e-mail me to let me know? My email address is . . . ."

This is a strategy inventRight coach David Fedewa developed. Most of the time, he says, someone does e-mail him back to confirm that his submission was received. This approach is so great, because now you know that someone has actually received your submission *and* you have a contact to follow up with. If the company is receiving a lot of submissions, it's important that you stand out. Doing this is one way of accomplishing that. It also creates a paper trail, which helps protect you.

It also doesn't hurt to call the company in addition to submitting your idea via its online form. Ask an employee what the company's submission procedure is. When he inevitably tells you to fill out the company's form online, thank him and ask, "Can you give me the e-mail address of the person who receives the form?" That way you have someone's contact information. You could also decide to call the company after you've submitted your idea online, particularly if the form you sign doesn't ask you not to. When an employee tells you, "Oh, we only accept ideas through our website," you can tell her that you have submitted your idea using the company's form. Then ask, "When can I expect a response?" It's very helpful to know what kind of time frame you're working with. The company could review new ideas biyearly! It's totally fair of you to ask what to expect.

The important thing to remember is, just like making a phone call to get in, you want to make sure someone is actually reviewing your idea.

You are trying to create a connection with a human being who can give you some feedback! Don't simply submit your idea and wait for something to come of it.

How to Get In via a Trade Show

I think attending a trade show is a fantastic way of getting your foot in the door, if you make the most of it. Trade shows are unique in that there are no gatekeepers—and everyone who's anyone in an industry is located in the same place for multiple days! Attending a trade show can get pricey (especially if it's out of town), but you should consider it, not as your first option, but as an option.

First of all, make sure you attend the right trade show. Visit the trade show's website to examine the list of who's attending. First, cross-reference your list of potential licensees with the list of attendees to make sure it's the right show for you. Second, don't bother getting a booth. Getting a booth is not only expensive, but it doesn't make much sense for product developers who are trying to license an idea. After all, it's not as if you can start taking orders. Instead, you should focus on walking the floor and approaching the booths of potential licensees to introduce yourself. When I attend a trade show, I get there early and map out which booths I'm going to hit and in what order. Then, when I walk up to a booth, I wait for someone to approach me first. I listen to what the salesperson has to say and compliment him or her on the company's products. Eventually, he will ask me what I do. That's when I introduce myself as a product developer and say that I have an idea the company might be interested in looking at. The salesperson is going to want to get you off his hands as soon as possible, so he can get back to selling, and introduce you to someone else from the company. I always make sure to get the business cards of everyone I talk to, so I can follow up later. If I work a trade show hard, I can come away with as many as dozens of business cards.

Make sure to dress the part, bring two pairs of comfortable walking shoes, and copies of your sell sheet and business cards everywhere! You never know whom you may meet, and when, or where. The more you dress up, the more seriously you'll be taken. It's worth it to make the effort.

Troubleshooting

If none of your efforts seem to be working, or you can't get someone to call you back, don't despair. You're just going to have to get a little more creative. Social media has made it easier than ever before to reach out to a specific person within a company directly, which is great. You could ask the operator to connect you with a specific person (a marketing manager, for example) or you could e-mail that person directly. If you choose to e-mail someone directly, one of the best ways to ensure that your e-mail is read is to write something engaging in the subject line. Your one-sentence benefit statement is perfect for this, because it will surely get the person's attention. This is a good idea even if you're cold e-mailing someone. After all, you want him or her to open your e-mail!

You can also use LinkedIn groups to look for leads. One of our international students got into a company by posting on the page of a LinkedIn group. She asked the group's members if anyone could provide her with contact information for a specific company. It worked! Another strategy is to ask the person you're trying to reach at the company to connect on LinkedIn after you've called him or her a few times. The same day you leave a voice mail, ask to connect. That way, the person will be forced to put a face to your name. As a last resort, you could use social media to ask a company if it looks at outside product submissions, such as via Twitter or its Facebook page. Ask who is the right person to direct your submission to. Someone will most likely get back to you.

Following Up

Getting your foot in the door is only the first step in what is often a long process. It usually takes a while—weeks, if not months—for a company to review your idea to see whether it's a potential fit for its customers and operations. So, I recommend waiting 7 to 10 days before contacting the person to whom you e-mailed your sell sheet to follow up. No one likes to feel hounded. However, after that, following up becomes extremely important. In fact, I cannot state the importance of following up enough. The truth is, people at these companies are busy. They're running around putting out fires! They may need to look at and be reminded of your sell sheet several times before responding to you. You're not bothering anyone, you're being a professional. A good policy is to reattach your sell sheet every time you e-mail the person. You don't want to make someone dig through his or her old e-mails to find out what you are talking about (which the person may not do).

While you're waiting for the company to go through its review process, don't just sit by the phone waiting for a call. Instead, pick it up and call other companies. If you've called all the companies on your list, start working on another idea.

If you don't hear back from a company that is reviewing your idea, call your main contact to check on the status of things. This is also a good time to ask whether the person has any questions and whether you can provide him or her with any additional information to help with the review process.

If You Get a No, Get Feedback

When you finally get an answer from the company, it will come in one of two forms: the company is interested, or it's not. If it's a yes, congratulations! It's time to move on to the contract negotiation part of the licensing process, which I'll cover in the next chapter.

It is hard to hear no. When you do, take a deep breath, and use this opportunity to ask why the company is not interested in your idea. If you receive a rejection via e-mail, take a few minutes to call your contact to thank the person for letting you know that your idea isn't a fit for the company, and then politely ask why. Most of the time, the person will gladly give you an honest and short answer. Maybe it's just the wrong time. Maybe the price point is too high. Maybe your idea is right for the market but not right for the company in question. Sometimes, you can use this feedback to change your idea to fit the market, or simply take your idea to a different company. For example, after learning that a toy idea of mine had been rejected because the company's product line had too many toys in that category, I was able to license it to a different manufacturer.

It is important that you get a yes or no, though. In many cases, you may have to ask for it. Who wants do that? No one! You're happy the company is reviewing your idea, period. No one likes to be rejected, but you need closure (in the form of a final answer) in order to move on. So make it easy for the employee to get off the fence. Ask point blank, "Are you interested?" For years, I avoided hearing no. But it's not good to let things linger. You want to confidently move on to your next project having gained as much knowledge as possible from your first go. And, you protect yourself by getting that no in print. Creating a paper trail is for your benefit, as you probably know by now.

HOW TOM LICENSED HIS IDEA IN TWO WEEKS

One of our inventRight students sent me an e-mail recently telling me that after calling four or five companies using my method, he was "amazed at how easy it was to get into companies and pitch my ideas!" He also reported that in the eight months since then, his "fear of making cold calls has vanished."

Once he started making those calls, Tom licensed his first product in less than two weeks. Although he had to call multiple companies before he finally got one to say yes to reviewing his idea, that company, Sportcraft, licensed his idea when the sales team got excited after watching Tom's YouTube video demonstrating his product, the Disclub.

In the beginning, Tom would write out a script, practice it, change it a couple of times, practice it some more, and then pick up the phone. Now, "the script is long gone," his confidence has soared, he's having "a blast" calling companies, and he's "on the way" to his next licensing deal.

Slip in Through the Back Door

Sometimes it is impossible to get in through the front door, especially with large corporations like Coca-Cola and Procter & Gamble. At best, it is difficult, and you often end up with the legal department. That's not necessarily a bad thing, but it takes longer and is more complicated, and if the legal department says no to your idea, you usually can't find out why. When the sentries at the front door are keeping you away from the people in marketing and sales who you need to talk with, you need to be creative and find other doors to knock on.

The following are some other ways to get your foot in the door.

Think Outside of the Box

There will be times when you just can't get through to anyone in marketing or sales. Do a little brainstorming to try to think of some other department or person in the company who might be interested in your idea. For example, when I was getting nowhere by asking for someone in marketing and sales at McNeil (makers of Tylenol and other consumer healthcare products) to pitch my rotating label idea, I was able to get in touch with someone in the design department who worked on graphics for labels.

Network Your Way In

Do you know someone who knows someone at the company? It doesn't even have to be a direct connection; the chain can be several "someones" long. You just need this connection to allow you to use his or her name when you call this contact within the company—or better yet, to refer you directly to that person. That is how I got into Procter & Gamble; the father of a friend of mine showed a crude prototype of my rotating label idea to the CEO of P&G while playing golf with him. Although that didn't result in a licensing deal with P&G, it led me to build a wall of patents around my idea; now other companies have licensed and sold more than 400 million of my Spinformation labels.

Start at the Local Level

If you can't get through the front door of the corporate office, call a regional sales manager, branch manager, or franchise owner and try to get that person interested in your idea. For example, I couldn't get through to anyone at PepsiCo headquarters to pitch my rotating label idea, so I got in contact with a local Pepsi bottling franchise owner. He liked my idea, and he was able to take it to some top executives at Pepsi and get them interested in it, too.

Knock on Their Ad Agency's Door

All big corporations have advertising agencies that brag about their clients to help attract new business. You can find the ad agency for any company by going to the agency's website, doing an Internet search (e.g., "Pepsi ad agency"), or browsing *Advertising Age* online (http://www.adage.com). Call and ask to speak to the person who handles new business; don't tell the operator why you're calling, only that you'd like to speak to that person. You'll usually be put right through, because the obvious assumption is that you're a potential new client and agencies are always looking for new business. Tell the account exec you have a product innovation one of the agency's clients might be interested in. If he or she bites, bust out your idea sell sheet. It doesn't always work, but once in a while it does.

This is exactly how I got into Coca-Cola. I knew that Primo Angeli, a large design studio in San Francisco (not far from where we lived) had its advertising account because the agency also represented E. & J. Gallo Winery, where my wife worked. I called the agency about my rotating label, and because it was close, I went there to meet with a few staff members. I showed them some samples, including a Coke bottle with my spinning label on it. They picked it up, spun it, and told me they'd be back in a minute. Five minutes later, the agency owner, Primo Angeli, walked into the room and asked, "Do you mind if we show this to our client?"

Sure enough, I got a call from Coca-Cola, and the next thing I knew, I was in Atlanta meeting with them. Although I did not get a contract at that time, the feedback I got at that meeting led me to redesign my label so it could be manufactured faster and at a lower cost. That enabled me to license my Spinformation label to Coca-Cola in Mexico as well as to Accudial and others.

Along the same vein, I've had success knocking on the doors of powerful companies' packaging design firms and equipment manufacturers. People are motivated by the possibility of new business. Give them a reason to want to show your idea to their contacts, and they will.

Try Pull-Through Marketing

Pull-through marketing is when you get the company's customers—the businesses that sell their products to consumers—interested in your idea and then they tell the company's sales and marketing people about it. One way to get your idea in front of a company's customers is to show it to buyers and distributors at trade shows. Another way is to call buyers at Target, Home Depot, PetSmart, or whatever other major retailer sells the company's products to see if they're interested in your idea. When a big customer tells a company, "Hey, I like this idea," the company will usually open the door and invite you in to show it your idea. I had an idea I wasn't getting anywhere with until I showed it to a buyer who wanted it—nine months later the product was available in stores. You could also trying getting testimonials from industry experts, celebrities, trade magazines, bloggers, and so on. Another option is to try to leverage the power of a national television program like *Shark Tank* or a contest like Walmart's "Get on the Shelf" competition. When my innovation won a Gold Award at the Edison Awards, my phone rang off the hook for a week afterward.

Crowdsourcing is a new, exciting form of pull-through marketing. In Chapter 7, I talked about how Eskil Nordhaug was able to harness the power of crowdsourcing to pique the interest of potential licensees. If companies just aren't hearing you, they will listen to the sound of hundreds of customers opening their wallets to order your product. Running a successful campaign isn't easy, but it could be worth it if you're willing to put in the hard work required.

If you were to ask a group of product developers whose ideas never made it to market why they did not, 9 out of 10 would tell you it's because they were unable to get their idea in to the manufacturers. If you were to ask what they did to try to get their ideas to manufacturers, you would learn that they made some of the simple mistakes you learned about in this chapter, like sending unsolicited e-mails, introducing themselves as an inventor, rambling and stumbling over their own words on the phone, calling the wrong companies, talking to the wrong people, not relying on their sell sheet to do the selling for them, not being prepared, and not being persistent.

But when you use the simple strategies and tools outlined in this chapter, doors open. When you call the right people at the right companies and say the right things, someone will let you in to show them your idea. Every week one of my students calls or e-mails to tell me he or she got into three, four, or more companies. The students are often shocked at how easy it is to get in using this approach. I'm not. I know it works. I also know that the more you do it, the easier and more effective it becomes.

PART SEVEN

Bring Your Ideas to Market

You've come up with a marketable idea, validated and protected it, researched potential licensees, and found the courage to call them. As a result, you've accomplished something many entrepreneurial product developers only dream of: you got the right people at the right companies to look at your idea. Now one or more of those companies has expressed interest in licensing it.

You're so excited and nervous, your head is spinning! *What royalty percentage will I get? When do I get paid? What about patents? What if the company wants an exclusive license? Do I have any say in what happens to my idea once the company licenses it? Should I arrange a meeting with the company? Should I call an attorney? What should I do next?*

First, take a deep breath or a long walk. Relax. Negotiating a licensing agreement takes a clear head and a good amount of time, but playing with the big boys is actually easier than you might think. All it takes is information and a few simple strategies. Let me show you the right way to cut a great deal, get your ideas to market, and live the licensing lifestyle.

17

Cut a Great Deal

THE CONVENTIONAL way of negotiating a licensing agreement is to hire an attorney to do it for you. As you may have guessed by now, I only follow convention when it's the best way of getting me where I want to go. If I can find a faster, easier, and cheaper route, I take it. And I have found that doing my own negotiating puts me way ahead of the game.

I actually like to negotiate my own deals, but I also like that it saves me money in attorney fees. Now I'm not suggesting that you negotiate a licensing contract without legal advice. I'm suggesting that you be the go-to person in all direct dealings with a potential licensee. Once you and the company have ironed out any issues and agreed on the main terms of the agreement, then it's time to bring in the attorneys.

Cutting a licensing deal is a lot like playing tennis. Various issues get lobbed back and forth until an agreement is reached. Just when you think all the issues have been resolved, you realize you've only played the first game of the first set and there is another whole match to go. If your attorney is playing for you, the costs add up quickly. Doing the negotiating yourself saves you money. It also usually makes the process go smoother and faster.

Another reason I prefer to do my own negotiating is that it enables me to better understand the potential licensee's business and to develop a relationship with a key player inside the company. As a result, any problems with the contract can be resolved more efficiently, and the deal we end up with is more likely to provide optimal benefits to both the company and me. The insight I gain also helps me ensure my product is brought to market and my royalties are paid promptly and properly, as well as gives me an advantage if I want to license another idea to the company later.

Cutting a great deal is all about knowing what a potential licensee wants and what you want, and then working together as a team to hammer out a win-win agreement. This usually takes anywhere from four weeks to two months. The more you know about negotiating a licensing deal, the better off you will be. Information is the most powerful tool you can bring to any bargaining table.

Leveling the Playing Field

Going up against a big company can be intimidating. The company has a whole team of seasoned experts on its side, and it's just you and your attorney, which I've just advised you to hold off bringing in until the ninth inning. The manufacturer is going to come to the bargaining table with a game plan, and its representatives are going to ask you a lot of questions. One of the first questions they'll ask is, "What do you want?" Regardless of how you answer, they're probably going to want to give you less.

I level the playing field by coming to the bargaining table with:

- A good idea of what I want and of what the company might want
- A good understanding of the company and its market
- My own questions
- The attitude that we are on the same team, rather than opposing teams, and that together we can work out a win-win agreement

I start preparing for the contract-negotiation process *before* I get the call from potential licensees saying, "We're interested in your idea." While they're reviewing my idea, I find out what they sell, how much they sell, and where they sell it.

Let's say a beverage company is reviewing my Spinformation label. Before we start negotiating a licensing agreement, I would want to know all about what the company produces. Does it sell soft drinks, energy drinks, bottled water, juice, tea, milk, beer, wine, hard liquor? Which national and international territories does it cover? Are its products sold by big-box retail stores, convenience stores, and/or specialty stores? Does it sell to commercial accounts? How many units of each product category does it sell annually?

You should have some of this information already from when you were studying the market, finding out how to manufacture your idea, and looking for potential licensees. But you'll probably need to do more in-depth research now to find out what, where, and how much the company sells.

Here are a few ways to find this kind of information:

- **Search the Internet.** For example, when I searched the keywords "Coca-Cola sales distribution," I got more than 80,000 results, including an Answers.com page stating the corporation markets "3,000 drinks under 500 brand names in some 200 nations" and citing the company's major brands, the location of each of its principal divisions, and its principal competitors.
- **Visit the company's website.** You can usually find product information as well as something about sales figures on the site's "About," "Corporate," "Products," "Brand," and "Annual Report" pages. For example, the "About" page of Kraft Foods says the company sells in more than 160 countries and has more than 80 brands; it also gives product and market information for each of its brands.
- **Ask people.** Call a sales rep at another company in the same industry, or call an industry expert, perhaps one who was recommended to you by a trade association. Ask about sales of a certain product industrywide, the market strength of the company you're researching, and where its products sell well and don't sell well, and so on. You can even call a sales rep within the company, tell him or her you're writing a business plan or a paper for a class, and ask about its different product categories (brands), sales territories, and sales volumes.
- **Browse trade publications and trade association websites.** Look for articles, press releases, reports, and announcements on

market data and stats for the industry, a product category, or a particular company.

- **Check online business directories.** These websites feature company profiles that sometimes include the information you're looking for.

You may not be able to find all the sales information you need. That's OK; you can ask the company for it later. What's important is that you have an understanding of a potential licensee's operations, products, and markets before you start negotiating a licensing deal.

Negotiating a Win-Win Licensing Agreement

I've been doing this for years and have had hundreds of companies interested in my ideas, and I still get a rush whenever I find out a company is interested in my idea. It's a great feeling! It can make you want to jump up and down and shout, "Yes! I'll take it! Where do I sign?" Go ahead and jump up and down, but don't say yes to anything and don't get too excited this early in the game.

Just because a company is interested in your idea doesn't mean you'll end up with a licensing contract. Deals fall out all the time. Don't expect to cut a deal right away, either. Licensing deals take time and a lot of negotiating. Although you may be the sole decision maker on your end, several people and departments are typically involved in licensing decisions on the company's end. I used to want to resolve everything in one conversation. Now I know that it may take several calls, lots of correspondence, and many weeks or months to work out an agreement. So I have learned to relax and be patient, and I try to approach the process as a team player and a problem solver. If your licensee is pressuring you to sign the agreement quickly, that is a red flag. I take at least 24 hours to respond to a question, without fail. I need time to think. A good licensee—one that has your mutual interests in mind—will recognize that.

Over the years, I've learned that when an agreement is too one-sided, it doesn't work out in the long run. For a contract to endure, both parties need to be giving up a little bit. At the end of the day, please understand that it's not going to be perfect. You're not going to get everything you want, but neither should the licensee. It's a give-and-take. Both parties are going to feel some pain.

It also really helps to have a big-picture attitude. What do I mean by that? Well, understand that there are going to be many details you will have to hash out, but you don't need to start talking about them right when you get that first call or e-mail. Instead, use your first communication as an opportunity to set things off on the right foot. Express your enthusiasm. Let the company know that you really want to make this work. Show the company that you're interested in working together because it's in *both* of your best interests.

Having a sense of humor goes a long way. Instead of becoming angry when you receive an e-mail that doesn't meet your expectations or when you feel that your potential licensee is being unfair, take a deep breath. A trick I use to defuse the situation is to read aloud an element of the contract that I think is clearly unfair. I'll say something like, "So, let me make sure I've got this right. You mean . . ." More often than not, a licensee will say with a chuckle, "Oh, yeah. I see what you mean. This is what we can do instead." The more you can laugh and keep things in perspective, the better your negotiations will be for it.

When companies are considering licensing your idea, they will often ask what you need, in terms of money, to make it happen. Sometimes they'll throw out a base offer: for example, worldwide exclusive, 3 to 5 percent (royalty), five years. But when I get that first phone call or e-mail saying, "Stephen, we're interested in your idea. How can we move forward?" I like to slow down the process. This is also an ideal time to ask important questions that will help me negotiate the best deal possible. So I usually respond by asking, "Do you want an exclusive license or a nonexclusive?"

Exclusive means the potential licensee wants to prohibit other companies from manufacturing and marketing your product. If the company wants exclusive rights, and most do, it is very important to define the parameters of this exclusivity. So the next thing I ask is for which territory or territories the company wants an exclusive. If the company has more than one category or brand in which my product might fit (which I already know because of my research), I also ask for which product categories or brands it wants an exclusive.

Early in the process, I also ask for sales information. I want to know the most recent sales volume of each product category in which my product will be sold. I want to know the company's sales projections for my product, broken down by sales territory, if possible. I also want to know the wholesale price it intends to charge for my product.

If the company is reluctant to give you this or any other information you ask for, explain that you just want to understand the company's business and how it intends to use your idea. If the company's employees still won't give you the information, then tell them you'll get back to them shortly and go research it yourself. It won't be hard to obtain. But most companies will be forthcoming with this information. It's a good idea to ask for this information early on because the company is much more likely to be forthcoming then than later on.

Take good notes during your research, make a record of every conversation you have with a potential licensee, and keep every piece of correspondence you send and receive from the company. Chances are, you will need to go back and forth several times before all of your questions and the licensee's get answered and before you come to agreement on all terms.

Before we take a closer look at how to address some of the most critical terms of a licensing agreement, I also want to stress the importance of a term sheet. Before you get too deep into the details of your contract, you need to determine whether or not you agree on the big picture. Think of working out a term sheet like dating. At this point, everyone is happy. But if both parties can't agree to the basic terms of the contract, how are you ever going to sign one? Big picture items include exclusivity, the length of the contract, distribution channels, royalty rates, and so on. Later on, after we've agreed to a term sheet and are moving forward, there are more sensitive topics (like minimum guarantees and improvements clauses) I will bring up. But when it comes to the term sheet, it's all about moving forward in a way that satisfies both of you. In general, it really helps to agree on a few things at first. Start out with the easy stuff. You want to get some momentum going.

You want your licensee to feel, "This is going to work!" After the company's employees have invested a lot of time, pulling out will be harder for them to justify.

Even though getting momentum going is important, time is on your side. I need time to think. So do you. Don't let yourself be rushed or pressured, and never agree to anything over the phone. If at some point the company wants to walk away, breathe. Everything is up for negotiation. The deal is never done!

Exclusive Rights

Most companies will want a worldwide exclusive guaranteeing that only they can manufacture and sell your idea. That's a good thing. You want an exclusive. An exclusive has a high value! But you should always ask the person you're negotiating with to define what is meant by *exclusive*.

From your earlier research, you may have learned that a potential licensee has strong sales in certain countries, isn't strong in others, and doesn't sell at all in others. It might be to your advantage to break the licensing deal into different geographic territories, with the company paying more for exclusive rights in its main territories, less for non-exclusive rights in its secondary territories, and reserving no rights in territories where it has no plans to sell your product. For example, the company may want exclusives in the United States, Canada, and Mexico, each of which is a huge market. However, the company sells very little in Mexico, where two or more other companies dominate the market. So rather than lumping all three countries into one licensing deal, you could negotiate an exclusive for only the United States and Canada. That way, you would have the option of licensing your idea to a different company with strong marketing and distribution in Mexico. I don't want you to get the wrong impression, though. Nine times out of ten, you are not going to be signing multiple licensing deals with the same idea. It does happen, and I have done it, but it is not common. Of course it's always a good opportunity to look out for!

The same goes for product categories: your idea may be suitable for categories in which the manufacturer does not sell products. That's why

I usually ask, "For which categories do you want an exclusive?" to which the company usually responds, "What do you mean by categories?"

Let's say I'm negotiating with a soda company to license my rotating label and the company says, "We want your label for all beverages." I would have to say, "Well, let's talk about that." The beverage industry is huge and includes several product categories.

If the soda manufacturer sells mostly soft drinks, water, and juice and only in the United States, Canada, and Mexico, I could offer it exclusive rights for those three product categories and in those three territories. If the company was coming out with a new energy drink and had recently acquired a large beer producer in Japan, it could counter that it wants exclusives in those product categories and in that territory as well.

You may also want to further define *exclusive* by sales channel. Does the company want to sell your product in only big-box retail stores like Target, Home Depot, Toys"R"Us, Walmart, and Costco? Does it want to sell your product in drugstores and supermarkets, too? What about convenience stores and specialty stores? What about institutional sales, such as hospitals, hotels, restaurants, schools, and the military? Maybe the company would be willing to limit its exclusivity to only major retailers and food service providers.

Will a company always agree to restrict its exclusive rights? Will holding back some markets work in your favor? Is there a substantial global market for your idea? I can't answer that, because every company, every product, and every deal is different. The only way to find out is to do your homework, discuss exclusives with the company, and decide what is in your best interests. Maybe the only way a company will license your idea is if you give it a worldwide exclusive. Maybe it's the only game in town, and no other company will be interested in licensing your idea. Maybe no one will want to take a chance on your idea outside the United States, and that's OK. The U.S. market is plenty big for most products. Whether the company wants an exclusive on all or some markets (or not), you should be compensated properly for the rights it is licensing.

Remember, the company isn't buying your idea outright. It's renting the right to manufacture and market your product for a specific market, during a specific period of time, and for a specific rate of compensation. Each piece of an exclusive has value, and you need to be adequately compensated for it. You can give away some value, but you can and should keep some value for yourself. One strategy I sometimes use is to hold back on certain countries the company wants and then later offer to give it those territories if it's willing to pay for the patents in those countries.

Here's another negotiating strategy that my students and I have had success with. Let's say a potential licensee wants worldwide retail rights to your idea but sells only to Walgreens drugstores. You could say something like, "I will give you an exclusive for all retail categories, even though you sell only in Walgreens." This lets the company know you are making a concession, that it's not a perfect deal for you, but it gives you some leverage in negotiating a higher royalty and higher minimum guarantees.

Remember, you're trying to understand the company's perspective. What does it need for the agreement to be successful? That should be an easy conversation to have! Don't lose sight of that. No company does everything well. They all have strengths and weaknesses.

Royalty

A royalty is a percentage of the wholesale sales of your product. Companies pay licensing royalties four times a year, once per fiscal quarter based on the previous fiscal quarter. Each payment is due and payable within 30 days of the last day of the fiscal quarter. For example, if the first quarter is January through March, the first-quarter royalty check would be due and payable by April 30.

People often ask me, "What is a fair royalty rate?" What's fair is whatever you can get—or the most you can get! I know that sounds terrible, but it is reality. Royalty rates vary somewhat from industry to industry. So find out the average royalty rate in your industry; a trade association or someone who has successfully licensed ideas in that product category or industry should be able to provide you with this information.

I know of many entrepreneurs who have killed deals by asking for an unreasonable royalty percentage. As a rule of thumb, 10 percent is too high and 1 percent is too low, though it depends on the product, the company, and the market. For most ideas, 5 to 7 is a fair royalty rate. What I usually do is start at 7 percent, and during negotiations, that figure usually works its way down to 5 percent.

Some ideas warrant a larger royalty. Of course, there are the big ideas owned by the Disneys of the world, but there are also situations in which a small idea can command a higher royalty rate. For example, if the company is going to sell a relatively small amount of your product and the profit margins are high enough, you might want to ask for 10 percent and settle for no less than 8 percent. The novelty business is like that sometimes. For example, a company may only want to license your idea for a few months during the Christmas season or some other shopping season (e.g., summer). Companies may license a seasonal product for a single season or for a few seasons.

Sometimes, a smaller royalty is in order: for example, if your patent doesn't issue or no intellectual property protection is available in that country or if sales volumes are very large. If my Spinformation label was on a beverage that sold billions of units a day, the licensing royalty could be a fraction of a percent. Your royalty percentage will also be less if you need to split it with someone else. For instance, I received a smaller royalty for the Michael Jordan Wall Ball because the royalty was shared between me and Michael Jordan.

Ultimately, the right royalty is the rate you're able to negotiate. Just be careful not to give away your idea for less than it is worth, and don't dig in your heels on a royalty that is deal-breakingly high.

Advance Against Royalties

Asking for a big lump-sum payment up front is the number one way entrepreneurs and independent product developers kill a deal. This is called "top-loading" a licensing agreement, and it's a lousy way to do business. It does not take into consideration the manufacturer's situation, signaling to a potential licensee that you are looking out only for yourself and aren't all that interested in reaching a win-win agreement. It doesn't exactly foster the kind of mutually respectful and beneficial long-term partnership that you want, or should want, to establish with the manufacturer that is going to be selling your product for years to come . . . and maybe license another of your ideas in the future.

Typically, though, some money needs to be paid up front as a gesture of goodwill. Most potential licensees will agree to pay a small advance. However, they will not offer it, so you will need to ask for it.

Here is what I like to do: in lieu of a big advance, I ask the manufacturer to pay for my patents. In fact, that is how I've paid for many of my patents. My attorneys filed them and I own them, but my licensees paid for them. While an advance is a gesture of goodwill, having a company pay for your patents is good business. It protects the company's interests as well as yours, and it helps incentivize and motivate the licensee to bring your idea to market so it can recoup the patent costs. If the company says no to a lump sum for your intellectual property, ask if it's willing to make that payment recoupable against future royalties. That way, the cost is spread throughout the year. Who would say no to that? You're looking out for both of your interests. A lot of deals are signed using variations of this concept.

Sometimes, the manufacturer will be willing to pay a small cash advance in addition to paying for your patents. It all depends on how big your idea is and how much money the manufacturer stands to make.

Minimum Guarantees

One of the most powerful bargaining chips you can use is something called minimum guarantees, which in a licensing contract is a type of performance clause. The minimum guarantee in a licensing agreement specifies the minimum amount of money (a dollar amount) the company will pay you the first year (or quarter), the second year, the third year, and so on, regardless of how much of your product the licensee actually sells. If it sells more than projected, you will receive more than the minimum guarantee for that year. If it sells less, you still get paid the minimum guaranteed amount for that year. If it does not pay the minimum guarantee, you get back the licensing rights to your product.

Without some sort of performance clause, the licensee could sit on your idea forever and never pay you, and you could be prevented from licensing your idea to another company. With minimum guarantees, if the licensee fails to bring your idea to market, you have the right to cancel the contract. If it does bring your idea to market but fails to sell the specified minimum quantity, you still get paid the royalty on that minimum-quantity amount.

Here's how I like to structure my minimum guarantees: I start out low the first year, increase it a little the second year, and hit them between the eyes the last year. Let's say that, back when I was asking for sales projections, the sales manager said, "We can easily sell $10 million worth the first year." I might say, "You said you could sell $10 million the first year, but if you can sell $2 million, that's good enough for me."

On a 5 percent royalty, my first-year minimum guarantee payment on net sales of $2 million would be $100,000. If first-year sales exceeded $10 million, I would receive more than $100,000, but if they were less than $10 million, I would still receive $100,000. The second-year minimum guarantee might be $150,000 (5 percent of $3 million), the third year $250,000 (5 percent of $5 million), the fourth year $350,000 (5 percent of $7 million), and the fifth year $500,000 (5 percent of $10 million).

When you structure your minimum guarantees this way, it puts the risk on the back end and gives the licensee more time to reach its own sales projections. It keeps the company focused on the minimum guarantees for those first couple of years rather than on the royalty amount. It also gives the company a strong incentive to get your idea to market and to put some muscle into marketing and selling it.

Many people think advances and royalties are the most important things. They're not: minimum guarantees are—both to you and the manufacturer. Without minimum guarantees, the manufacturer could sit on your idea and delay bringing it to market or never do it. Minimum guarantees lock in the deal much tighter, and they guarantee your idea will be brought to market or that you will be paid the minimum amount and get your rights back if it is not. That being said, you should wait to bring up minimum guarantees until later on during negotiations. Understandably, companies don't like them. When you do bring up guarantees, use the phone rather than e-mail to do so. It will go better (as discussions about all touchy subjects do). I've also found that licensees respond better when I speak about minimum guarantees in terms of units, rather than dollars (even though they mean the same thing!). For example, rather than saying, "$2 million net sales," say "10,000 units." You get the idea.

If the company will not agree to a minimum guarantee, you can sometimes negotiate an "inside/outside date" instead. This provision states that the company agrees to bring your idea to market no sooner than a specified date and no later than a specified date, and if the company fails to comply with that provision, all rights revert to you. Although this is better than nothing, it is far from ideal. Without minimum guarantees, the company can retain licensing rights to your idea even if it sells only one of your products within that time frame. So I don't recommend this option until and unless you've exhausted all other potential licensees *and* tried but failed to include minimum guarantees in your contract.

Improvements

This is extremely important, but it can sometimes be a prickly point. So I usually slide it in a little later in the negotiations process, after the manufacturer and I have reached agreement on the other major terms of the licensing deal. I always ask for ownership of any improvements that are made to my idea. The licensee "rents" the exclusive right to manufacture and market my idea, and if that involves the company making improvements to my idea, that's fine with me. But the company has to pay for the patents, and the patents are all in my name. I own my idea lock, stock, and barrel.

This "improvements clause" came in handy a few years back after I had negotiated and signed a licensing contract with a large label manufacturer. For about a year, I worked with a gentleman there whom I thought was my ally and was trying to bring my rotating label idea to market. What he was really doing was trying to get around my patents; he actually filed a couple of patents on top of my technology. But he didn't read the fine print in the licensing contract: the clause stating I owned all improvements. The contract gave his company the right to manufacture and market my Spinformation label with his improvements—but only if it hit its minimum guarantees.

Audits

The last thing you'll want to request is the right to audit the licensee's accounting records if you suspect you are not being paid what you're supposed to. Auditing a company's books does not foster trust, and licensees do not like this.

So how do you get an audit clause into your contract? Well, like every other aspect of negotiating a deal, you make it fair to both you and the licensee. Here is how you do that: you ask for the right to audit the licensee if you suspect a discrepancy between how much of your product is being manufactured and sold and the royalty checks you are receiving. Then—and this is where the fair part comes in and why the company will likely agree to this clause—you agree to pay for the certified public accountant (CPA) if no significant discrepancy is found. If the CPA finds a serious error that resulted in a loss of, say, 5 percent or more in paid-out royalties, then the licensee will have to pay for the CPA's audit. If there is a discrepancy, ask your licensee to pay not only the difference, but also interest on the difference—that's what is fair.

Put It in Writing

I know I've said this before, but it bears repeating: it is so important to have a good paper trail of the entire contract negotiation process! I keep copies of every piece of correspondence exchanged between a potential licensee and me. During every phone conversation and one-on-one meeting (which are rare), I take good notes, and then I send a follow-up e-mail that sums up what was said and agreed upon.

Then once a potential licensee and I agree on the big picture, I write up a one-page term sheet and send it off to the manufacturer. This says to the company, "I think we can work together, and here are the terms we have talked about." Sometimes, the manufacturer and I will have a few more conversations about the terms, and the proposal will go back and forth a couple of times, with items being crossed off, changed, or added.

Working out the main terms of the licensing agreement with the manufacturer and putting it in writing will save you a significant amount of money on attorney fees and improve your chances of closing a deal. It says to a potential licensee, "I think we can work together." The licensing proposal can then serve as the basis for creating the actual licensing contract.

That's when it's time to get the attorneys involved. Drawing up a licensing contract is expensive, and many companies have a standard licensing agreement. Let the company pay for the contract, and then have your attorney review and redline it. When you first read it, it will be one-sided. Don't be taken aback by that. The company's lawyers wrote it! I like making them throw the first punch. That way, I know what they want. Always make sure to bring in your licensing attorney to look things over. Even though I negotiate upwards of 95 percent of my contracts, I would never sign anything without having a licensing attorney comb it over first.

HOW A LITTLE GUY USED KNOWLEDGE TO PLAY TOUGH WITH THE BIG BOYS

You're excited that a company is interested in licensing your idea, understandably. But it really does pay to slow things down! There are lots of nuances you need to be aware of, and that takes time. For one, you must read the language of your contract very carefully. One of my students invented a very clever innovation. She knew that scissors are often misplaced, frustrating those who need to use them. (This is certainly true of my own household.) So she designed a stationary cutting device that sticks on the wall—allowing users to cut whatever they need to cut without having to waste time searching for misplaced scissors.

However, in her contract, her potential licensee included a provision stipulating that its contract only applied to one of her patents. In other words, if that patent didn't issue, it wasn't going to pay her. We discovered that the licensee was carefully tracking the office actions (which the USPTO makes publicly available online) of that patent as it worked its way through the system to see if it would actually be issued. So I encouraged her to file more patents and to include a provision in her contract stating that it applied to all future intellectual property as well. She informed her licensee's representatives that she was applying for more IP "to protect their interests." The key word there is *their* interests. She outsmarted the big guys this way, and you can too.

Even experienced professional product designers need to know how to cut a good deal, to be prepared for the give-and-take that it usually involves, and to be in control of the contract negotiation process. You should, too. Chances are, the draft contract will be lobbed back and forth and amended at least a few times. Rarely do you get everything you want, but then, neither does the licensee. With a good licensing contract, both sides feel a little pain but end up with what they need and want the most. Don't fight all the issues at one time; make a couple of changes during one go-around and a couple more the next. Just keep moving the ball down the field, and before you know it, you and your licensee will be signing on the dotted line.

18

Living the Dream

WHEN PEOPLE find out what I do for a living, they often wonder how successful I really am at licensing ideas to companies. They have a hard time wrapping their head around why a large corporation would want to rent an idea from someone like me—a lone entrepreneur working out of a small office, with only an office manager. They question how I could possibly come up with an idea that a large company's own product development and R&D people could not. They can't imagine why a big company would even open its doors to a small fry like me.

When they find out how successful I've been at this game, that I've been able to cut great deals with dozens of corporations on more than 20 of my ideas, that the royalties have enabled me and my family to live the life of our dreams in a very beautiful place, including graduating from college debt-free and traveling—they want to know how they can get companies to license their ideas, too.

"Just come up with a good idea and do the right things to get the right company to license it," I tell them. Then I give them a quick rundown of how to do that, the steps we've covered so far in this book, like studying the market, validating and protecting your idea, pitching your benefit statement and sell sheet to potential licensees, and cutting a great deal.

"That's it?" they ask. "Sounds simple."

"It is simple," I'll say. "But there's one more step to creating the licensing lifestyle. This is a numbers game. So you have to keep the ideas—and the royalties—coming."

Now I'm going to tell you how to do just that.

A Marriage Made in Heaven?

In a perfect world, every deal you cut with a potential licensee would result in a win-win licensing agreement that never needed to be amended. The licensee would quickly and adeptly bring your idea to market. It would pay all your minimum guarantees and all royalties to which you were entitled, in full and on time, for the length of the contract. Sometimes it happens that way. It is just as likely that you will need to keep your hand in the game, or at least your eye on it, to ensure that your licensee doesn't sit on your idea, try to design around your idea, or neglect to pay every dollar due to you.

The least likely of these scenarios to happen is for a licensee to design around your idea to avoid paying you royalties. As I've said before, most companies need and want ideas from entrepreneurs like you and me to compete in today's innovation-driven global marketplace. Trying to intentionally rip off independent product developers is not in their best interests. If you negotiated for an improvements clause in your licensing contract, they wouldn't get away with it, anyway—if, that is, you knew about it. That's why you need to police your licenses, as I will explain how to do in this chapter.

The most likely of these scenarios to occur is that the licensing contract will need to be amended. During the processes of developing a product and figuring out how to package, manufacture, sell, and distribute it, any number of circumstances can arise that require a change or addition to a licensing agreement. So you'll need to be flexible, but you also need to be smart. If you maintain a good working partnership with the company after the honeymoon, you won't be blindsided when your licensee wants to amend the contract. You'll also be in a better position to ensure that the amendment is really necessary and works for you as well as the company. For example, if the company has a legitimate reason for wanting to reduce its minimum guarantees, maybe you agree to that—because in exchange, the company agrees to limit its exclusive to one country or to a certain product category.

As for the odds of a company licensing but never manufacturing and marketing your idea, that risk is greatly reduced by writing minimum guarantees into your contract. Because the licensee has to pay the minimum guarantees whether or not it hits its sales projections and because it can lose its licensing rights if it does not pay your minimum guarantees, it behooves the company to get your product to market. But it sometimes takes a while to do that. Sometimes glitches—in design, patenting, manufacturing, packaging, or distribution—delay the process. And sometimes markets change during the process. So you need to stay on top of the process and help in whatever ways you can after the honeymoon is over.

Then there's the matter of money, and money matters a lot. You need and deserve to be paid, and your licensee is legally obligated to meet the advance, royalty, and minimum guarantee terms of your contract. It's also legally obligated to pay for your patents, if that clause is written into your contract as well. Rarely does a licensee delay or withhold monies it owes to a licensor or for patents. When it does happen, it is usually due to an oversight or a mistake that can be resolved by contacting the company and discussing the matter. Sometimes, though, the licensee does not have the resources to pay up, and once in a blue moon, you'll run across a company that is deliberately trying to stiff you. Whatever the case may be, you need to police your licensees so that you'll know about any discrepancies and can take appropriate action to resolve them.

A licensing partnership is a lot like a marriage. It only works when both parties are working toward a common goal. If it's a good marriage, there is an understanding of and respect for one another's needs and wants. There is a willingness to resolve differences and problems, and there is a spirit of give and take.

If it's a bad marriage—well, the sooner you recognize that, the better. Then the only good resolution is usually to end it . . . as fairly and peacefully as possible. Sometimes that means going to court and letting a judge or jury decide. More often, though, if a licensee fails to bring your idea to market within a reasonable period of time or to make your minimum guarantees and royalty payments, you can just cancel the licensing agreement.

After the Honeymoon

Contrary to popular belief, your responsibility for the success of your idea doesn't end after you've signed a licensing contract. There are still myriad reasons why your idea might not make it to market, and there are many things that can go wrong once it does. No one is going to be a more passionate advocate for your idea than you are, and you no doubt have some design, manufacturing, or marketing expertise to offer, too. If you're working in conjunction with the licensee, the likelihood of your idea making it to market is much higher. Staying involved with the company also puts you in a better position to work with the company to amend the licensing contract if things change or don't work out as planned.

Now, some people (especially those who think of themselves as inventors) want to license their idea and have nothing more to do with bringing their product to market. Others want to control, or at least have a say in, every aspect of it—from how the product is designed to how it's manufactured, packaged, marketed, and sold. Likewise, some companies will want you to go away and never contact them again, while others will be receptive to and appreciative of your advice and assistance.

In my mind, there is no question as to whether you should be involved. It's simply a question of determining the appropriate nature and level of your involvement. And that depends, to a large extent, on the company you're dealing with and on the relationship you've built with it. That's one of the reasons I like to negotiate my own licensing terms: it helps me better understand how the company operates and to strengthen my relationship with the product manager or some other key person within the company.

During the negotiation process—and before that, when I'm trying to get my foot in the door and showing a potential licensee my idea and discussing it with company employees—I ask a lot of questions, do a lot of listening, and take good notes. By the time we've signed a licensing contract, I usually have an idea of how I might support the licensee in bringing my idea to market. So I offer a specific type of assistance, or I simply ask the product manager, "How can I support you in this?" At the end of the day, I want my idea to see the light of day. So I try to offer the licensee whatever assistance I can to make that happen.

You can ask for a fee for your services, and sometimes you can write your role into the contract. But I volunteer my assistance free of charge, and I usually wait until the contract has been signed to broach the topic. Sometimes companies take me up on my offer, and sometimes they don't.

If the company does not want me involved, I don't press it. However, I might offer my help later if I see the company struggling with something. When Disney was launching a new beverage called Twist 'n' Chill that featured my rotating label technology, I sat in on some of the product development meetings, and I could see the staff was having trouble coming up with creative content for the label. So after one of the meetings, I quietly asked the project manager if I could help with that. Sure enough, he took me up on my offer, and I was able to help move things along.

One way to stay involved with your idea is to add some "brand standards" language to your licensing agreement. For example, you could try to negotiate to have final approval of all products derived from your idea as well as final approval on packaging. Most companies will not agree to this. When my partner and I (at Hot Picks, my one foray into manufacturing) licensed intellectual property from Disney, the contract included many stipulations on how we could represent the brand. It also included a clause stating that Disney had to give final approval of all products before they went into production. You may be able to negotiate with your licensee for similar stipulations—but it's a long shot.

Most of the time, it's better to just offer to help if and however the licensee needs it. You can help your licensee in many ways. You can give design assistance or manufacturing advice. You can refer the company to a materials vendor or a packager. You can offer to participate in any promotional activities the licensee has planned or to send a press release to your mailing list. Often, I will offer to try to get the media to write a story about the product and me, as the product's developer. You can even open a promotional door for the licensee, as I did when

I got Accudial, which licenses my Spinformation label, on the television show "The Doctors." In that case, I was totally behind the scenes; I got the ball rolling and then turned it over to Accudial's PR people.

The important thing to remember is that when you license your idea to a company, it's the licensee's baby now. Yes, you still own the intellectual property, but the company owns the product—and the company is in charge of getting it to market. So you probably won't have much say, if anything, in the product's name, packaging, and final design nor in how it's manufactured and sold. If you want complete control of every aspect of your idea, then licensing is not the game for you. I know it's hard to relinquish control of your creation. I had a hard time with it at first too. But I became used to it and soon came to love creating and selling my ideas, even if a company ended up changing my idea in a way I wasn't completely comfortable with. My kids used to ask, "Dad, why isn't your name on the product?" I would tell them, "The only place my name needs to be is on my check."

So if the company wants you to be involved, great! Do what you can, but take a supportive role. Be careful not to overstep your boundaries, never act as a rogue player, and always give credit to the project manager or whomever you are working with. When the company sees that you're a team player and that it can count on you, it will appreciate your contribution and work even harder to make sure your idea is a success.

If the licensee doesn't want you to be involved, step back and let the employees do their job. Check in once in a while, and offer your assistance again if you really feel they need it and you're confident you can help. But don't be a pest. Respect their authority. And focus on collecting your royalty checks and creating new ideas.

Policing Your Licenses

Among the most common questions I hear from people new to licensing their ideas are, "How do I know how much of my product the licensee is really selling?" and "How do I make sure the licensee pays me what it promised to?" There are some simple ways to police your licensees to make sure you receive all the royalties to which you are entitled.

One way is to include an audit clause in your licensing contract, which I told you about in Chapter 17, and then send in an auditor to audit the company's books if—and only if—you suspect the company is selling more of your product than it's paying you royalties for. This is actually not a simple way to police your licensees. It's risky, and it's expensive. An audit is a major imposition to the licensee; it takes up a lot of time, especially if it's a large corporation, and no company likes someone going through all its accounting records. If no serious discrepancy is found, you'll have to pay the cost of the audit, which can be quite expensive. However the audit turns out, it could also put a serious strain on your relationship with your licensee. So I strongly suggest you audit a licensee's books only if you have some kind of evidence indicating a discrepancy between what's being sold and what you're being paid, and only as a last resort. And be prepared to lose money if you are wrong.

There is another way to police a deal that is much simpler and won't cost you a dime: keep your eyes and ears open. Pay attention to what your licensee is doing in the marketplace. Does it have any new products? Is it selling in new product categories or new territories or new stores? Which of its products are selling well? How is your product selling? Browse the company's website, read trade magazines, go shopping, search the Internet, and talk to industry experts. Talk to the company's sales reps, and don't be afraid to ask them which products are selling well and how your product is selling. Salespeople love to talk about these things!

If while scanning the market you discover something you think is awry, call your licensee and calmly try to get to the bottom of it. Do not accuse the company of wrongdoing; instead, tell your contact what you discovered and ask him or her what's going on. Maybe you found your product in a Walmart in New Jersey, and to the best of your knowledge, you've been receiving royalties only on convenience store sales west of the Mississippi. Or maybe you found that the licensee is using your idea in a new product that you were unaware of and are pretty sure you aren't receiving royalties for.

Most of the time, it's either a fumble or a dropped ball, an unintentional screwup. And it can usually be resolved or explained with a phone call to your licensee. In those rare instances when a little foul play is going on, once the company realizes you're paying attention and expecting it to pay up, it will usually be quick to correct course and unlikely to repeat its "error." If the problem is bigger and nastier than that, you'll need to get your attorney involved.

Many years ago, I licensed my Michael Jordan indoor basketball game to Ohio Art. I was very happy with the good job the company was doing keeping the Michael Jordan Wall Ball in Walmart, Toys"R"Us, and other stores around the country for years. A few years into the licensing contract, I was strolling down the cereal aisle at my local grocery store looking for clever ideas on the backs of cereal boxes, and I saw a mini-version of the Michael Jordan Wall Ball on a box of Wheaties. The first thing I thought was, *Wow! What a great job Ohio Art is doing marketing my idea.* The next thing I thought was, *Why am I not getting a royalty check for this mini-version of my idea? The company mentioned nothing about this to me!*

After I finished freaking out, I called my contact at Ohio Art and politely asked why I wasn't getting royalty checks for the mini-version of my idea. The guy stumbled a little, "Ah, well, we must have overlooked that. I'll talk to accounting and make sure you get a check for that." That's all it took to resolve the problem: a two-minute phone conversation. I didn't need to yell. I didn't need to threaten an audit. I didn't need to file a lawsuit. I just had to call, and the royalty checks for the mini-version of my idea started coming. I never even found out if they did it on purpose.

The thing is, some companies are so large that one hand doesn't know what the other arm is doing. Occasionally, someone will get lazy or try to pull a fast one. So you have to police your deals to make sure you know what the licensee is doing with your idea and that you're getting paid for it.

It's also a good idea to survey the marketplace to determine whether a potential licensee that's sitting on your idea, or one that passed on it, has brought that idea to market without your knowledge—and without paying you. It doesn't happen often, but when it does, it can be brutal. It happened to me once.

MY ONE AND ONLY COURT BATTLE WITH A LARGE CORPORATION

So many people are afraid of having their ideas ripped off, and patent attorneys feed on that fear. I don't like using the terms *rip off* and *steal*. A better word might be *infringement*, and most of the time it is unintentional. I have submitted thousands of ideas over the last 30 years, and I have had only one real problem. I now believe it could have been avoided.

I had a master license for my Spinformation label technology with CCL Label. That company sublicensed it to a company called Kenilworth in Ireland. Lego, a privately held company headquartered in Denmark, contacted Kenilworth asking for samples and a quote to use this label on a new toy called Bionicles. After we signed nondisclosure agreements and my office made samples, Kenilworth gave the quote and samples to Lego. Then all communication stopped.

About 12 months after our conversations ended, I returned from a six-month trip around the United States with my wife and three kids. My son's birthday was approaching and he loved Lego, so my wife purchased the new Bionicles product for him. I remember this like it was yesterday. I was out in the garage, and Janice came out with this toy in her hand and a strange look on her face. She said, "Steve, you won't believe this, but the new Lego that I bought our son has a spin label on it." My heart sunk to my feet. The first thing I did was call my attorneys.

At the time, I had multiple patents and many patents pending in many different label formats for this technology. Apparently, Lego's engineers tried to design around my patents, not realizing I also had patents pending.

I felt violated. I took it personally, and I let my emotions take over. I ended up suing Lego in federal court in San Francisco, California. My attorneys took my case on a contingency basis, since they had written all of my patents. To litigate a patent infringement case can cost upward of $1.5 million. Most attorneys won't take on a patent litigation case unless there are at least $20 million in sales. So this is not an option for most independent product developers.

continued

It was a long, painful process. The first day in court, I remember seeing *Stephen Key Design, LLC, et al. v. Lego Systems, Inc., et al.* and thinking, *I have arrived*. I also remember watching all the attorneys from Lego and my attorneys argue over words, over interpretations of words. Instead of using gloves, they battled with words, and the judge acted as the referee.

I signed a document limiting what I can say about the case. I cannot reveal the terms of the settlement; I can only say that we settled on terms that are confidential after three years of litigation. Lego never took a license from me, and they stopped using the rotating label.

I think it was all a misunderstanding, and if my emotions and their emotions hadn't gotten in the way, I think we never would have gone to court. We would have worked it out.

Most of the time, it comes down to miscommunication between product developers and potential licensees. Sometimes companies are designing the exact same product you are, and you are not aware of it. Sometimes they don't have knowledge of all of your patents or patents pending. That's why it's smart to stay in touch with potential licensees and maintain involvement with active licensees. It's also smart to try to resolve any problems calmly and rationally by talking with one another. Once you get emotional and get attorneys involved, no one wins.

Keep the Ideas—and Profits—Coming!

No one wins at this game by beating a dead horse. Nor does anyone win by giving up too soon. So what do you do after you've shown your idea to many of the potential licensees on your list and none are interested? When do you walk away from an idea?

To be completely honest, the majority of the companies that review your ideas are going to reject them. You have to get up to bat many times before you hit a home run. But let's say you've submitted your idea to 20 companies and they've all rejected it. Before submitting it to another round of potential licensees, you might want to reassess your idea to determine whether you should revise and resubmit it or just let it go.

Remember in Chapter 16 when I advised you to ask potential licensees why they had rejected your idea? Did they say it was wrong for them at that time, or for that product category, or for that industry? Was it too difficult or expensive to manufacture? Did they say the technology was too advanced or too passé? Did they give you any specifics about how you might improve the idea? Were they able to recommend another company, product category, or industry for which your idea might be a fit?

Industry experts are another good source of information for evaluating why your idea was rejected. Maybe the market has changed since you developed your idea; maybe it's in a lull. Attending trade shows, reading trade magazines, talking to industry leaders, and studying the market will help you understand the market as well as the marketability of your idea.

Sometimes you can use this information to fix your idea and then resubmit it to the same companies that rejected it or submit it to other potential licensees. Sometimes you just need to keep trying—to submit it to 10 companies if you've submitted it to only 5, to 15 if you've submitted to only 10. If you've tried all the midsize companies on your list of potential licensees, try the big corporations and the small manufacturers. If the idea is solid and you believe in it, you just need to keep knocking on doors until there are no more to knock on.

Other times, when you take a step back and look at the evidence, it becomes clear that you're just spinning your wheels. It's time to move on; let go of your idea and find another one. Corporations don't expect all of their ideas to pan out, and neither should you.

Don't be one of those nutty professor types who spends years and years and thousands upon thousands of dollars "inventing" something that can't be manufactured or sold. Don't cling to an idea that isn't working and that no company wants to license. Get good at letting go, and put your talent and your time where the market is. Thousands of companies out there are willing, able, and eager to license your ideas. Keep the ideas coming, and the profits will follow. I guarantee it.

What's fantastic about this game is that anyone can play it! You don't need to quit your day job or get a degree in design, engineering, or marketing. You don't need to build fancy prototypes and file expensive patents. You don't need to dream up some revolutionary new technology. You don't need to go into debt, give up your freedom, and launch a company to manufacture and market your idea yourself.

Anyone can create and license ideas following this simple 10-step strategy:

1. **Study the marketplace.** Go shopping, attend a trade show, talk with a guru, and consult with your mentor to find a simple idea with big market potential.
2. **Innovate for the market.** Use your creativity to add value, novelty, and pizzazz to an existing product.
3. **Prove your idea.** Do your homework to validate that your idea will sell and can be manufactured at the right price points.
4. **Prototype your idea.** Bring your idea to life using fast, inexpensive, and effective ways of creating a model or other visual representation of your idea.
5. **Create a one-line benefit statement.** Articulate the greatest value that your idea offers to potential licensees and their customers in one concise and compelling sentence.
6. **Create a one-page sell sheet.** Show potential licensees the benefits of your idea, a visual representation of your idea, and a short infomercial in a powerful one-page ad.
7. **Protect your idea.** Protect your intellectual property with an inexpensive provisional patent application.
8. **Get a company to say yes.** Get your foot in the door and your idea in front of potential licensees by mastering the art of getting in.
9. **Cut a great licensing deal.** Use the right information and the right attitude to negotiate a win-win licensing agreement with a potential licensee.
10. **Keep the ideas and profits coming!** Work in partnership with your licensees, police your licensees, and move on to your next idea. Keep innovating, and keep selling your ideas.

All you need to create the life of your dreams are these 10 simple steps for bringing ideas to market—and one simple idea. Then another simple idea. And another simple idea . . . You get the idea.

19

The New Opportunities for Inventors

I THINK IT'S an extremely exciting time to be a creative person. There are more avenues to get your ideas out there today than ever before, and even more importantly, fewer gatekeepers. It doesn't matter where you live or even how well you speak English. If you have an Internet connection, you can participate! I think we're on the cusp of an explosion, really. So many factors have contributed to this new reality, including the widespread use of social media and the Internet, the advent of crowdfunding, the birth of the freelancer economy, the increasing affordability of prototyping techniques, and our growing ability to effectively communicate with manufacturers overseas. The simple fact is that you don't have to start a business to bring your ideas to market. Nor do you have to work your way up a corporate ladder.

It's not only a few companies that are actively seeking out new ideas; an entire product marketing industry is taking shape as we speak. I am going to discuss some of the new opportunities available to inventors in this chapter with a particular emphasis on how you can make the most of them.

Quirky

A recent *New York Times* article described Quirky as "exhibit A for the case that a digital-age renaissance of the small inventor is not only possible but underway." Quirky is unique in that it is striving to be so many things at once—in that way, it embodies the merger of all these cultural shifts that are taking place. Ben Kaufman, the company's 28-year-old founder and chief executive, calls it a "modern invention machine." I had the pleasure of interviewing Ben years ago and have watched Quirky grow with interest.

So what is Quirky? The company encourages inventors to submit their ideas to the site. Then its community of more than one million users votes for the ideas it likes best and thinks have the most potential. At a publicly broadcasted meeting, a group of industry experts decide which ideas to move forward with. Fewer than 10 ideas (out of the thousands of submissions Quirky receives each week) are presented; typically, half of those get the go-ahead. The company's community of "influencers" is encouraged to weigh in again, this time on the product's design. Approximately one out of the five ideas that make it through the expert round actually sees the light of day. Quirky manufacturers and markets the products that make it through all of the rounds. More than 400 Quirky-generated products have been brought to life so far. Two of its newest partners are General Electric and Mattel, and Quirky says a handful of other companies are slated to join its corporate partnership program in the future.

For all of the work that it does (essentially, the same work that a licensee would do), Quirky pockets 90 cents of each dollar of product sales. The other 10 cents is distributed among the community of inventors who contributed to the product's design—leaving the inventor who came up with the original product idea about 4 cents of that.

Because Quirky is so competitive, I do not believe that it is the best avenue for most of your ideas. But I think the site is an interesting experiment and has value apart from licensing your ideas. For example, Quirky doesn't require that submissions be protected by intellectual property. If you have an idea for a product that cannot be protected with intellectual property, I think Quirky is a great option to turn to. As I've said over and over again in this book, the best form of protection is getting to market first anyway. And in that way, Quirky excels. One of my students, Jared, a full-time inventor who has been submitting his ideas to Quirky for years, said that the company took his idea for a product that neatly organizes unsightly power cords, the

Plug Hub, from sketch to store in eight months. Quirky took Cordies, a desktop cord manager, from sketch to store in a mere four weeks. That's fast. On the other hand, when you submit an idea to Quirky, it enters the public domain. When you choose to publicize an unprotected idea, there's always the chance that someone else could beat you to the punch.

I think Quirky is an interesting avenue for those ideas that you have, but do not (or cannot) put any effort toward attempting to license on your own. Once you submit something to Quirky, it's out of your hands. You no longer have any influence over its development, because it's subject to the whims of the community at large. I also think becoming a part of Quirky's community would teach you a lot about innovation quickly. You could watch case study after case study play out. What do the ideas that succeed on Quirky have in common? Why are they compelling? What makes them stand out from the thousands of other ideas? If you made a commitment to submit one idea a week for a year, like Jared did, I believe you would become a much better product developer.

If you want the ideas you submit on Quirky to stand out, it's important that you make them as engaging as possible. Focus on creating titles, taglines, and thumbnails that are compelling and explicit. When someone clicks on your thumbnail image for more information, reward him or her with more information, such as a digital rendering or sketch. You should also make your pitch timely. Why is your product idea needed now? How does it capitalize on what's going on in the market?

Shark Tank

I would be remiss if I did not address ABC's hit reality television show about pitching investors in this new edition. Do you watch, *Shark Tank* every week? I do. As an entrepreneur, what's not to love? It's exciting! You and I are not alone. Since the show premiered in 2009, it has become incredibly popular. Nearly 8 million people tune in each week to watch entrepreneurs pitch their product businesses to a panel of potential investors. There are different versions of the show all over the world, like Canada's *Dragons' Den*. Part of the reason I enjoy watching the show is because there are so many parallels between pitching a shark and selling a potential licensee in real life. For one thing, both are extremely risk-averse. They need to be convinced that your idea is worth taking on. There are benefits to appearing on the show regardless of whether or not you're offered a deal—like a staggering amount of exposure. I personally know a few entrepreneurs who have appeared on the show exclusively for the exposure. As I'm sure you've read, businesses that are featured tend to explode afterwards, regardless of whether a shark makes an offer. Be careful what you wish for though. To meet demand, you will need to be prepared.

However, I am wary of inventors who peg their hopes on making it big on *Shark Tank*. That is an unrealistic goal, to put it mildly. They remind me of the inventors I've met who want everything done for them. I want to talk about it though! What does it *really* take to succeed on *Shark Tank*? I poured over episodes and success stories to give you my perspective.

If the following is true of your product, you may be a good fit for the show:

- It is already being sold in the market.
- It has a clear benefit.
- It is easily demonstrated.
- A large market exists for it.
- It has a high profit margin.
- You have established perceived ownership over it.
- It fits into one of the shark's area of expertise.

As you've probably noticed, there is a good bit of overlap between what it takes to succeed on *Shark Tank* and what it takes to succeed at licensing your ideas. The critical difference is that to succeed on the show, you need to have a product that is already being sold in the market. The important thing to understand about *Shark Tank* is that its producers not only want to tell a success story, they want to tell a success story *quickly*. They want to be able to say, "Look at what a positive impact the shark has had!" It's part of their storytelling and branding.

But as you know by now, bringing a product to market is anything but a quick process. Therefore, to win big on *Shark Tank*, you need to already be in business. Unlike a licensee would though, it's not as if a shark is going to run your business for you. Manufacturing, marketing, and distribution—those are all still on you. (Frankly, I think one of the biggest benefits of partnering with a shark isn't necessarily their financial resources, but their extensive list of contacts.)

It's not enough to simply be in business, though. I also want you to understand that getting picked to be on *Shark Tank* is as much about you as it about your product. Do you long for your 15 minutes of fame? Do you think you have a personality that will leap off the screen? Does your product have a thrilling origin story? The casting director has plainly said that he has passed on great ideas simply because they weren't presented in an exciting enough way. Never forget that *Shark Tank* is explicitly about entertainment.

In my eyes, *Shark Tank*, like Quirky, is simply too competitive to peg your hopes on. In 2013, 40,000 entrepreneurs applied to be on the show. Out of those, a mere 180 actually made it. A few walked away with investment deals. I would never discourage you from trying to appear on the show, but it's a long shot—the longest of shots, really. However, I think there's a lot of value in watching the show. Doing so will force you to think about the economics of any business. What are your manufacturing costs? What is your overhead? What is your profit margin? These are all extremely important considerations for any entrepreneur. As you enjoy the show, think about your own point of difference. What skills do you lack? What skills do you have? You will also learn a lot about pitching! And pitching is an absolutely indispensable skill.

Crowdfunding

I've touched on this throughout the book, but I think crowdfunding is one of the most exciting new developments for independent product developers and entrepreneurs. I mean, think about it. For the first time, we consumers have a voice. And our voices are powerful!

Crowdfunding has enabled us to directly express what we want to see on the market. Creators have more freedom to work on the projects they want to and believe in. To me, that is the most wonderful thing on the planet. It's changed everything.

I think crowdfunding and licensing can be quite complementary. As I mentioned earlier, if you're unable to convince potential licensees that your idea has merit, you could run a crowdfunding campaign to prove that demand exists. You could decide to preemptively run a campaign (like Eskil did) before ever showing your idea to a potential licensee with the hope that it would garner you a higher royalty rate, which is totally plausible. Ultimately, at the end of the day, if you run a successful campaign, you're in a more advantageous position when it comes to negotiating. Another one of my other students, Kevin, asked for a mere $10,000 when he ran his campaign. Meeting that goal was enough to convince a company to license the idea from him.

There are a lot of resources available about how to run a successful campaign, so I'm not going to detail them here. But suffice it to say that running a campaign isn't something you should decide to do on a lark. For a campaign to benefit you, it needs to make a splash—which requires a lot of planning and foresight. For one, campaigns live or die by how many people fund them. How are you going to get the word out about your campaign? In reality, you will need to build up an army of support months in advance to get the reaction you're looking for. At a minimum, you should reach out to industry bloggers and magazines to alert them about your product and its campaign. You should also consider getting testimonials from industry experts. Remember, only a small percentage of the people who hear about a campaign actually fund it. And secondly, you will need to make sure all of your presentation materials are top-notch. People fund ideas that they can truly visualize and get behind. I don't mean to dissuade you—I just want your campaign to kill it!

Just recently, one of my former students ran a campaign that raised nearly $450,000 for his product PancakeBot, the "world's first pancake printer." Miguel had already found a licensee for his product (after years of working on it, I might add). Together, they decided to run a campaign to get the word out. It was an incredibly smart decision.

Since the product is still being fine-tuned, they're able to take into account the comments and requests backers have made. This is just one example of the myriad of ways crowdfunding can be used to test the market.

DRTV

The direct-response television industry has always been a popular avenue for inventors to bring their ideas to market, but increasingly, it's one of the hottest industries licensing ideas. Have you heard of the Snuggie? What about the Magic Bullet? These days, it feels as if every retail store I walk into has an "As Seen on TV" section—and it's usually prominently displayed. Products advertised on DRTV are increasingly being sold at retail, which is causing the industry to grow and expand. One of the things I like about DRTV is that companies operating in this sphere move extremely fast. If you submit an idea to a DRTV company, you can expect to receive a response much sooner than you would typically. For that reason, I recommend submitting your idea to one company at a time. (All these companies, and there are only about five right now, know one another.) Another reason I like this industry is because these companies don't require patents. As you know, I think companies that require an idea submission to be patented in order to review it is foolish. However, you should have protected your idea with a PPA before proceeding.

There's a lot of money to be made, but you need to be careful. If a company demands that you pay for the commercial, or that you have to make it yourself, be wary. That's a red flag. Avoid them. If your benefit is strong enough, they will test your idea. In my experience and that of my students, they test extremely thoroughly, actually. If you license your idea to a DRTV company, you can expect to receive about a 3 percent royalty on wholesale, and 1 percent royalty on direct sales, aka sales made by phone. A common minimum guarantee is $250,000. However, it's safe to say that in this sphere, everything can be negotiated.

DRTV companies are very specific about what they're looking for. Your product will need to have a 5 to 1 ratio. In other words, whatever your product costs to manufacture, it will have to retail for five times that much. Price points are very important in this industry, and there isn't a lot of wiggle room. In general, products in the cookware, personal care, auto, and pet industries are particularly successful.

When you approach a DRTV company with your idea, it is imperative that you show them a short infomercial about your idea. Like I said earlier, your video sell sheet should always be brief and to the point. This is the format they're familiar with. Watch the promotional videos on the websites of DRTV companies such as Allstar Products to get a better idea of what I mean. Again, it's not that your video needs to look as good—it's that it needs to follow the same format. To determine whether or not your idea is a good fit for DRTV, study up on existing DRTV products. What does well? It's all out there.

20

If I Were to Do It All Over Again: The Need for Product Scouts

Aᴼᴛᴇʀ 30 years in this business, I sometimes wonder what I would do differently if I were to do it all over again. And the answer is, I would become a product scout. The fact is that companies in all industries need ideas. They're desperate for them. Today, a company's success depends on its ability to quickly bring new products to market. Few companies can do that solely from ideas they develop in-house. Like you know by now, this is where open innovation comes into play.

But many companies don't know how or don't have a good system in place for finding those ideas. Likewise, many independent product developers don't know how to license their ideas, and some would simply prefer hiring someone to "rep" their ideas to licensees for them. I know, because I often receive messages from product developers asking me to recommend them a product scout. This scenario creates a huge opportunity for people to profit from connecting innovators with manufacturers. As a product scout, you find great ideas and then find the right companies to license them. In return for your services, the company pays you. Every time a company sells a product you scouted, you make money. There are certain personalities I think are beautifully suited to this kind of work. Do you thrive on being a connector? Do you like to manage people and projects? Are you capable of seeing the big picture? If you answered yes to these questions and want to work with the most innovative people and companies in the world, this could be the job for you.

The reason I would try to become a product scout is because I believe in the power of the multiplying effect. The multiplying effect also applies to licensing, of course. It's part of what attracted me to this business. When you license an idea, you earn income based on every product that is sold. Once your idea is out there in the world, you no longer have to do very much (if anything) to make money. But, I now realize that the ideas don't have to be mine. After all, I know each of the steps. I know what it takes to succeed at this game. And, truthfully, I'm not that creative—not nearly as creative as many other people are. But connecting talented designers with companies that are looking for ideas? Now that excites me. I think that if you have an entrepreneurial spirit and great selling skills, you can do this. If you have a passion for products, even better!

What Scouts Do

I like to say that product scouts are akin to unicorns—they just don't really exist. That's not completely true, but what I mean by that is: there are just not that many people out there who are connecting creative people and their ideas to companies that are looking for new products. People often message me to ask if I can recommend them one, and for the most part, I am unable to. I think that is going to change, though. I hope so, anyway. The opportunity is enormous and only going to grow. So I'm going to tell you how I would go about doing it.

First, you should know that there is a difference between product scouts and licensing agents. Licensing agents share a percentage of their clients' royalties, whereas product scouts are paid by the companies they scout for. Because individual inventors pay licensing agents for their services, licensing agents fall under the category of "invention promotion services" and are subject to a specific set of rules established by the American Inventors Protection Act of 1999. (Which is a great thing, because there are so many invention promotion firms out there that are scams, and that take advantage of inventors.) I would prefer to become a product scout rather than be considered an invention promotion services company. There are a number of different ways you could structure your payment. It could be a per-project, one-time fee. I would prefer to be paid royalties or by commission. (In other words, I'd agree to be paid on the back end.)

The main reason independent product designers would hire a product scout is because they don't have the expertise to license their ideas to companies themselves. And like I said, many product designers would choose to work with a licensing expert because they want to focus on creating ideas rather than selling them. In either case, they'll expect *you* to be the licensing expert. After all, that's what they're paying you for. The more you know, the more successful you'll be.

As a product scout, your success depends on three things:

- How many of the ideas you scout out *get licensed*
- How many of those licensed ideas *get to market*
- How *well those ideas sell* on the market

So it is vitally important for you to become a licensing expert—that is to say, a master at finding marketable ideas and getting them into the marketplace. That's the only way you're going to be able to convince designers to let you pitch their ideas to companies, and that's the only way you're going to be able to convince companies to bring those ideas to market. In fact, I think you will need to work the 10 steps yourself to truly succeed at being a product scout. The only way to know how to do something is to do it on your own. There are no shortcuts! You'll be better at identifying good ideas if you do. And having worked the steps will give you credibility in the eyes of designers as well as potential licensees.

Becoming an expert takes time. Help yourself out by sticking to one industry in particular. My advice, especially when you're first starting out, is to focus on an industry you're familiar with, a market you're interested in, or a product category you're passionate about (ideally, all three!). You will want to learn as much about the history of innovation in that industry as you can, as well as come to know all of its players. There are immeasurable benefits to sticking to one or two industries. Your success as a product scout will depend largely on the relationships you make and maintain. If you stick to one industry, you will become an expert in it. You'll know what's hot, what's going to be hot, and most of all, what kinds of products companies are looking for. That is priceless information. Finding your niche and looking for ideas there first is ultimately a more efficient, productive, and profitable use of your time and talents. It increases your chances of finding good ideas and getting them licensed. It takes less time to scout, research, and network in one or two industries than in three, four, or more. At least some of the work you do for one idea will be useful for other ideas. Success builds on success. For example, if three or four of your clients have big hits in the novelty and gift industry, it will be easier for you to secure other novelty and gift designers as clients and to get novelty and gift companies to open their doors to you. Markets also change constantly and quickly, and it is imperative that you stay plugged into new and emerging trends.

That does not mean you need to, or even should, limit yourself to one market. Feel free to go scouting wherever you might find good ideas that interest you. It's just significantly easier to get started when you narrow your search. When you've decided on an industry, start studying it intensely. The more familiar you are with a market, the easier it will be for you to find ideas and the more likely you'll be able to recognize a marketable idea. Studying a specific market will also increase your likelihood of finding one great idea after another, which is critical to your continued success as a product scout.

This does not mean you need to be an expert in every industry you want to work in. You just need to know the market well enough to make good judgments about an idea's market potential. To familiarize yourself with a market, do the same things that designers and inventors do, or should do, before they design a product: go shopping. Talk to retailers and consumers. Search the Internet. Read trade publications. Go to trade shows. Check out the websites of trade associations and major manufacturers in that market.

After narrowing down my focus, I would begin building relationships with open-innovation companies so that I could ask them, "What are you looking for?" Then I would go out and find product ideas that meet their needs.

Focus on Ideas You Can License

I think one of the most challenging aspects of becoming a successful product scout would be finding great ideas. That's why I would focus on finding and working with talented designers (like from the country's top design schools) who are frustrated and really just want to focus on designing ideas rather than licensing them. Be selective about which ideas you choose to take on. Just because an idea is clever doesn't mean it will sell. If an idea is too much of a departure from other products in the market or if the technology is too new or complicated, you could invest a lot of your time and hard work only to discover that no company wants to license it. Taking on an idea that you have doubts about or that you don't have good reason to believe can be manufactured and sold is a waste of your time and only gives false hope to the designer or inventor.

That does not mean you should limit yourself to only ideas with big markets and a huge profit potential. In fact, I think that's a bad strategy, because ideas that are that hot tend to be few and far between. To be a successful product scout and to maximize your income, you need to find as many marketable ideas as possible and get them to market as quickly and easily as possible. Like I've said before, a simple idea—a small change to an existing product—is the easiest to license. Home runs are often hit with a new twist on an old idea. Just make sure the time you spend on an idea is commensurate with its profit potential.

I've found that some designers can talk for a long time but still not give a clear vision of what their idea is. Sometimes, the idea simply isn't ready yet, and the product developer has more homework and legwork to do. To maximize the return on your time, you need to manage the process and get the inventor working for you. That's why it's important to evaluate an idea *before* you agree to take it on and to control the process every step of the way.

First, you should let designers know up front that you only take on ideas you think you can license. Tell them that in order to make that determination, you will need them to provide you with certain information before you will discuss their idea with them. Then use a checklist or submission form that specifies the information you need to evaluate the idea. At a minimum, designers should provide you with these four items:

1. A brief description of their idea stating its features and benefits. Ask them to limit this *benefit statement* to one or two sentences. Give them a couple of examples, such as "I have a five-dollar ballpoint pen that writes at any angle, including upside-down, and writes as smoothly as similar pens that retail for 5 to 10 times more," and "I have a lightweight hammer that hits nails straight every time."
2. A drawing or a computer model of their idea, or a photograph of a prototype of their idea.
3. A list of stores, catalogs, or websites that might sell their product.
4. Whether or not they have applied for intellectual property protection. (See Chapter 10.)

Some designers will balk at sharing this information. Just explain why you need it and assure them you will hold it in strict confidence. If they provide the information, move forward with the evaluation process. If they don't, let it go. This will help you pick out designers who are serious about getting their ideas licensed and willing to go the whole nine yards with you. In fact, you will probably need more information while you assess the idea. Again, be very specific. The designer's responses will help you determine whether the idea is ready to be licensed and how much work you'll need to do to license it.

You will also need to craft a well-written standard NDA for free-lancers to sign that they feel comfortable with. In terms of publicizing yourself, I would stick to a sophisticated looking website. If you advertise your services too strongly, you will start receiving a heavy volume of ideas, which isn't ideal. You're in search of quality, not quantity.

Get It in Writing

Once you and a designer decide to work together, you'll need an agreement that authorizes you to present his or her idea to potential licensees and spells out the terms and conditions of the agreement, including your compensation. These are legally binding documents, and every situation is different. So I strongly recommend that you consult with a legal professional for all contracts.

To become a great product scout, you'll also need to understand the language of licensing agreements to keep both of your clients happy. Designers will want to work with you if you are an ally to them (and again, they're coming to you because they don't want to put in the time or effort themselves to learn this information). So it would behoove you to befriend licensing attorneys as well.

Mine the Talent at Art and Design Schools as Well as Design Firms

These schools are where some of the most creative people around learn how to bring their ideas to life. If I were a product scout, this is the first place I would look for innovative ideas and creative talent. Art and design schools are a gold mine of great ideas.

Some years ago, I was asked to speak at the Art Center College of Design in Pasadena, California. There are schools like the Art Center College across the United States, and they are the premier design schools in the country. The Art Center College of Design teaches classes in 12 different disciplines—everything from industrial design, packaging, and graphic design to website development, transportation design, and more. Students pay up to $200,000 to go to these schools; they are the cream of the crop.

Mateo Neri, an instructor at the school in Pasadena, teaches students how to bring a product to market the old way, by starting a business. Mateo found me and asked me to speak to his classes because he discovered that the students did not want to start companies in order to bring their ideas to market. He realized they needed help licensing their ideas.

When I went to the school to speak, I was blown away when I saw their gallery of ideas. They were some of the most innovative and creative ideas and products I had ever seen. Mateo told me that all of those prototypes, drawings, and ideas were thrown away at the end of the semester. I was heartbroken. I saw such potential in many of the ideas. I knew we had to do something to help these students.

I would also go after industrial design firms. Founders of big design firms are often frustrated that they are paid per project and do not collect royalties from their innovations. I have always enjoyed working with design firms when I have had the opportunity, because the talent is so incredible. They're a hotbed of new innovative ideas—many of which tragically sit on a shelf because they aren't exactly what a client wants and there's no time to find them an alternative home. That's where you come in. Finding the top design firms is easy: Google them. I also recommend contacting their trade association, the Industrial Designers Society of America.

HOW WARREN HELPS BRING OTHER PEOPLE'S IDEAS TO MARKET

For 20 years, Warren Tuttle worked in the housewares industry, first as a buyer for a major New York City department store, next as the designer of his own line of gourmet cookware that sold in food stores, and then as the owner of an upscale housewares store. About 16 years ago, Warren decided he wanted to bring not only his own but also other people's innovative houseware ideas to market. In his first five years as a product scout, the products Warren was responsible for brought in more than $300 million in sales.

Eventually, Warren partnered up with Lifetime Brands (LB) to bring in product ideas from outside the company. At the time, LB had an internal research and development (R&D) team of 40 people, and the external product development program was the first of its kind. In less than two years, Warren brokered 21 licensing deals between LB and independent product developers. He has since partnered with the power tool division of Techtronic Industries—the largest producer of power tools in the United States—to help oversee its open-innovation program. His latest venture, Access Innovation Solutions, is dedicated to scouting ideas for the DRTV industry. He also continues to develop and license his own ideas.

continued

Warren attributes his licensing success to his extensive knowledge and experience in the housewares industry, which he says has given him the "ability to assess new ideas." He also studies the market, keeps abreast of what's going on in the industry as a whole, and maintains a high profile with product developers and inventors. Some of his connections date back 20 to 30 years, and he's always networking and scouting new ideas. Consequently, people constantly refer inventors and product developers to him, to the tune of 1,200 to 1,500 leads a year.

Because of his market expertise, Warren Tuttle knows a winner when he scouts one, and that has resulted in licensing royalties for both Warren and the people whose ideas he has helped bring to market.

To play this game, you don't need to be a creative genius. You don't even need to come up with your own ideas; you can play—and win—by connecting people with great ideas to the companies that want to license them. If you have a passion for innovative products, a penchant for selling, and some licensing expertise, you, too, can reap the rewards of the licensing lifestyle by becoming a product scout. That's the beauty of the licensing lifestyle.

Index

About the Authors

STEPHEN KEY has been a successful entrepreneur and award-winning product developer for more than 30 years. He has licensed more than 20 of his ideas and has nearly two dozen patents to his name. His products have been sold by major retailers throughout the world as well as endorsed by basketball great Michael Jordan, *Jeopardy* host Alex Trebek, and superstar singer/songwriter Taylor Swift.

Stephen's innovative Spinformation® rotating label has been licensed for use on many products, including Nescafé coffee, DeKuyper liqueurs, and Rexall Sundown Naturals. SpinLabel Technologies, Inc., a Florida-based company, purchased his patent portfolio in 2011. His third book, 2015's *Sell Your Ideas With or Without a Patent*, details how to use intellectual property strategically for profit.

He and his partner Andrew Krauss have been educating entrepreneurs and inventors for more than 13 years as the cofounders of inventRight. He recently partnered with Youth Entrepreneurs, a non-profit 501(c)(3) organization that teaches business and entrepreneurial education in 41 high schools across Kansas and Missouri, to develop a free program about licensing.

Recognized as an outstanding leader in the field of innovation, Stephen has appeared on national television numerous times, including the CNBC show *The Big Idea with Donny Deutsch* and as an expert guest on *Dr. Phil*. He was also a consultant during the first season of the ABC reality TV show *American Inventor*, created by Simon Cowell.

Stephen is among the most well-read contributors on Entrepreneur .com. He is also the author of a popular weekly column about licensing, "The Licensing Lifestyle," for Inc.com. National magazines, newspapers, and authors such as Tim Ferris (*The 4-Hour Work Week*) regularly consult him for his insights.

Stephen joined Make48, a new event competition whose mission is to provide a fun, entertaining, and educational vehicle for everyday people to showcase their ingenuity, in 2015.

Stephen lives in Glenbrook, California, Lake Tahoe's oldest community, with his beautiful wife Janice. The Keys have three children, two of whom graduated from the University of California at Berkeley and the youngest of whom is currently pursuing a law degree from the University of California, Davis.

Colleen Sell is a writer and editor who specializes in applying the art of storytelling to all forms of media—from books to blogs to branding content and beyond. She is the author, coauthor, or ghostwriter of more than 20 published books; the anthologist of the bestselling, 40-volume Cup of Comfort book series; and the former editor-in-chief of two award-winning print magazines and a digital magazine. Her articles and essays have appeared in dozens of publications, and she has edited more than 150 published books.